Advance Praise for
Bridging Troubled Waters

"*Bridging Troubled Waters* weaves together striking analyses of cases and stories with a sensitive and reflective meditation on the challenges of community building and peacemaking. Instructors, students, and practitioners of all kinds will find fresh insights and approaches here."
—*John Forester, professor, Department of City and Regional Planning, Cornell University*

"*Bridging Troubled Waters* illustrates and illuminates the value and importance of creativity in dealing with the complexity of conflict. It helps us explore how to employ our whole selves—our minds, hearts, and souls—in approaching conflict."
—*Chris Carlson, coexecutive director, the Policy Consensus Initiative, Santa Fe*

"This is a must-read for the practitioner as well as the academic. A brilliant approach to conflict resolution that is certain to shift the thinking of those who are still operating from twentieth-century approaches. This is a necessary addition to the library of all conflict resolution educators and practitioners."
—*David E. Reagan, psychology and communications instructor, Camosun College, Victoria, British Columbia, Canada*

BRIDGING TROUBLED WATERS

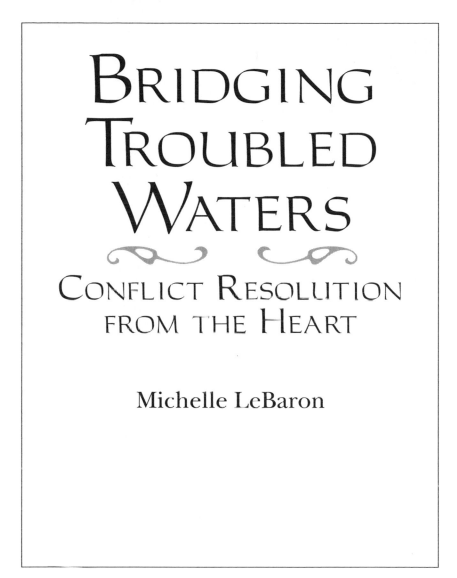

BRIDGING
TROUBLED
WATERS

CONFLICT RESOLUTION
FROM THE HEART

Michelle LeBaron

JOSSEY-BASS
A Wiley Company
www.josseybass.com

Published by

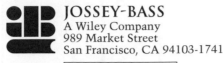

JOSSEY-BASS
A Wiley Company
989 Market Street
San Francisco, CA 94103-1741

| www.josseybass.com |

Jossey-Bass books and products are available through most bookstores. To contact Jossey-Bass directly, call (888) 378-2537, fax to (800) 605-2665, or visit our website at www.josseybass.com.

Substantial discounts on bulk quantities of Jossey-Bass books are available to corporations, professional associations, and other organizations. For details and discount information, contact the special sales department at Jossey-Bass.

We at Jossey-Bass strive to use the most environmentally sensitive paper stocks available to us. Our publications are printed on acid-free recycled stock whenever possible, and our paper always meets or exceeds minimum GPO and EPA requirements.

Jossey-Bass also publishes its books in a variety of electronic formats. Some content that appears in print may not be available in electronic books.

Library of Congress Cataloging-in-Publication Data

LeBaron, Michelle, date.
  Bridging troubled waters : conflict resolution from the heart /
Michelle LeBaron.—1st ed.
      p.   cm.
Includes bibliographical references and index.
  ISBN 0-7879-4821-7 (alk. paper)
  1. Conflict management. 2. Interpersonal conflict. I. Title.
HM1126 .L4 2002
  303.6'9—dc21   2002002222

FIRST EDITION
HB Printing   10 9 8 7 6 5 4 3 2 1

CONTENTS

FOREWORD

I still remember how shocked I was when a colleague suggested that we begin a training program in South Africa with song. It was 1994. Key political and national groups were engaged in appalling violence, and in many cases their songs were their war cries. How could this be a safe and constructive way to begin a workshop to train people as election monitors? My colleague even suggested taking the group out to the street to give them real-life experience applying some of the skills we were teaching. I was apprehensive, to say the least!

To my surprise, beginning with songs and taking to the streets turned out to be wonderful ways of helping parties connect from their deepest and most personal selves. They shared extraordinary, unanticipated, and, for some, very frightening experiences that softened the ground, allowing them to be more expansive and spacious with one another and to feel much more prepared for the hard world that awaited them as election monitors. This experience stayed with me, motivating me to explore what my right brain might have to say about conflict resolution training and practice.

As I reflect on my more than twenty years as a professional third party and trainer of third parties, I recognize that I've prided myself on dancing as fast as I can, juggling the many balls of management, training, and intervention. I know that I often do the "right thing," intuitively, when working with parties in serious conflict. I may take a sharp turn when needed or say just the right thing to help parties find ways out of confining and limiting corners. This beautifully written book helps me understand how and why I do these things. How did Michelle LeBaron know that I needed it just now?

This past year has challenged me to move even further outside my comfort zone, exploring new possibilities in my work. I recognized, talking recently with a close colleague, that it's often easier to focus on ideas and the person speaking to me with my glasses off. Moving away from the sharp focus of the intellect to the wisdom of my intuitive self offers me a way forward, a way to approach conflict resolution "outside the box."

Yet the experience of being outside the box means that there are few maps to point the way. How do we teach ourselves to be more intuitive, more sensitive, maybe more courageous in doing our conflict resolution work? How do we make our creative and brilliant interventions a little more predictable and understandable? How do we embrace the art as well as the science of conflict resolution work? A good step is to read *Bridging Troubled Waters* and explore, with Michelle, what it means to work from our hearts.

This book is written elegantly; it clearly comes from her heart. Characterizing conflict as "the sand in our oysters," Michelle encourages us to stretch outside our linear mode of moving from positions to interests. She invites us to cultivate "texture" and "maneuverability" in our practice, to use our whole selves to help move "from rigid to fluid, from knotted to relaxed." We help parties take the next step by paying "exquisite attention" to "the insistent tapping of what we know but have forgotten." Using rituals, metaphors, and stories, we find ways around the divides that keep parties engaged in long and bitter struggles. Her language helps us to feel, as well as see, her vision of going broader and deeper.

Michelle leads us into a theory of conflict resolution where relationship is at the center. She nudges us to look for unexpected connections among parties, drawing on our own and our clients' imaginations. She holds a mirror for us to see ourselves and the richness of our own lives as a fruitful part of the web that connects us all. Working from this place, we help parties transition through what seem to be inescapable mazes of anger and confusion.

The power of Michelle's stories helps us achieve new levels of understanding. Drawing on the richness of metaphors and symbolism, we see ways to move parties out of the narrowed, flattened, and unimaginative places that their conflict has dumped them, into a "spaciousness," where they can catch a glimpse of what just might be possible. We find, through new stories (or new ways of telling old stories), how an adversary might be able to accept a little of a counterpart's perspective, enough so the need to be right is held in abeyance. While they may not have reached a win-win solution, this picture is closer to what is achievable in working with today's frighteningly complex disputes. In this way, the book counters the critique of conflict resolvers as pie-in-the-sky optimists, revealing the progress that is possible when we work together from our minds and our hearts.

Even as we trace our successes in providing intuitive and imaginative leadership, we are cautioned to stay mindful. My favorite of Michelle's many quotations is a Sufi saying: "Trust in God but tie up your camel." With words from an exalted collection of wise people, including philosophers and psychologists, potters and poets, mediators and meditators, Michelle reminds us to remain humble and learn from our failures. Knowing it is possible for us to be utterly wrong, we are wise to bring a sense of humor and a spirit of lightness to our work.

Michelle also encourages us to remain true to our values and convictions, invoking moral courage to balance the tension between advocacy and our roles as third parties. She urges creativity, asking us to find innovative and thoughtful ways to help achieve change, inviting us to explore many ways of knowing as resources. As we commit ourselves to being more open to opportunities that may be shrouded, welcoming more connected ways of being with each other, we help ourselves and our clients to replace old stories of hatred and hurt with hope and heart.

MARY MARGARET GOLTEN
Boulder, Colorado
May 2002

To the first artists in my life,
my grandparents Luella and Neal,
and to my children,
Daniel, Emily, Genevieve, and Justin,
who carry on their artistry

PREFACE

An achingly beautiful piece of music marks the dawn. Another day begins and, with it, a changed existence. It is an existence that invites creativity, that requires love and courage and constant attention. At its heart is relationship—relationship with ourselves, with others, with that which is bigger than ourselves, whether we call it Spirit, Universe, or Nature. Now it is up to us. We must give our best, with fierce dedication, all the while realizing that change is constant and our sight limited. We step out into the morning, walking with loss and joy and courage left to us by those who have passed.

When I began writing this book, my father was well. A few months later, he had a stroke and slowly died. In grieving his loss, I came to a new appreciation of relationship. In missing him—our talks, our affection, our laughter, our differences—I realized that I missed his spirit most of all. There is no one else in the world who carried that same spark, who knew me in the acorn that became the tree, who loved me into being with the depth and the dreams of a father for a daughter. Though one of us was liberal and the other conservative, though one of us favored development and the other conservation, we were family.

For a time, this book lay fallow. How many ways we reorganize ourselves inside when loss visits us. Sadness saps energy and interest. The slightest breeze blew me from course. I took on too many other things and told myself I was too busy to write.

But then it came to me, gradually, as the rising sun pigments the sky before it can be seen. The book *wanted* to be written—an affirmation of the multidimensional gifts of relationship and their central role in our lives, in our creativity, and in our conflicts. The book stands, an artifact of devotion despite difference; it stands in contrast to the many books and articles that would persuade us that creativity is a solitary act and that conflict can be solved by reason alone. It breathes, homing back to the place where life begins, where our first significant moments are marked in their warmth, unpredictability, and familiarity.

Following the breath, we come back home again. Home, after all, is about relationship. Home is where we come to know ourselves through the first caring relationships that sustain and grow us. It is where we go to rest, to hear ourselves, to sort ourselves out, to regenerate, to be heard, to listen. It is a place where we let go of image and distraction, where we surround ourselves with what is precious, with nourishment, beauty, and love. We are authentic at home, deeply connected to what matters to us. We observe ourselves in the safety of home, uncovering habits that limit us and planning ways forward.

This book is about bringing our creative, authentic selves with the capacity to love others to the work and play of conflict resolution training and intervention. It is a book that challenges boundaries erected between who we are and what we do, between constructed, reasoned approaches and imagination, intuition, and felt experience. It is a book that invites us to explore our creativity, not as a course in self-improvement or a series of techniques but as a core relational capacity for our work—a capacity that is already well developed.

This book is written from the heart about using the heart and all of its "partners" (our physical, imagining, spiritual, and emotional intelligences) in addressing conflict. It is a book about courage, meaning, and creativity. It is not comprehensive; these are big subjects. It is not written in the spirit of criticism of existing practices, though it may seem so at times. It seeks to be an "and," not a "but," in relation to what conflict resolvers already do. It is meant to invite a dialogue, to pose new questions, to begin the process of unfolding answers. It is meant to engage, to stretch, to disturb our "givens" in the spirit of asking, "What else?" It is offered in the spirit of positive contribution, from the hope that authentic inquiry will lead to more generative ways of moving forward together.

Bridging Troubled Waters introduces a robust and holistic approach to conflict. We begin where much of the theory and practice we now rely on leaves off. Like a hand pulling back the curtain from those parts of us that have been hidden away from our conflict processes, this book reveals ways we can use more of ourselves in addressing conflict. Moving beyond the analytic and the intellectual, it situates our efforts at bridging conflict in the very places where conflict is born—relationships. From relationships come not only conflicts but connection, meaning, and identity. *Bridging Troubled Waters* is about bringing the strengths of relationships into the light, making them accessible to conflict resolution practitioners, teachers, people in organizations, parents and others who want to engage conflict and bring about positive results. I invite you into a relationship of inquiry, of dialogue, following sparks that may arise. Sparks are those ideas that catch the light, inviting us into remembrances, explorations, and connections with those underground rivers that nourish us. As we talk, won't you get yourself a cup or plate of something delicious and join me for some stories? They are stories about us—what we do, what we choose, and what happens to us in spite of our choices. They are stories about life as a source of inspiration for work and work as learning in our lives. They are stories about journeys and sharings and wonderings. Will you add yours as we go?

One more thing. Where there are sparks or trails of light leading us to ideas we want to pursue, there are bound to be "skraps"—*sparks* spelled backward. Skraps, as you might imagine, are the opposite of sparks. Sparks make us want to go toward something. They invite, intrigue, illuminate. Skraps come from places in us that have experienced pain, loss, or confusion. They are connected to feelings of discomfort, aversion, or sadness. We tend to move away from them. Both sparks and skraps strike emotional and physical chords in us that give us clues about what is important, unfinished, or available for us at any given time. Notice them. Follow them. Ask what they have to show you.

I invite you to keep something nearby to write on as you read. Note things you already do that relate to the ideas in the book. Record questions, concerns, disagreements, ah-hahs. Note sparks and skraps to consider later. This practice will give you a baseline for later reflection, a place from which to continue dialogue with friends and colleagues, and a place to unfold your relationship with *you,* which makes everything else possible. I hope that you will find the dialogue rich, intriguing, and useful.

MICHELLE LEBARON
Fairfax, Virginia
May 2002

ACKNOWLEDGMENTS

A book is an invitation to conversation, inspired by many other conversations. To those who have shared their ideas, surprises, and insights with me, I am deeply thankful. Leslie Berriman, now of Conari Press, helped birth the idea for the book and get it launched. Alan Rinzler, at Jossey-Bass, has been the best editor I could have asked for: unfailingly supportive and astute in his comments in a way that caught the spirit of the book and made it stronger. Venashri Pillay provided superb research assistance and helped get the book ready for publication. Karen Bhangoo was there to help it all come together. David Elliott engaged me in creative inquiry about how the ideas in the book inform training and practice. He helped me stay focused, supported me to innovate, and reminded me that climbing mountains requires sustained effort long before panoramic views are experienced. For all of this, I offer my appreciation.

My colleagues encouraged me, even when my ideas were unusual and challenging. To Craig Darling, Mark McCrea, Sara Looney, Amr Abdalla, HoWon Jeong, Mary Clark, Daniel Bowling, Larry Hoover, Oscar Nudler, David Potter, George Renwick, and Sheila Ramsey, my deep thanks. Without you, many things would never have been tried. I also acknowledge those whose lives and work have been a continuing inspiration: Laura Chasin, Jim Laue, Fanchon Silberstein, Andrew Acland, Jean-Nicolas Bitter, Ann Baker, Mary Margaret Golten, Lena Moore, Juliana Birkhoff, Zena Zumeta, and Lorna Irvine. My thanks to the faculty of the Institute for Conflict Analysis and Resolution, whose patience during the writing process I appreciate.

My students from George Mason University, the University of Victoria, York University, American University, and many other places, have enriched and stretched my thinking beyond the bounds I imposed. I cannot name all of you, but my thanks are no less personal.

Good conversations continue in the minds and hearts of participants long after they are over. For the ways many people contributed to starting and continuing these conversations, I am thankful. Omissions and failures are my own; credit for the ideas is shared.

M. L.

Bridging Troubled Waters

PART ONE

Creative Ways to Bridge Conflict

Conflict has been with us as long as human history has been recorded. Conflict resolution is a much newer phenomenon. It makes sense to approach conflict thoughtfully, with a set of carefully chosen tools to minimize its destructive potential. The field of conflict resolution has generated a set of tools, as well as a number of approaches that are informed by theories and empirical findings. Many of these tools come from a rational, problem-solving orientation. They are useful in uncovering interests that fuel positions and helping parties improve their communication. But they do not always work to bridge cultural or worldview differences.

Cultural differences exist in every society, as each of us is a multicultural being. In the global village of today, we constantly encounter diverse ways of naming, framing, and addressing conflict. To successfully bridge these differences, we need approaches that work on the symbolic level—the place where we make meaning, telling and retelling stories about our people and our lives that give coherence and form to our history and our relationships. It is the place where identity is forged, day after day, in the fire of conflict and the glow of connection.

In bridging conflicts intertwined with different ways of understanding self and other, life and loss, creativity is called for. We need a wide range of tools to touch the many parts of us engaged in conflict: emotional intelligence to address hurt; imagination and intuition to dream new ways of being into reality; body awareness to find those parts of ourselves that know what to do when our minds are frozen by fear or pain; and spiritual resources to reveal connection when we have experienced only separation in the past. These tools all come to life in relationship.

Problems do not exist apart from the relationships that give rise to them. Conflict resolution practitioners are challenged to use resources centered in relationship, drawing on our capacities for caring and connection, even as conflicts magnify our capacities for distancing and for inflicting pain. Besides being the context from which conflict arises, relationships are also sites of resilience, connection, and collaboration through which resolution or transformation can come about. Relationships thrive on mutuality and respect for difference, so processes centered in relationship draw on a wide range of ways of knowing and being. When we draw on a range of ways of knowing, we invite creativity into our midst.

Bridging Troubled Waters begins with an exploration of what it means to center our conflict resolution processes in relationship. It is an invitation to a dialogue about creativity and an exploration of what creativity looks like in conflict resolution practice. It is an opening to shared inquiry into how we can invoke a range of gifts, perspectives, and capacities in the difficult work of bridging the differences that divide us. We begin with a mountaintop view, showing us connections among creativity, relationship, and conflict.

CHAPTER ONE

From the Heart
A Creative, Relational Approach to Conflict

Conflicts happen, leaving us with knotted stomachs, furrowed brows, shaky knees. They stress us and stretch us—they show us what we value even as we stand to lose it. Conflicts are significant emotional events. They happen in relationships, calling on our creativity and all our ways of knowing. To address conflicts constructively, we need intuition and imagination to navigate the nuances of conflict's terrain. We need our bodies, sensitive instruments that both receive and send signals reflecting our deep, inner wisdom. We need our emotions in active dialogue with our thoughts, giving us cues to action. And we need our spirits, sources of resilience, strength, and purpose.

In this chapter, we explore the resources of relationship, beginning with a letter to Madeleine, an experienced mediator. Building on this foundation, we examine the topography of conflict processes, climbing six metaphorical mountains to discover the creative gifts available to everyone who finds themselves in the midst of conflict.

Dear Madeleine Mediator,

Where did you get your ideas about conflicts? How did you learn to solve them? Can you help me learn, too? When things get complicated by history or hurt, how is it best to move forward? What do we rely on when things really feel tough? How do we proceed when the people in conflict come from different cultures? Can you look into your bag of tools and tell me what helps?

Yours sincerely,

Curious Caitlin

Dear Curious Caitlin,

You have some good questions. And I have the answer to each of them. In every case, relationship is the answer. I got my ideas about conflicts in relationships with my family, classmates, and communities. I learned what I know about solving them through relationships with my teachers—some formal, traditional teachers and some I met on the path. I learned that when things are complicated, the only way through is by building and growing relationships. We can rely on them when the going gets tough; we can change them and even wish them away, but they are important for our progress.

Conflict is just relationship on a bumpy road. When we look into a relationship, we can almost always find good in it that can help us make it through the bumps. When people come from different cultures, they need to build relationships to feel comfortable with each other and get things done. This works well when they remember that their ideas about how to do things are part of the relationship, but not all of it.

A relationship is two rivers coming together. Neither is ever the same again. And this is good. Think of the mighty Mississippi when it is joined by the Missouri. How much stronger they are after joining. So are we. Relationships strengthen us, give us mirrors to see ourselves, test us, and help us feel good. They keep us looking, laughing, and discovering new things. Sometimes when they are hard or painful, other relationships can help us learn about what to do. We call these other relationships *mediation,* which is a word for someone who makes sure that the rivers don't dam up and miss the chance to become great.

Relationships are precious, Caitlin. I know that yours will teach you everything you need to know.

Love and best wishes,

Madeleine

Relationships. They are the crucibles from which we come, shaped and sometimes scarred, but shining. They teach us about the world and how to be in it. They give us a multitude of messages about conflict, including what it is, how it happens, and what to do about it. When we need help with a conflict, we generally seek it through relationship. The helper must develop a relationship with us in order to help. We may resolve the issue that brought us or transform our understanding. Whatever we do, it will happen through relationship.

Eastern cultures understand this a little bit differently from the way dominant cultures in the West do. In Japan, for instance, a great deal of effort is directed to maintaining harmonious relationships and avoiding the open rupture of conflict. Smooth relationships prevent possible damage, disruption, and loss. There is an awareness that repair is never complete—that once the water of the relationship has spilled onto the floor, it can never be fully recaptured. There is also a shared desire for harmony to extend beyond individual relations to the smooth functioning of collective relationships.

I mention this not to valorize Eastern cultures and denigrate my own but to suggest that there is a golden nugget in this perspective. The nugget is the value placed on relationship. Although we may contend that pursuing harmony and muting conflict impedes the resolution of conflicts that exist beneath the surface or that a focus on collective cooperation can result in a tyranny toward conformity, the value of relationship stands on its own merits. In our individualistic, busy, efficiency-driven society, relationship is not always given the credit or the emphasis it deserves.

Of course, everyone values relationship. We all depend on it for survival. In our conflict processes, we build rapport with parties and emphasize the importance of building functional relations in parenting, in work life, and in communities. This book asks not *whether* but *how* we value relationship. How are relationships resources for our processes? How can we tap our relational and creative capacities in addressing conflicts? Relationships have emotional, physical, imaginative, and spiritual dimensions. Do our processes welcome these as equal partners with logic and rationality? What qualities of attention and relationship—to ourselves and to others—do we bring to our work?

I have a friend named George. Like several other friends, he will live in this book through stories. I hope he won't mind. It is through relationship that I learn. George brings a rare quality of attention to his relationships. As a consultant to companies around the world, he travels a great deal, and he needs to be available to a variety of people when he is in far places in the world. But he does not use e-mail. George invites his clients to phone or to fax to set a time, and then he phones back. They have conversations in real time, with voices that convey emotion, senses, and nuance. He wants to center his work, as he does his life, in relationship.

I don't want to get too far from my point, but being around George is different from being around others. When I am with him, he is fully available. He is not distracted by the things going on around us, nor do I notice him disappearing into his mind to consider some problem or issue he has been working on. He gives himself to the relationship as it unfolds in shared time. When we part, I feel as though I have received a rare gift. It is a gift of connection and relationship. It teaches me, encourages me, and calls me to pay attention to relationship as the foundation of everything else in my life.

When I say "relationship," I mean it in a spacious way. I mean my relationships with others and also my relationship with myself. Effective mediators and trainers cultivate interior dialogues and qualities that sustain their own being and doing in the world. They connect their work to their sense of purpose and meaning. They are meaning-making creatures; they create stories, invent metaphors, and rely on rituals. All of these connect us to others, to our own past and future, and to that which is bigger than any of us.

Relationship as the foundation of conflict bridging is not only individual and interpersonal; it is transpersonal. Whether we find meaning in nature, a deity, or energy within and around us, this dimension also feeds our work. We will explore ways to nurture all of these relationships in the pages of this book. Doing this is increasingly important in our fast-paced lives.

All of us are busy. I pack many things into every day, tending to family, teaching, writing, advising, mediating, exercising, driving, going home, shopping, making phone calls, e-mailing, going to the market, selecting clothes, planning. The list is longer than I ever finish. Relationships are too often rushed, fit-in, condensed into the too-small space on the list for the day. I struggle to slow down, to welcome the surprises and gifts that arise in conversation, family time, and meetings. Somehow the speed and efficiency that should leave us more time to relate leads us to take on more things, actually leaving us less time for relating and creating. We see this reflected in our conflict processes.

The Topography of Conflict

If we were to map our conflict processes, they would look more like a corridor than a diverse biosphere. We operate in a fairly narrow band of approaches, drawing on fewer resources than we have to offer. Our conflict practices mirror our individualistic and technically oriented culture. In professional settings, we devote defined lengths of time to staged processes that are designed to create closure. Out of our need for order, we restrict movement by sitting around tables, approaching conflict with the problem-solving parts of our brains. We break things down into bits to understand them. When there are strong emotions, we think of ways to manage them. Seldom do our process maps contemplate whole people and their relationships, with all of their varied artistry, grace, and wisdom. Even less do our processes take the symbolic level into account—the level where meaning is made, perceptions shape reality, and identities are defined and redefined in the dynamic dance of relationship.

Figure 1.1 depicts three levels of conflict and the kinds of strategies we have devised to bridge them. In the early days of the conflict resolution field, we noticed the integrative potential of "win-win" solutions. Conflict was seen to arise from competition over resources and differences over material things. To address it, we devised analytical frameworks, problem-solving approaches, and logical, staged processes. Success meant getting to "yes" about the material matters at issue. People needed to be separated from problems so they would not personalize issues and make them more difficult to resolve. This advanced the theory and practice in conflict resolution by substituting scientifically ordered thinking for "jungle theories" in which wits and luck had been the tools.

In a second wave of theory and practice, it was recognized that conflict does not arise in a vacuum. It arises from poor communication, often exacerbated by poorly designed systems and unequal power. Third parties were trained to employ a range of communication strategies such as active listening, using tools like restating and reframing in a staged process framework that is designed to manage and moderate emotional intensity. They were admonished to balance power, although the ways to do this were not always clear. Hoped-for outcomes included enhanced participation by all parties, better understanding, calm discussions, and acceptable outcomes. This advanced theory and practice by bringing attention to communication as the conduit for conflict resolution. But still, our capacity to generate lasting results was limited.

Conflicts do not arise simply because of differences over issues or miscommunication. Some of the most difficult conflicts we face have well-defined issues and have been the subject of countless efforts at calm communication. Despite attempts to extract people from problems and promote rationality, more conflicts have surfaced, emerging out of unaddressed roots like nested Russian dolls. This is because conflicts are indivisible from the relational context in which they arise. As depicted in the third level of Figure 1.1, they are bound up with the stories we tell, the ways we order and structure our thoughts and our feelings, and the cultural messages that shape our perceptions. They calcify and keep us stuck, or they shift, energizing our lifeblood with new ways forward.

If we want to bridge differences durably and respectfully, we cannot use a strategy centered in problem solving or in improving communication alone. We have to begin by acknowledging that our logic and common sense about how to communicate arise from our own ways of knowing—the ways we make meaning of our lives. These ways are influenced by culture, personality, context, and a whole system of knowing called our worldview. Along with cultural and personality differences, our worldviews are present in

Figure 1.1. Levels of Conflict and Conflict Strategies

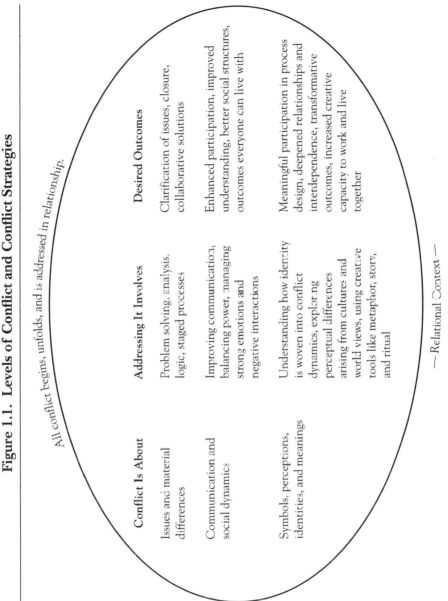

All conflict begins, unfolds, and is addressed in relationship.

Conflict Is About	Addressing It Involves	Desired Outcomes
Issues and material differences	Problem solving, analysis, logic, staged processes	Clarification of issues, closure, collaborative solutions
Communication and social dynamics	Improving communication, balancing power, managing strong emotions and negative interactions	Enhanced participation, improved understanding, better social structures, outcomes everyone can live with
Symbols, perceptions, identities, and meanings	Understanding how identity is woven into conflict dynamics, exploring perceptual differences arising from cultures and world views, using creative tools like metaphor, story, and ritual	Meaningful participation in process design, deepened relationships and interdependence, transformative outcomes, increased creative capacity to work and live together

— Relational Context —

conflict, even when everyone at the table looks the same and apparently comes from a shared context. A look at the abortion conflict or any other deeply rooted social conflict makes this clear.

As we realize that ways of being and seeing lead us to understand conflict differently, we see that we can neither conduct an analysis nor design and implement a process without inquiring into the cultural and perceptual frames of those involved. If we proceed without this inquiry, we impose our own culturally shaped ideas of process and appropriate skills on others. Seeking to make conflicts manageable, we may extract and compartmentalize them in a way that makes sense to us but may not be shared.

If we want to truly bridge differences, we begin not with formal analysis but with stories, metaphors, and shared experiences. Parties cannot tell us directly about their cultural ways of seeing or worldviews; much of this is outside conscious awareness. Believing that surfacing ways of seeing is central to bridging conflict, however, we learn about them through inviting in as much context as we can. Conflict lives in the stories we tell about ourselves and others, in the ways these stories shape our identities, and in the options we perceive. As stories are told and experiences are shared, relationships deepen and interventions emerge that fit organically with the parties and their contexts.

In composing the next wave of conflict resolution practice, practitioners and trainers need to access a range of resources rather than rely on limited approaches to bridging conflict that focus on logic and communication. As creative and relational beings by nature, we have emotional, imaginative, physical, and spiritual gifts that assist us in the central human task of getting along. Using them, we welcome diversity; we build a range of cultural ways of being and navigating conflict into our processes. As we resist circumventing the rhythm of our conflicts through premature problem solving, we use inquiry, dialogue, and imagination to shift relationships. As troubled relationships are shifted through sharing stories, dreams, and other facets of ourselves, we clear our minds and hearts for effectively solving the problems that divide us. Stories, dreams, and shared experiences are the tributaries that lead us to the river where connections are more visible. Sometimes we discover them in places we had not thought to look.

Tributaries Leading to the River

More than a quarter of a century after she had taught me the same subject, my seventy-seven-year-old friend Meredith came to guest lecture in my "Psychology of Personality" class. You could see the looks on the faces of my twenty-something students. Who was this gray, stooped woman in the faded sweater, and what would she have to say that would be contemporary enough to touch their world? Hearing that she had taught me before they were born only intensified their apprehension. They settled in with unobstructed views of the clock.

Meredith arranged herself stiffly in the chair with a writing table attached to it. The chair seemed ill fitting and rigid, rude to her arthritic joints. She spoke with a voice slightly raspy, uneven. She knew their discomfort and dubiousness. She had voiced it herself to me earlier: What could she have to tell them? It was true she had practiced as a psychologist for fifty years and taught as long, but these days she felt invisible and increasingly dismissed by others. She began with the questions she had prepared.

"Are you more like a daisy or a rose?" she inquired. Silence. One or two of the more vocal or compliant ones volunteered an answer. "Why?" Meredith asked. More silence. She moved on. "Are you more like the city or the country? Like a mountain or a valley?" There was a spattering of answers, uncomfortable laughter, incredulous looks. She persisted. "Are you more like a computer or a quill pen?" No embarrassing psychological meaning having been unearthed in relation to the earlier questions, a few more students ventured answers. Most of them chose the computer.

At this point, it must have occurred to Meredith that they had been born after quill pens were no longer everyday currency, because she offered her own explanation. "I am more like a quill pen," she demonstrated, holding her third finger in the air with her others tucked under, revealing the bump that decades of holding pens had produced. Holding the pose, she slowly moved her hand so that everyone in the room could see the pronounced bump on her raised third finger.

This gesture was met with muffled giggles that matured into laughter and broke out among even the most reticent students.

Meredith looked out at her audience mystified, then down to her third finger, then out of the corner of her eye at me. And then she joined them, with deep belly laughter from the lower register on a tenor sax. When the mirth subsided, she apologized for giving them "the finger" inadvertently and moved into her presentation.

The entire climate in the class had shifted. Someone who would do what she had done, even inadvertently, and then laugh about it could not be all bad. Meredith knew to follow the tributaries of surprise and interest to the relational river. Now students sat in postures of openness and interest. They listened, participated, offered ideas. They asked questions about her practice. Meredith had changed for them, from someone outside their world to someone they welcomed in. A stranger still, she had come into relationship with them and this changed everything.

Their stereotypes and assumptions originally coalesced into a kind of groupthink that yielded the conclusion: "She's not one of us." Only after judgment had left their minds were they able to draw on the spirit of curiosity they had brought to earlier classes. After the incident, they referred to her affectionately as "that lady who gave us the finger," going out of their way on campus to greet her and introduce her to their friends. They had come into relationship with her, and it had changed them all.

Relationships as Resources

Relationships are the places where conflict arises. They are more than locations of blame, hurt, and pain. Problems cannot be solved without the energy and the resources of the people who created them. The question then becomes how to engage people with each other constructively so that problems can be addressed. As we saw with our Y2K computer problems, changing one piece of programming code necessitates other changes. We have to work at the level of the relational system to get results. Where are our problems if not in relationships with people? Where are the resources to address them if not in the relationships? Where is the will to sustain transformation or resolution if not in the relationships of communities, families, work groups?

When we think of relationships, we tend to think of them narrowly. We mediate between two people rather than involve their staffs or their families. We help spouses divide marital property without inquiring about the role extended family members or children may play in decision making. We seek to separate and moderate people and their relationships, structuring our processes by invoking ground rules and turn taking. What would happen if we stopped to consider how these relationships developed and grew and invited the same resources in to address the conflicts that arose in the process? How would our conflict practice change if we saw relationships not as extractable entities but as woven into cultural and worldview contexts that give them texture, richness, and intrinsic worth?

As relationships begin and deepen, we draw on many creative resources. We experience physical, emotional, imaginative, and spiritual connections. We do things together; we feel for and with each other. We share visions and possibilities, cultural and personal ways of knowing, weaving them together with our past. Looking for similarities, we find connections rather than differences. When our relationships through work and play are meaningful, we experience synergy, energy, and inspiration.

At the same time, focusing on relationship when it seems to be disintegrating rather than flourishing is difficult. It means going against the momentum of our thought processes, the ones that help us feel OK, justified, right, or angry. The difficulty is that these thought processes also work to narrow or flatten our resources in conflict. We become defensive, self-protective, closed. From this state, we do not have access to the resources that flowed so freely during the development of our relationship. It is just plain uncomfortable to be in the muck of unresolved emotions, unsalved hurts, and tumbling dreams. Our response to this discomfort has been to construct processes that largely operate in a thin band, drawing on a finite set of communication and structuring tools. Sometimes these processes insulate us from our full potential for exploration, inquiry, discernment, and discovery.

It is true that relationships are complex and unpredictable. No matter how much we may wish to control them, we cannot. Our relationships are stories brought alive. Like anything living, they change. Some changes move us in the direction of openness and exploration. Others reinforce our separateness, our differences, and our boundaries. How can mediators, facilitators, and trainers help, given this complexity and the difficulty of accessing expansive creative tools from a constricted space? Sometimes relational complexity leads us away from creative tools, daunted by the many variables. We prefer a process arising from our needs for certainty, calm, and closure to the dance of uncertainty that may or may not produce alchemy.

Add all of this complexity to real pressures of time, results, cost, and accountability. We exist in a far-from-perfect world, and we need to get things done. Most of us are uncomfortable enough with conflict that we want to get things done quickly. In our focus on speed and efficiency, we may not see relationships for the sources of resilience they can be. What would happen if we grounded our processes in this resilience, using creative tools to build new containers for damaged relationships?

After all, the cost of neglecting relationships is considerable. In personal lives, it leads to fragmentation, loss, and disorientation. In communities, it leads to disintegration, conflict, and violence. In our world, it leads to paralysis, waste, and the loss of countless innocent lives. Let's consider what happens when we place relationship at the heart of our study and practice of conflict, to inform what we see, what we do, and how we approach it. Will you imagine this with me and join me in inquiry about the capacities and tools that best support a creative, relational approach?

Capacities for Relational Processes

Imagine a process that draws on all of our relational capacities—a process in which emotional fluency is valued along with incisive analysis; our powerful capacity to envision is paired with symbolic actions that help build the scaffolding to get there; there is lots and lots of room for divergence along the way to closure or transformation or whatever we define as outcome; and creativity breathes life into "givens," thus inviting originality, genius, and attention to "chance" references and ideas.

Analysis, reason, and logical problem solving may help address conflicts, but they are not all we need. Not only are they situated in particular cultural understandings but they obscure other parts of the picture. To use them alone is to be like the woman who took a transatlantic cruise after saving for years. Each evening she hid in her room, eating the cheese and crackers she had brought from home while other passengers dined on exotic delicacies, accompanied by fine music in exquisite rooms. Only at the end of the voyage did she realize that meals were included in the price of her passage. She had missed a part of the voyage she would have enjoyed immensely, narrowing her experience because of her mistaken assumption. Logic and reason are like the seascapes she loved; they are an essential part of the picture. But the whole can be even more satisfying when our full range of relational capacities is available to our processes.

Bringing emotional, spiritual, physical, and imaginative resources to conflict gives us many more routes to resolution or transformation. Our processes also become accessible and useful to a much wider range of people. Not only are these resources important for building and sustaining good relationships, they validate different ways of learning, knowing, and approaching conflict. They help us bridge cultural and personality differences; they help equalize power; they broaden the wisdom available for changing the form and dynamics of conflict.

Educators know that presenting material in different modes, at different paces, in ways that promote interaction and reflection is effective in promoting learning. Visual, auditory, and kinesthetic learners are served when some material is presented in their preferred format. So conflict resolvers and trainers who think broadly of their processes draw on all the senses, as well as on their capacity for emotional intelligence, spiritual meaning making, physical movement, and creative imagination.

There is sure to be resistance to doing things differently. Bureaucratic cultural expectations color our processes, leading to expectations of traditional formats and meetinglike settings. Many of us are uncomfortable with conflict, with its emotional intensity and relational complexity. Developing creative and multimodal tools requires that we "do" and "be" differently, situating relationships at the center of our approaches. In all of this, we will face challenges from within ourselves as we question our givens and step a degree or two out of our comfort zones. We will also face questions from parties and trainees who want and need to get to the point, to arrive at yes, to leave the discomfort of conflict behind.

In our diverse world, cultivating comfort with paradox and ambiguity is fast becoming a life skill. We already draw on it in conflict interventions, telling parties we have to go slowly at the beginning to go fast later. We suggest that broadening the conversation through investigating interests will advance our ultimate aim of finding specific solutions. We can also open the possibility that there are a variety of complementary ways to shift through conflict. We need two kinds of resources: our human, relational capacities and an array of tools. These relational capacities include our abilities to feel and sense, dream and envision, physically enact, and create and discover. As we have seen, we draw on these capacities as we build relationships. We will explore how these capacities can inform our conflict processes, bringing texture, maneuverability, awareness, and results.

From these capacities arise an infinite number of creative tools. They range from the dramatic, like psychodrama (acting out situations for therapeutic reasons), to the ordinary, like the universal act of telling a story. They touch our senses, referencing physical, emotional, and spiritual experiences. They speak to us of the underground rivers that connect us, building a foundation of relationship at the center of our processes. We explore three of the most basic, yet most powerful, tools in this book: story, metaphor, and ritual.

This book is about using these capacities and tools to enhance our practice and achieve success in our teaching. It is about strength and resilience in relationships as a resource in our work, even when it is hard to see where we are going. It is about noticing times that stand out for their brilliance, their poignancy, or their surprise. Can you think of times when something unexpected or out of the ordinary happened in a mediation or a classroom? Times when you or others were especially creative? Where were the sparks and the skraps in these moments?[1] What stood out as particularly shining or tarnished? What has this shown you about relationship and conflict? What has it shown you about creativity? My experience is that these sparks and skraps arise unplanned. I do not program them; I cannot predict them. I only learn from the serendipity they deliver or from the discomfort they cause—discomfort that leads me to change an approach next time.

Sparks and skraps have topographical reality. Sparks are the hills we stand on from which we can see a long way. Things fall into perspective. Relationships grow closer. Creativity flourishes. Thoughts and feelings are integrated. Skraps are the valleys from which the summit seems remote and difficult. Distances are hard to judge and distorted. Relationships may be strained and creativity seems inaccessible. They are the "ouch" in the classroom, the dart in the mediation. They hurt.

Conflict is mountainous terrain. It happens in human relational systems that are bigger than we are. Mountains happen. This book is about climbing, playing, reaching the summit, and exploring. It is about accessing creativity in the valley and empathy on the peak. It is about developing repertoires that span the altitudes and reach to the depths. It is about curiosity, hope, and grace in the face of conflict.

Seven Mountains: Principles of a Creative, Relational Approach to Conflict

To conflict we bring energy and the capacity to solve problems using all of our resources. We bring tools to help us make the journey. At last, we seek the grace of acknowledging that we could not have made it by ourselves. Conflict is a relational journey. Curious about ways to enhance our work and play, we traverse seven mountains that are central to a creative, relational perspective.

1. Circle Mountain: A Holistic Approach

We are now at the point in the development of the conflict resolution field where we need to reexamine and refocus. For years, we have worked to develop staged processes and communication skills training modules to help people become fluent with conflict resolution. We had to do so if we were to bring awareness of the positive potential that conflict brings and of the possibility of handling it in ways that yield integrative solutions and less animosity than previous approaches. We had to formulate structures that could be taught easily, in a language that made conflict a part of our everyday lexicon. This is the phonics of bridging conflict.

It is now time to balance phonics with whole language, to look at the meaning and the sense of what we are doing and ask these questions:

- How is relationship a resource in our work?
- What are the core capacities for third parties and trainers in conflict, and how do these complement the approaches that we already use?
- How can we infuse conflict resolution or transformation with creativity?
- What helps us bring our whole selves into the service of addressing conflict?

I have taught in this field for fifteen years. When I began, I was enthusiastic about the discovery of a constructive way to approach conflict. I taught principled negotiation and helped many lawyers, judges, counselors, scientists, scholars, and others learn to distinguish an interest from a position. It excited me to see the paradigm shift that took place. It excites me still to participate in questioning the ways we have done conflict in the past and proposing new ones that respect and honor relationship.

Increasingly, however, students in my classes tell me that they leave with more questions than answers. This is because I have come to believe that one of the most important jobs we have as educators and intervenors is to get the questions right. This means wondering what else we might bring to the project rather than traversing the same ground. I hope, as the poet Rilke[2] suggests, that we might collectively live into some of the answers. I wonder:

- Are there ways we can draw on ourselves and our relationships in addressing conflict that we have not yet conceived?
- Are there sectors where creative, relational practices have evolved that could inform other sectors and groups of practitioners?
- Where are questions being generated that can inform and focus our explorations in new ways?
- How can we integrate creative, relational tools into our practices?

As a field, we have achieved wide exposure for our conflict resolution and transformation ideas. Few people are confused these days about the difference between *mediation* and *meditation*. Mediation services are available in many communities, schools, and workplaces. At the same time, the many trained mediators we have produced have not eliminated intractable conflict. Differences in class, ethnicity, race, gender, and other identities seem to be intensifying rather than diminishing. What does a mountaintop view of our field show us about what else we can do and how else we can be?

This book seeks to contribute some answers. It looks to build trails up the mountain that respect the ecosystem and suggest themselves from the terrain. No superhighways are contemplated. Rather, climbing Circle Mountain is a process of integration, of gathering wisdom along the way through openness to diverse ways of seeing, doing, and being. It is to acknowledge where we have come, how we have affected systems around us and how they have affected us. As we do this, we will see that change occurs through relationship, that our hearts have contributed, along with our minds, to our greatest successes.

2. Heart Mountain: Relationship as Resource

As we have seen, relationship is both the medium in which conflict sprouts and the soil that births and sustains resolution. Putting relationship at the center of our processes situates us so that we can see the many resources it offers. This does not mean, as one of my colleagues worries, that we should all sit around and sing "Kumbaya." There is too much tumult, too many barriers, for that to work. When we center our response to conflict in relationship, we are called to authenticity and openness. Conflict was never successfully addressed by welcoming in only the treble clef. Our whole range of experience becomes a resource for our processes, drawing on many ways of knowing, being, and relating that are learned through pain and loss as well as joy and connection.

Because we are different culturally and personally, no one of us has a prescription that can be swallowed whole by others. We can only work together, devising ways that fit particular times, groups, needs, and understandings. As we work, we create a relational space in which shifts and change can happen. We always work within boundaries. Part of our job is to discern where the boundaries are, how they both inhibit and support progress, and ways it may be possible to shift them.

Boundaries are important to the healthy functioning of relationships. In their absence, there may be confusion, waste, and even resentment, exploitation, or injury. Boundaries facilitate safety and spontaneity by letting us know limits. They free us to explore, relate, and inquire within a safe space. As a facilitator, teacher, and mediator, I engage everyone in naming, setting, and maintaining boundaries so that learning can take place. I try to get everyone on the same page, or at least in the same book. This is not always easy. Difficulty with initial boundary setting signals a need for more relational work before engaging the substance of issues.

Some of the hardest conflicts arise when different relational expectations are brought to a process. I remember when a friend taught a week-long course about women and global leadership some years ago. She is an accomplished scholar, and many of the students came with high expectations, born of reading her work. It happened that they were all women. But there the similarity ended. Some of the women believed that a course of this nature would, at long last, invite all dimensions of their identities into the room. They could engage in spiraling dialogue, sharing their experiences as mothers alongside their experiences in the boardroom, all in a seamless web. They resisted structure, as well as all but the most relaxed boundaries and most attempts to focus their participation. They were there for the journey, unconcerned about destination.

Others came to challenge themselves with theories and facts in the service of advancing their career paths as global women leaders. They grew impatient at prolonged sharing. They wanted to move through material, not into it. And they wanted to leave their multifaceted identities at the door, coming together as learners with a common, focused objective. These women resisted experiential exercises, especially as the course went on and they encountered more and more of what they perceived to be diversions from the agenda.

One particularly challenging day, my colleague asked her class to form small discussion groups. As it was warm and sunny, they dispersed outside the building. It took her some time to realize that she had not told them when to come back. Surprised at her lapse in clarity and boundary setting, she realized that the struggle to bridge the two kinds of agendas in the class was more wearing than she had known. She found them, scattered on the grass, and invited them back into the classroom.

Part of what saved the course was my friend's awareness and articulateness about the process. When she did reassemble the class, she engaged them in dialogue about how to proceed. She shared her genuine frustration at the level of conflict among class members and resistance to nearly every suggested activity. Together, class members negotiated a way of proceeding that balanced the concerns of those who wanted to explore with the needs of others for information and closure. Although the trail had switchbacks, the women did make it up the mountain. On the last day of class, they brought my friend a beautiful hand-potted bowl to symbolize their full learning experience—a remembrance of their now-precious relationships.

Seeing the class together after their final meeting, I was amazed at how close they seemed and how much affection was demonstrated among those who had acted earlier in quite adversarial ways to each other and the instructor. The affection lasted; many of the women remained in touch with each other and with my friend in the years to come.

Relationships strengthened in the fire of conflict can be resilient and enduring. For those of us engaged in helping to build and hold relational containers, it is important to remember that the process is not a straight line. We see ourselves through the mirror of relationship in ways we cannot when we are alone. Relationship shows us our blind spots, our weak points, our surest strengths. Our most important job in conflict may be to find a way to hold the mirror high so that as we see ourselves, we also see the choices we make in seeing. Exercising choice, we look for places where our hearts are partners with our minds in engaging relationships. This is the journey of Heart Mountain.

3. Magic Mountain: Welcoming Surprises

All dimensions of relationship are realized most expansively in the creative process, which calls us to attention, invention, and change. All of us are fluent in these processes, though some of us have built fences around the realms in which we show it. We ask ourselves *whether* we are creative (and many of us answer no) rather than *how* we are creative. We think of creativity as a thing we either have or do not have rather than as a process available to all of us. How do you manifest creativity? How do you be creative? When you bring a creative moment to your awareness, what comes? Take a moment to notice the feelings, thoughts, and physical sensations that are present. Now consider what it would mean to experience the same vitality in the midst of conflict.

Engaging creative processes requires suspending judgment at least temporarily, substituting a spirit of inquiry and openness to outcome. Judgment will shut down creativity every time, just as it stopped members of my class from relating warmly to Meredith. Judgment has nipped more creative possibilities in the bud than lack of time, funds, or imagination ever could. Turned inward, judgment inhibits individual creative expression. We second-guess ourselves, minimize our contributions, and mute our voices. Critical judgments also build fences between us and others. Believing we know, we do not inquire. Thus we quash possibilities for transformation and even peaceful coexistence.

When we suspend judgment, we acknowledge that other ways of being and knowing exist alongside our own. We get genuinely curious about how these work, how they lead to ways of seeing and being, how they translate into behaviors. As we do this, our ways of being with each other and with conflict shift, opening new possibilities and revealing again the importance of relationship as a learning place, a place from which quests, tests, and gifts arise.

Recently I taught a course titled "Spirituality and Conflict." The course was broad and general and covered a variety of topics from forgiveness to resilience—from an exploration of cultural ways people make meaning to an examination of reconciliation commissions and processes. How could I join with the class to hold all of this together in a coherent whole? How could I

- Introduce and define the topic of spirituality in a way that included everyone yet was not so broad and abstract that it could not be grasped or integrated?
- Convey the universality in the topic and invite expansive thinking yet create boundaries for comfort and clarity?

- Engage participants in a way that would make the creativity inherent in spirituality and the spiritual component of creativity apparent?

Before the class began, I saw a friend who is a docent at a modern art museum. I shared with her my judgments about modern art and my fear that, if I suspended them, I would be left only with my lack of understanding and frustration. I had dealt with this by avoiding modern art exhibits. If I had thought of connecting art to my class, it would surely have been Renaissance pictures of angels before any piece from the twentieth century. "But Michelle," she said in an excited voice, "modern art is all about spirituality. That is why there is so much space. It invites us to go within, to explore meanings and meaning making!"

Together we generated an idea. Rather than a traditional meeting for the first class, we met at the museum. With her gentle leadership, we walked, watched, and listened our way into dialogue about spirituality, conflict, and creativity. Surrounded by the stark whites and grays of the museum walls, ceilings, and floors, we found warmth and connection. Encountering paintings and sculptures that would have intimidated or put us off in the past, we found surprises and insights.

We began in front of an egg-shaped piece resting on the floor, covered in pure, deep-blue pigment. It was quietly lighted, a symbol of life and paradox. It seemed deep and shallow, concave and convex at once. Setting aside our initial anxiety about not understanding it, we began to share our responses. The piece elicited feelings of attraction and awe, fear and distancing. It was an inviting cocoon. Or was it bottomless and frightening? Some saw nobility, others intensity, others ambiguity.

This experience led us to a dialogue about the paradoxes of conflict and our ambiguous feelings about approaching it. The theme of spirituality wove through our observations, touching issues of boundary and mystery, infinity and simplicity, transformation and loss. As we moved to view other items in the gallery, we built on these themes, reflecting on the different messages conveyed by the artists about spirituality and existence. Were they communicating the importance of transcendence or of humble acceptance? Did the pieces speak to releasing attachments or of creative connection to our world and each other? Our exploration created sparks that enlivened later conversations and a quality of relationship among us that made learning deeper and more productive.

Only later did I reflect that the whole experience mirrored the creative process. It began with an opening, sparked by my initial suspension of judgment about modern art. Together we moved through exploration and inquiry to insight and integration. We composed our experience in the moments together, releasing our thoughts, feelings, and imaginings into the museum space. By the time we left, we felt much closer than when we had come. We felt the satisfaction of having explored without reducing, of having shared without contesting, of having entertained paradox without retreating. Every participant agreed that this had set a generative tone for the class, where there would be plenty of time later to weave theories into the pattern of our experiential web. We had set a rich table for ourselves, one loaded with textures, visions, scents, and sounds. And so we made ourselves available to surprise and experienced creative synergy that arose, not from any one of us but among us. This is the gift of Magic Mountain.

4. Goldmine Mountain: Involving Our Whole Selves

We have said that effectively bridging conflict is at its heart a creative, relational process. Creative processes call for the active engagement of all of our parts:

- Our physical selves, who enact relationship and creativity, receive discernment, provide direction, and embody flexibility
- Our emotional selves, from whence comes resilience, interpersonal facility, empathy, clarity, and hope
- Our imagining selves, who visualize, hear, taste, and touch possibilities into reality, giving our intuition form
- Our spiritual selves, who connect us to larger contexts and to meaning making and exploring mystery through the natural world and that which we cannot touch

Each of these capacities is explored in a separate chapter; each is connected to, or coexists with, the others. Our peak experiences draw on all or many of them together. Our conflict processes, as we have seen, tend to underuse and underappreciate them. Yet our conflict stories are full of references to these facets of our experience. One story comes to mind.

We were outside Dublin, meeting to work on issues relating to the Palestinian-Israeli conflict. I was part of the facilitation team for this gathering of diplomats from around the world. It was the early 1990s, and the region was unsettled. What would happen if a group of people who understood international relations and the skills of diplomacy came together in dialogue about Israeli-Palestinian issues? For the first two days, nothing much seemed to happen at all. Rhetoric was familiar, as issues of identity and security were spoken about in the guise of confidence-building measures. Sessions were sometimes intense but more often verged on tedious. Someone has said that watching mediation is a bit like watching paint dry. It is hard to see it happening and it takes a long time. In this workshop, it was worse. I was not sure that any paint was sticking to the walls at all.

On the third day of this five-day workshop, a trip had been planned. We loaded ourselves onto buses and headed up the east coast of Ireland to Belfast. Organizers thought that seeing another deeply divided society would give us food for thought or at least reality therapy. In fact, the visits we paid to an organization dedicated to bicommunal housing and the sites of bombed buildings had less impact than the hours we spent being jostled in the bus. On the bus, we learned that one of the participants was a novelist. He wrote every evening after work for four or five hours and had produced several books. Another raised horses. There was talk about children, spouses, cars, and traffic. We shared stories about travel disasters and childhood dreams, about New York City and the streets of Cairo. When we arrived back in Dublin, the relational climate among us had shifted.

Over the remaining days, we worked together with energy and imagination. We did not solve the complex issues involved, but we engaged in authentic conversations and exchanged ideas that were followed up after the workshop. The physical act of taking a bus trip got us out of our problem-solving minds, tapping our emotional intelligence in the service of building relationships. We had shared dreams, and this helped us take an imaginative look at our subject, the conflict between Israel and Palestine. We had shown each other parts of our lives that matter deeply and so shared some small part of our ways of making meaning.

What did we learn from all of this? Should we always take bus trips together when trying to address problems? Prescriptive and narrow as that is, it is not as wrong as it might sound. Designing opportunities for movement and relational engagement, as well as for sharing dreams and purposes, is important in our processes. Taking a break and moving our focus away from a problem that we have tried hard to solve without a breakthrough is an important step toward a creative outcome. In so doing, we share parts of ourselves that become relational resources to our processes. We literally share who we are in the service of what we are trying to do. This is the gift of Goldmine Mountain.

5. Noble Mountain: Being Our Teachings

What images come to mind when you hear the word *noble*? Perhaps you remember a person, perhaps a piece of art or a place. Is it the Grand Canyon, stretching out in endless possibility, or the Milky Way splashed onto a magnificent desert sky? Is it a black-and-white image of Gandhi or Mother Teresa, gazing at you in calm sureness, or is it a painting by Georgia O'Keefe, inviting you into the delicate heart of an exquisite flower? Nobility conjures awareness of the big picture. We call an act noble when it serves others. We feel admiration and appreciation for noble acts. They inspire us to stretch ourselves, to be leaders, to listen to that which calls us.

Leaders in conflict resolution bring sets of techniques and understanding of processes but, most important, they bring themselves. Without the self, none of the other things are useful. We saw at Goldmine Mountain that we enhance our processes by bringing all of ourselves. Noble Mountain asks that we consider how vision and purpose direct the selves that we bring. At Noble Mountain, big-picture questions reveal themselves as we climb. What is our purpose? How does our work relate to our purpose? Beyond this mediation or that process, what is our vision for ourselves, for others, and for our world? The questions persist, moving to deeper and deeper levels. It is not enough to say that our purpose is to help and our work as mediators or facilitators is helpful. When we have climbed our last mountain and look back at all the others, what will be the thread that holds them together? What unique gifts do we bring? How do we bring them? What is the legacy we live into every day? These are big questions. Having climbed several mountains already, you may wonder why these questions are necessary here. Does a book about conflict resolution really need to treat such weighty topics? For two reasons, the answer is yes.

First, as we tell our clients, we really need to know where we are going if we want to arrive there. Purpose provides focus, fuel, and feeling to our journeys. Second, our dominant culture surrounds us with values of consumerism, pleasure, and quick fixes. Just below the surface, there is a hunger for meaning, community, and connection with others; we seek connection with the natural and spiritual worlds, with ourselves. Knowing our purpose is a way of deepening our relationship with ourselves. As we do this, we are better able to engage relationships with others, including those who are different from us. This is because comfort and clarity with ourselves leaves us with less of a need to change others. As we attend to our own internal voice and walk our own purposeful path, we can be of service without bringing our unmet needs to the table and imposing them unconsciously on others.

Articulating our purpose brings focus to our actions, calling us to decision and discipline about what fits and what does not fit well. Duane Elgin, in his book *Voluntary Simplicity,* quotes Richard Gregg, who originated the term *voluntary simplicity:* "Voluntary simplicity . . . means singleness of purpose . . . an ordering and guiding of our energy and our desires, a partial restraint in some directions in order to secure a greater abundance of life in other directions. It involves a deliberate organization of life for a purpose."[3] To see the value of this, we look at the alternatives.

Have you ever had the kind of morning where you set out to do one thing and never got to it? There is the phone call that interrupts, the kitchen drawer that needs tidying, the dog who won't take his medication, and the agenda to prepare for tomorrow's meeting. Walking past the mirror, you see that your hair needs attention. On the table is a half-written letter you had promised yourself you would get out. The morning disappears into fragmented doing, none of it wrong, all of it at some level necessary. But the "one thing" lies unfinished, perhaps not even started.

Sometimes we treat purpose like this: it is something we plan to get to after we clear up everything else that demands our attention. And so it waits for a time when, climbing Noble Mountain, the questions come back again in ways they cannot be ignored. Then we call a time out and commit to exploring our purpose.

We can learn about our purpose through self-reflection and dialogue with others, as well as by watching ourselves in the world. What do we try to do, to be, in our interactions with others? Do we want acknowledgment, harmony, victory, security, or connection? Do we seek adventure, creativity, joy, solace, or certainty? How do the things we care about manifest themselves in our relationships with others, with the natural world, with spirit? We may want many of these things, but we can't pay attention to them all at once. Our habits of attention lead us to look for and cultivate particular things in our lives and pay less attention to others.

Richard Leider has been working with leaders to discern and realize their purposes for many years. Most often, he reports, purpose involves contributing to someone or something outside the self. It may be "bringing joy to others" or "being a small part of making others' lives big." For the past few years, my answer to this question has been consistent. My purpose is to live creatively in relationship with others, the natural and spiritual worlds, and myself, sharing and receiving gifts of discovery and connection. A primary way that I share my gifts and facilitate discovery is through writing. When days go by and my writing is neglected, something inside feels "off." I have an internal alarm that starts to ring when life gets too busy to attend to a core part of my purpose. It calls me back to the computer, sometimes late at night or early in the morning, to write a letter, to add to a book, to let my thoughts take form on paper.

Try asking yourself this question, or get a friend to help by asking you repeatedly: What do I want to do and be in the world? Once you answer, pose the question again. If a friend is helping you, ask the person not to comment or share views but simply to thank you for each response and ask the same question again. This is not our ordinary way of conversing, and it may feel awkward at first. As the question is posed again and again, you will get beneath the quick, ready answers to deeper answers. What stands out as important to your life mission, your purpose? Your answers may surprise you. After doing this, consider how the ways you have set up your life and work match your purpose.

My goal here is not to prescribe a particular purpose. Recognizing diverse ways of knowing and of making meaning suggests that there are an infinite number of purposes. Each of us can only discover purpose for ourselves. Others cannot impose it. Naming purpose ourselves and keeping it in everyday awareness is a powerful step toward realizing it. Noble Mountain represents many different purposes. If we could survey people in the field of conflict resolution, we would find many reasons for involvement. This is excellent news; it means that we can serve diverse people in diverse ways that fit with our wide range of purposes.

We teach others that conflict-bridging skills are life skills. We magnify those skills through engagement in creative, relational processes. It follows that we cannot draw artificial boundaries between what we do in our work and how we are in other facets of our lives. As I seek to engage disputing parties in creative invention, practicing at home with my children and partner helps. It helps not just in expanding and strengthening my repertoire but in contributing to the alignment of my purpose with all facets of my work and play. As there is alignment, there will be congruence, and I will grow in my capacity to do imaginative and creative work from the solid foundation of Noble Mountain.

A story about Gandhi speaks powerfully of this. He was asked by a mother to tell her child not to eat sugar. "Come back in two weeks and I will tell him," he assured her. She did as he asked. When she returned, he spoke to her child about the ill effects of sugar and the benefits of abstaining. When the mother asked why he had requested two weeks, he told her that he had to stop eating sugar before he could ask anyone else to do so. Gandhi knew the power of congruence. Through congruence—living his principles in his actions—he changed systems and upset injustices.

Daniel Bowling and David Hoffman,[4] two leaders in our field, have written persuasively about the personal qualities needed in conflict intervention and training. They suggest that once we have mastered conflict resolution skills and an intellectual understanding of processes, our next developmental task is to develop and integrate personal qualities of clarity, awareness, and centeredness. As they acknowledge, there are many paths to these qualities.

This is reinforced in another book in our field, Deborah Kolb's book *When Talk Works*.[5] She shows persuasively that mediators and facilitators are diverse in their approaches. What each of them brings is a strong, authentic personality, creativity that fits with their way of seeing and being, and ways of building influential relationships. Although Kolb's work does not explore *purpose* explicitly, the clarity and coherence demonstrated by her interviewees suggests its presence. Third parties in Kolb's book match their work in the world with what they care about internally, thus manifesting congruence.

We live in a time when ideas about congruence are countered in popular culture. Politicians and other leaders would have us believe that it is possible to segment our lives, to be ruthless or unfaithful in one setting and compassionate and trustworthy in another. Without entering this philosophical debate, I will share my personal answer. It is my experience that I am more at peace and therefore more effective when my purpose and my actions are aligned. Alignment brings energy and clarity to my work and play.

Thinking of this takes me back to an early summer afternoon. I was sitting in my ample office with the window open. A breeze wafted in from the manicured green lawn, bordered by neatly trimmed pink and mauve azaleas. It was quiet and my work on patients' files was proceeding. My life in general seemed settled and secure since I had accepted the job of patient advocate at a large mental hospital. True, I was not experiencing much success in changing conditions at the hospital or achieving releases into supportive communities for my clients. I was working in a system where control and power were centralized, where my clients were impoverished not only financially but also in life choices. It was hard to see how an atmosphere of collaboration could be cultivated in the midst of such a huge and powerful bureaucracy. Protracted litigation and efforts to change legislation loomed ahead; it was a difficult and adversarial road.

Then the telephone rang. I was offered a new position, directing a research project in conflict resolution and culture at a university in another city. To my surprise, I heard myself accept. The acceptance came from deep inside of me, from the place where I was crystal clear about my purpose.

Earlier that year, I had visited a psychotherapist for one session, seeking to clarify my career direction. It had become very clear to me that my heart was in conflict resolution rather than the adversarial practice of law; I wanted to creatively and collaboratively bridge differences in relationship with colleagues and clients. The new opportunity fit this purpose elegantly, so I stepped into a career that has given me space to create and contribute in relationship with many others I deeply admire. This taught me the importance of knowing and clarifying purpose as I go along. It is hard for us to be congruent when we have a fuzzy idea about what we are aligning with.

When there is not alignment, tension arises. Sometimes I live with that tension because there are external pressures to proceed. It is matter of degree; I may do something I know is not central to my purpose because I am asked or because it is important to another. This works as long as it is not opposite my purpose and as long as it does not violate any deep belief. Sometimes the tension arises because I have not been clear enough about my purpose in taking on a project, only realizing later that it is taking me away from my purpose. Most of us do things that are not central to our purposes, and we sometimes feel ourselves out of alignment. And still we can be effective. We compose our lives around themes, and the themes shift, changing the way the light shines on our purposes in a dynamic and intriguing dance.

The journey up Noble Mountain has a fluid quality. It is neither extreme nor rigid. It just asks us to keep our purpose in view and to ask questions of alignment and congruence of ourselves as we climb.

6. Mirror Mountain: Transcending Limitations

At the summit of Noble Mountain, we come to see our purpose and its power to illuminate our actions. On the way down the mountain, we encounter obstacles and tests that challenge our resolve and our clarity. These obstacles can obscure our view of connections—connections between ourselves and others, our experiences and their impact on our lives and work, our histories and what they lead us to perceive as well as what they may obscure. Recognizing these connections is the gift of Mirror Mountain.

Some of the obstacles have their roots in our early histories as peoples and as individuals. As we seek to engage our creative purpose, many of us have to grapple with the limitations of our beliefs about ourselves. Whatever the stories we tell ourselves, they have a great deal of influence on our actions and effectiveness in helping others in conflict.

A Chinese Canadian woman came to my workshop on creativity and conflict transformation. She was respectful and earnest, speaking when asked and otherwise silent. I asked the class to work individually, remembering and writing down the messages they had been given about creativity as children. An astonishing number of participants had received messages from parents, teachers, and others about limitations on their creativity. I asked them to draw a picture of creativity in their own lives as they would like to imagine it. What would it look like? What colors would it be?

She did the activities intently. Slowly her face seemed to relax and she set down her pencil. She related the story of how she had moved from China as a young girl with her immigrant parents. They had opened a Chinese restaurant in western Canada. While her brothers were involved in after-school athletics, she helped at the restaurant. It was a given; she was needed. Her life was busy and full. She learned that it took a lot of hard work to get ahead.

She remembered how, as a little girl, she had loved to draw. Late in elementary school, she was given a scholarship to a summer art program. There she drew animals and flowers, earning the praise of her teachers. At the end of the program, she had a portfolio of treasured pictures of shaded charcoal, pen-and-ink, and pencil sketches. She put them in the basement of her parents' home. They stayed there during all of her school years. They stayed while she went to the university and when she married. When she visited her parents, she often disappeared downstairs and got them out, just for the pleasure of seeing them again.

She was close to tears as she said that she wanted to redraw the lines of her life, to reclaim that part of herself who had fallen outside the boundaries of schoolgirl and family helper. It was a passion that called her through the years since she had drawn two decades before. She felt relief to articulate it and energy to pursue it. She was living a script of security and self-deferment, but her art still called her to relationship. It called her to a relationship with her creative self, with her capacity to extend herself and expand her experience. Later she told me that the art had made a difference in her relationship with her husband and in her work. "I feel opened up inside," she confided.

Reflecting on this experience, I saw again that creativity is a sensitive area for many of us. Imagining that it is something we "are" or "are not," our wish to be creative seems like the desire to change our height or our blood type. Considering it narrowly, we see it in others, not ourselves. Setting it apart, we do not integrate it into our everyday selves. We know intuitively it is important to bridging conflict and to living a satisfying life, yet we are threatened by our perceived inadequacy and unsettled by our uncertainty about what creativity is and how it might manifest in our lives. I am reminded of Marianne Williamson's words, as quoted by Nelson Mandela in his acceptance speech when he became president of South Africa: "Our deepest fear is not that we are inadequate. Our deepest fear is that we are powerful beyond measure. It is our light, not our darkness, that most frightens us. We ask ourselves, Who am I to be brilliant, talented, gorgeous, fabulous? Actually, who are you not to be?"[6]

As we climb Mirror Mountain, we remember that what we see outside ourselves is a reflection of who we are inside ourselves. We can live into spacious ways of being, using our physical, emotional, imagining, and meaning-making capacities. As we magnify our creative capacities, we are better able to assist others in bridging conflict.

7. Invention Mountain: Creative Tools

Cultivating our capacities for relationship and creativity, we discover new ways of engaging with others on Invention Mountain. The toolbox for a relational approach is bottomless. We can reach in at different times and find surprises among our tried-and-true favorites. We may reach in and find it empty during one panicky moment. Grounded in a relational approach, we know that it is never empty. Sometimes we find the needed tool through letting go of our idea of what a proper tool should look like. Sometimes we find it by posing the question to those with whom we are working. For they bring their own wisdom, whether or not they know it. Sometimes we find it by chance. At least, we call it chance. Together we will explore how we can prepare ourselves to be favored by chance through personal preparation and fluency with creative processes.

No plumber goes out to fix broken pipes without a wrench; no attorney attends a meeting without a pen; no dancer heads for the theater without her shoes. Conflict bridgers need fundamental tools, too. In addition to the communication and structuring skills we have developed, we need our capacities for relationship and our fluency in creative processes. Our tools give us what we need to respond with resourcefulness, spontaneity, and ingenuity to conflicts:

- *Metaphors*—direct links from language to experience and back again
- *Stories*—containers for meaning and relationship since before language was invented
- *Rituals*—new and traditional ways to mark, change, and contain new stories, identities, and relationships

Our creative processes are animated through language, both verbal and nonverbal. From language we build stories enlivened by metaphors or images. Stories stimulate empathy and build connection. From connection we bridge experiences of separation and conflict. Rituals help us cross the boundaries between the world we know and the world we imagine. They help us move through conflict, with the changes in identities, roles, and meanings that conflict brings. Sometimes metaphors, rituals, and stories help by stirring things up enough for new meanings to emerge.

I was giving an intensive course on creativity and conflict to a varied group of people with widely different levels of experience in conflict work and seriously different perspectives about creativity. Nothing undermines a course on creativity more than an atmosphere that is flat and unengaging, just as nothing undermines our effectiveness as third parties in conflict more than exhibiting our own unresolved conflicts. The morning was going slowly, and it was difficult to find places where relational bridges could be built that would allow for exploration and discovery in the group.

After a break, I asked the participants to come back into the room and introduce themselves to each other. They had already done this, of course, sharing names, contexts, and learning goals. This time, I requested that they introduce themselves as someone they have dreamed of being. There were no other instructions, except that the dreamed person was to be as complete as possible in demeanor, affect, speech, and presentation. As they introduced themselves, I asked them to talk to us about creativity and how it related to their ways of being in the world.

What happened was amazing, to me and to them. We met a professional hockey player, an award-winning gardener, a dancer, a writer, a waitress, and an inventor; before there had been lawyers, judges, and consultants. They introduced themselves in completely different voices, complete with accents, new intonations, and body language to go with them. Freed from their usual identities, they exuded confidence and certainty about their art, their work, their lives. Creativity was something they knew well, but they needed to shift their stories, their images of themselves, to express it. The new introductions became a ritual for these expressions, an invitation to share parts of themselves usually kept hidden.

This foray into metaphors and stories through an informal ritual made room for many new conversations among us. Flexibility flourished among us, where self-consciousness and image had dominated. The exercise powerfully underscored our role in creating ourselves in the world, minute-by-minute. Our identities come from the identities we live into being every day. Together the creative tools of metaphor, story, and ritual help us compose the worlds we envision. To use them, it is helpful to consider some things about creative processes and how they work. First, come down from Invention Mountain and take a rest, savoring the journey.

Gifts from the Mountains

We have visited seven mountains—mountains that symbolize the principles of a relational approach to conflict. Although we may have wanted to stay longer, we did not linger. We took the chairlift up and down, seeing the view but not getting muddy or winded. We will have opportunities to climb each of the mountains as we go forward, to taste the air freshened by local flora, to experience ourselves in connection with ideas and stories. Woven into the chapters that follow, we will visit

- Circle Mountain, beginning and ending our journey in integration and connection, recognizing many ways of seeing and knowing

- Heart Mountain, inviting us to mindful and heartful relationship in the service of bridging conflict
- Magic Mountain, drawing us to stay open and alive to discovery and surprise
- Goldmine Mountain, where the winds whisper that we need all of our physical, emotional, imagining, and spiritual selves to do this work
- Noble Mountain, reminding us why
- Mirror Mountain, engaging us in seeing and surpassing our limitations
- Invention Mountain, offering us ways to be the creativity we envision

As we do, we will draw on creativity as a relational resource. Before we begin, a few words about creativity and relationship.

The Relational Nature of Creativity

There are thousands of books about creativity. Sadly, many of them reinforce narrow ideas about the subject. Anthologies about creativity collect the voices of accomplished painters, authors, and scientists, perpetuating the idea that creativity is about mastery. A myriad of books provide steps to creativity, suggesting that it is reducible to a series of techniques. When the techniques get usurped by other attractions or demands, they are relegated to a shelf in the garage next to the dusty rowing machine, and we continue as before.

Although these books may be limited, they are surely correct in their message that we can all develop our creative capacities. The question is how to proceed. Creativity is the process of bringing something new into being. It involves all parts of us: our beliefs and attitudes about ourselves and others, as conditioned by experience; our physical, mental, emotional, and spiritual states; and our ways of paying attention. It also involves relationship, whether fleeting or long-term, before, after, and during the creative process.

Most books on creativity treat it as an individual pursuit. Let's take a moment to examine that assumption. Bring to mind a time in your life when you felt inventive or imaginative, when you were involved in bringing something new into being. What was the process like? Can you locate the sensations you felt then in your body? How did you feel about the activity? What were your thoughts? Take a moment and explore these questions in writing or a drawing that evokes your experience. Celebrate your creativity by naming and marking it.

If you have difficulty thinking of such a time, remember that creativity need not be the invention of electricity. Use these questions to help:

- When did you feel enlivened or energized?
- When did you mediate, facilitate, or train in a way that went especially well?
- When did you feel particularly close to someone else?
- When did something happen that surprised you or led you to change your point of view about an issue or another person?
- What was happening at these times that brought something new into being?

Once you have brought a creative time to mind, consider these questions:

- Where did the idea come from, how did it arise?
- What role did others play in your first brush with the ideas or activity, either through interaction, casual encounter, or remembered contact?
- Did you carry them out in a solitary way, or in connection with others?
- How did contact with others, with the natural world, with dreams, or with spirit inform or shape your work?
- When the process came to closure, how were others involved?
- If there was a product of your work, did you share it?
- If there was no product or you did not share it, how did the creative experience affect you?
- How did it affect your relationships?

I notice that my creative moments always have to do with relationship. When I struggle with writing, enduring confusion and the voice that asks why I am trying to write at all, I remind myself through conversation. The conversation may be with a friend or colleague who understands and supports what I am doing; it may be a conversation with myself in which I go back to the purpose I had for writing; it may be a conversation with Spirit as I walk along the beach, asking with genuine inquiry what comes next. At some point, the creative process extends beyond me and my ego boundaries, refuting the image of the tortured composer or painter working endlessly in isolation. Even in these cases, creative work is conceived and shaped through relational experiences, and it is eventually played, shared, and experienced in relationship with audiences.

Creativity happens in relationship, in the multidirectional exchange between us and our environment. To engage creativity is to pay exquisite attention, to let our agendas be shaped by interactions and relationships with other people, ourselves, Spirit, and the natural world. Picasso said, "I do not seek, I find." Mozart wrote the last movement of the G-major Concerto for Piano and Orchestra after hearing a starling singing in a street vendor's cage. Antonio Stradivari came upon a pile of broken, waterlogged oars while walking in Venice one day. From these he made some of his most beautiful violins. A woman blocked in writing her dissertation found an article open in a study carrel addressing exactly the point she found puzzling. How have chance encounters, conversations, disclosures, and discoveries made a difference to your creativity?

Creative intelligence makes itself at home in the world. The first step in cultivating creativity is to be sure we are not so attached to outcome or design as to block out the daily wealth of gifts—gifts we might call accidents or chance. This means that we cannot be dogmatic about processes but must constantly adapt them and ourselves to the creative possibilities that present themselves. In doing this, we model the very flexibility and spirit of inquiry that parties need to shift conflicted relationships to those more generative.

Creativity—bringing something new into being—involves releasing the old, whether the old is an idea, an assumption, a value, or a way of ordering life. It is therefore central to conflict, which requires bringing something new into being to be resolved or transformed. We open ourselves to the creative process, releasing our ideas about outcome. This is why techniques are not the whole story. Creativity is neither a straight line nor purely an individual act of volition. It is a relational process in which we make ourselves available to synchronicity in whichever form it appears.

We open ourselves to relationships, not only with a canvas or a musical score but with each other, with our natural world, and with vast unknown parts of ourselves. All are rich sources of inspiration, motivation, and unique ideas.

Creativity, Courage, and Conflict

Seeing this, we can understand why it is so difficult to engage creativity in conflict. Conflict involves narrowing ways of seeing, not expanding them. It may mean fierce attachments to ideas, identities, needs, and interests, rather than elasticity and inquiry. When in conflict, we are in a perceptual corner. If we could easily use creativity to get out, we would. We don't like to think of ourselves as attached to pain and narrow vision, though these may feel more known and secure than alternatives in the midst of deep conflict.

Engaging creativity is an act of energy and courage, as Rollo May reminds us. Courage is not the opposite of despair. We will encounter despair along the way in any creative endeavor, and this is to be expected. Normalizing despair and discouragement is critical to our work in bridging conflict. We may not be able to quickly get to yes. We may find our way to some maybes or some things to try along the way. Some will work; others may not. Courage and creativity is about continuing through despair.

To do this, we need to cultivate relationships with ourselves that sustain us, even as relationships with others are tested. May observes that a "chief characteristic of this courage is that it requires a centeredness within our own being, without which we would feel ourselves to be a vacuum . . . [E]mptiness within corresponds to an apathy without, and apathy adds up . . . to cowardice."[7] Conflict resolution and transformation teachers, trainers, and third parties who cultivate a rich and reflective inner life will have more creative resources to offer their clients. They will also model creativity. This congruence between a professed value and a way of living is powerful indeed. Throughout this book, we will talk about developing, maintaining, and enhancing a creative relationship with ourselves.

May, writing more than thirty years ago, outlines several dimensions of the courage to create. Because they are powerfully in accord with the ideas in this book, I want to mention them here.

Listening with the body. Sensitivity to our physical being is central to our relationship with ourselves and each other. The body is a means by which we empathize and communicate with others. It is an instrument of discernment that cues us about ways to engage and help. It provides important information about our level of depletion or fullness and how this can enliven or impede our work. It is with our bodies that we enact our ideas, so our bodies are important vehicles for creating and anchoring change. We develop these ideas further in Chapter Two.

Aligning ourselves against violence. In May's assessment, alignment against violence comes from moral courage, from allowing ourselves to feel outraged at others' pain and inhuman treatment. To take an interest, to devote energy to drawing attention to violence and developing alternatives, is an exercise of moral courage. It is to remember the questions of Noble Mountain that ask us how our work connects to the world outside ourselves. It is an essential step on the creative path. Many conflict trainers and third parties come to their work from a philosophy of nonviolence and a commitment to peacemaking. Keeping fairness and justice in the equation as we design and implement conflict resolution and transformation programs is a way of demonstrating our empathy for those in conflict. We consider the role of empathy in Chapters Three and Seven.

Relating to others with intimacy. When we enter a relationship with another, we do not know where it will lead. This is true whether the relationship is personal, collegial, or professional. Choosing to invest in relationships is an act of courage in the face of risk, which is always present because relationships are systems. When one part of the system shifts, all parts of the system shift.

We can enrich our practices by bringing the understanding that relationships are systems. As one member of a family, community, or workplace changes, ripples affect everyone. This is true of even small or incremental changes. We can help parties in conflict remember that their conflict did not arise in a day and it may take time and patience to address. Because change happens in systems, it is always to some degree outside our control. We offer ourselves in the service of change, while maintaining openness to form and outcome.

We are most effective when we offer ourselves in ways that are authentic and genuine. Authenticity deepens our relationships with others. This involves another level of risk because we are making ourselves vulnerable by keeping less hidden. It can also stimulate fear, either the fear of losing the relationship or the fear of absorption. As we intervene in conflict, we will see both kinds of fear manifest. It helps to know that these fears arise naturally in deepening relationships. Engaging with each other in spite of fear or distrust is a kind of courage central to a relational approach to conflict.

Following our deep convictions while maintaining an awareness that we may be wrong. Commitment is healthiest when it is not without doubt but in spite of doubt. People who are absolutely convinced that their idea is the only right one are not open to change or truly mutual relationships. Bridging conflict requires both. For every idea there is another perspective. As these perspectives are shared in relationships, something new can be born. We aspire to this statement attributed to Leibniz: "I would walk twenty miles to listen to my worst enemy if I could learn something."[8]

A relational approach to conflict involves listening—not active listening or any other listening technique. It involves listening with every fiber of our being, both to that with which we feel in accord and that with which we feel discord. It means listening for connection, not agreement. It means listening for humanity and artistry, not evaluation and comparison. It means finding a space within ourselves that is open to relationship, with all of the surprises, gifts, and challenges it brings us. In the service of relationship, we tap our physical, emotional, relational, and spiritual ways of knowing and being. We use stories, rituals, and metaphors to help us uncover what has meaning for us, communicate it to others, and shift when we encounter conflict.

Sometimes we lose sight of the trail, getting lost in the brush, fearing the onset of night or a coming storm. Addressing conflict relationally is about staying together in all conditions, not idealizing relationship or minimizing its damaging possibilities but firmly situating ourselves in openness, inquiry, and commitment to purpose. Preparing to be surprised, we work toward shared goals. Trusting individual and group wisdom, we marry analysis to intuition, imagination to logic. We invest in creative possibility experienced through relationship within, with others, and beyond ourselves.

Along the way, we will generate new questions to be answered in future books, in processes that are never recorded, and in quiet moments never spoken. Following Rilke's advice, we live our ways into answers, step-by-step. Sometimes we come upon breathtaking moments in the form of sweeping views or tiny wildflowers. Sometimes we simply continue, watchful and open. Coming back, we are refreshed and energized. This is the gift of time in the mountains.

PART TWO

Creative Ways of Knowing as Resources for Bridging Conflict

From the peaks of seven mountains, we have seen conflict as a relational process. Whether we aim to resolve, transform, or manage conflict, the resource we need most is our creativity. When committed to creativity, we recognize that no two expeditions up a challenging mountain are the same. Conditions and dynamics vary, and change is a constant. Although we endeavor to bring what we need for the journey, we inevitably end up improvising and using tools in ways we had not anticipated. Our ability to respond to changing conditions and our resilience when challenged are central to our success on the mountain.

When facing conflict, we need flexibility, resourcefulness, creativity, and the willingness to examine the lenses through which conflict is seen. Conflict is not only about material things or communication difficulties; it arises from different perceptions and ways of assigning meaning. Because conflict is experienced differently, depending on how we compose our identities and make meaning, conflict practitioners increasingly recognize that neither a discrete set of skills nor any one formula or process "fits all" for bridging conflict. Third parties and educators are best prepared when they access a range of capacities drawn from diverse ways of knowing.

In Part Two of *Bridging Troubled Waters,* we traverse four ways of knowing that complement analytic, intellectual ways of knowing well developed in our scholarship and practice. Emotional ways of knowing, often avoided as untrustworthy, volatile, and troublesome, are explored in Chapter Two. Emotional ways of knowing can enrich our capacities to address conflict constructively.

As we develop our emotional intelligence, we recognize another underdeveloped resource for conflict processes: somatic intelligence, the subject of Chapter Three. Somatic intelligence—the wisdom of the body—provides essential information as we navigate conflict, making it possible to enact new roles and transition through change. As we develop ways of engaging somatic intelligence in our processes, we encounter another set of resources: intuitive and imaginative ways of knowing.

Intuitive and imaginative ways of knowing, the subject of Chapter Four, tap our capacities to attend to and welcome insights that come through channels we cannot trace. Both imagination and intuition draw on somatic and emotional intelligence, where our feelings and sensations act as catalysts and guides for process choices. Together, imaginative and intuitive ways of knowing help unwind conflict, generating new ways forward as we engage in creative collaboration.

Each of these ways of knowing overlaps with connected ways of knowing—a topic explored in Chapter Five. Connected ways of knowing remind us that conflicts are part of relational webs and that all of us have access to many ways of knowing, being, and connecting as we seek to address them. We may become stuck in patterned, limiting ways of seeing and being when in conflict; connected ways of knowing remind us that there is always a bigger picture. We expand our time horizons, our understandings of self and other, and our perspectives about place and purpose, remembering our interdependence and our sense of what deeply matters. As we rely on connected ways of knowing to expand our awareness, we bring new hope that it is possible to bridge the conflicts that divide and separate us.

Difficult conflicts always engage us emotionally. And so we begin our exploration of ways of knowing with emotional intelligence—an important and often-neglected resource.

CHAPTER TWO

Emotional Ways of Knowing
Negotiating the Labyrinth

Ours is an excessively conscious age. We know so much,
we feel so little.
D. H. LAWRENCE

Emotions. They are common to all human experience; they are a frontier in science. They are our earliest ways of knowing ourselves and connecting ourselves to others; many of us get suspicious of them as we age. What if emotions were vitally important in addressing conflict? What if they were cues to action: powerful, instinctual, and helpful? Emotions, when understood for the riches they offer, when put into a place where they are neither discounted nor in absolute control, can provide key information and insight to guide our actions. When conflict arises, whether we are a party or a third party, we need insight, information, and an approach that takes all of our strengths into account.

Emotions, felt through the body, are one of our most direct sources of strength and energy. Yet they are only beginning to come out of the closet where they have been secreted while reason, logic, and analysis have stood at center stage.

In 2001, I gave a public lecture attended by three hundred people. As it was hosted at a university, some of the people were academicians; others were community members of a variety of ages and diverse backgrounds. During the lecture, I questioned the prevailing logic that would screen emotions out of our conflict

45

processes, suggesting instead that emotions may be helpful guides in achieving change and revitalizing relational connections.

At the end of the lecture, a cluster of graduate students spoke to me with tears in their eyes. They told variations on each other's stories, reporting how their academic careers had involved shelving important parts of themselves, including their feeling selves. As they were encouraged to see things analytically and dualistically, rational logic trumped feelings. This stood in stark contrast to the ways the rest of their lives worked. The academy sought to extract, isolate, and fragment knowledge through disciplines, scientific methodologies, and an emphasis on mental logic. Their actual lives worked quite differently, woven together in complexity, held together with the glue of feeling, connections, and intuitive knowing.

This experience led me to reflect further on our conflict processes and training approaches, exploring how they have been influenced by academic culture. Despite gaps between theory and practice, many of the ideas that support our training and intervention come from psychological and communication theories. These theories have been developed in the fire of the academy, held up to rigorous standards of peer review and scientific proof. Emotions, notoriously difficult to measure or quantify, have only recently been studied in depth. It would be an understatement to suggest that emotional ways of knowing have found little acceptance in academic disciplines. Conflict resolution is not unique in sharing this. There is great potential for our theory and practice to be enriched by the work of those who have studied the important role of emotions as dimensions of intelligence and interpersonal competence.[1,2]

Our practice is already enriched immeasurably by emotions. Not only are they cues to the intensity and nature of the feelings of others but they give us important information that informs our process choices. Listen to experienced groups of trainers and third parties. They describe diverse approaches, based on theoretical roots that often go unarticulated. When they describe how they know which decision to make at key moments in training sessions or interventions, they commonly use expressions like "I had a gut feeling about it," "I followed my intuition," and "it just felt right." Almost all of them communicate a reliance on ways of knowing informed by emotions.

Recent advances in physiology and neurological science have helped us understand more about emotions. As Daniel Goleman carefully traces in his book *Emotional Intelligence,* new brain imaging technologies have shown us many things that were locked away from human understanding for centuries. Although he may be overly optimistic in his claim that science is now able "to map with some precision the human heart,"[3] these scientific advances have done much to challenge our limited view of what constitutes intelligence and to suggest complementary ways of knowing that stand together with rational analysis. Taken together, these findings support an approach to conflict that looks again at emotions for the richness and the wisdom they offer.

In this chapter, we consider some of the findings from the past decade relating to emotions: what they are, how they function, and how they inform our behavior and relationships. Then we turn to the question of how these understandings inform our practice as trainers and third parties in conflict. My objective is not to argue for an emotion-centered method of practice but for a balanced approach to practice in which emotions are neither dominant nor discounted.

What Are Emotions?

Would you know an emotion if you met it in the road? Some people would, and some would not. Everyone experiences emotions, but there is wide-ranging awareness about our own and others' emotions and the degrees to which we express them. Scientists tell us that emotions are impulses to act—instant and instinctive ways to handle life that kick in before rational analysis has had a chance to function.

Physical Expression of Emotions

Love is the first emotion most of us experience. Psychologist Ian Suttie[4] suggests that love is a primary drive arising from the desire for social give and take and responsive relationship. Suttie studied dozens of mothers and infants and noticed that nursing babies gaze at their mothers' faces, often getting loving glances in return. Soon infants start smiling as they suck, sometimes dropping the nipple in delight when they get a response. In this first playful exchange between mother and child, the baby gives the only thing it has to give: love through its body. This is the beginning of creativity in the child's life, grounded in reciprocal feelings of connection and attachment.

What Suttie and others point us toward is the primary importance of loving feelings in the earliest exploration of our identities. This psychological perspective echoes centuries of spiritual teaching about the centrality of love in the human experience. Not surprisingly, physiologists tell us that loving feelings release a bodywide set of reactions that generate a general state of calm and contentment, facilitating cooperation. Other emotions have different physiological effects. Fear and anger are attended by a high level of physical arousal, making possible the classic fight-or-flight response. When we are surprised, we raise our eyebrows, actually increasing our field of vision and making it possible to take in additional information to inform our response to an unexpected event.

Emotions are expressed physically, using the hundreds of muscles in the face as a primary medium. Around the world, sadness, happiness, fear, love, and disgust look the same. This lends credence to the idea that emotions are a part of our human genetic legacy, arising from biological imperatives. Emotions may be enacted, received, and privileged in different cultural contexts differently, but they are part of all human experience.

Emotions are surely present in any conflict of consequence. Although it is obvious that family and community conflicts involve a range of emotions, it is also true that organizational and commercial conflicts are influenced by emotions. Emotions are a part of living; we can no more excise them from our experience and our relationships than we can make it to the moon without a spaceship. They are part of us; they inform us, motivate us, delight us, and depress us. Although there are no subjects in school called "emotional fluency," those of us who have developed some fluency are better able to manage our relationships and our conflicts.

Emotional Styles

Someday we may consider understanding different emotional ways of being as important as learning styles (such as visual, auditory, or kinesthetic preferences) and conflict styles. It is true that some of us are more aware of our emotions, more able to name them, more reliant on them, and more intensely involved in the emotional realm than others. Consider these examples: Alice loses a favorite pen and is upset and distracted for days, searching for it in the same places again and again, not feeling quite "on" because of her frustration. José also loses his pen. Although it is the only thing in his possession that had belonged to a well-loved grandparent, he shrugs philosophically and tells a friend that if it was stolen, he hopes the thief gets as much pleasure from it as he did. Both Alice and José are in situations that could be emotional; Alice apparently experiences emotions with different intensity and triggers than José.

What is your experience of emotions? Are there times when a past painful memory is evoked on a perfectly good day, and it changes your mood like a blue lens over the sun? Are there also times when feelings of elation or joy are so pervasive that you do not notice dangers or difficulties? In both these cases, feelings arise and change our experience of the present, our behaviors, and interactions. The picture is even more complex when we realize that emotions are not just individual but arise in relationship; they are shaped by culture and can be transmitted from one person to another without speech.

Bring a strong emotion to your awareness now, whether positive or negative. Is it related to another person or a social situation? Chances are it is. Like creativity, emotions are relational. Love, fear, betrayal, and joy happen in and through our relationships with others. When we encounter conflict, emotions tend to intensify. These emotional triggers may act like a vortex, gathering force from real, anticipated, imagined, feared, or remembered aspects of the relationship and past relationships.

Themes of betrayal, anger, and hurt—all common to conflict—arouse strong responses in all of us, though we express them differently. What is your response when you are in the vicinity of such strong emotions? Are you like the male partner in a couple's workshop whose wife was expressing her disappointment with him? When asked what was in his awareness, he reported that the thing in the room that kept drawing his eye was the exit sign. Or do you feel the emotions along with the speaker, losing your own agenda? Do you tend to go toward them—welcoming them, exploring their depths, bringing them into the air where they can breathe and take on life? Or perhaps you feel tense, concerned about the effect of the emotions on you or others, or vaguely uncomfortable. Try this story as a way of exploring your emotional responses.

You are riding public transit at the end of a long and taxing day at work. Your mind is in a reverie, lulled by the rhythmic movement of the train. In front of you, a couple sits with their heads leaning on each other, talking quietly. Suddenly, one of them jumps up, shouting, "You didn't!" in a loud voice. Tears are flowing and the accuser's body is taut, towering with quivering rage over the still-seated partner. And you feel . . . how?

Of course it is a shock when the emotional tone apparently changes so suddenly. You may feel embarrassed to be so close to an intimate confrontation. You may feel judgment about the propriety of the behavior; you may be intimidated or afraid. You may want to run, or help, or just listen to see what happens next.

As long as you're here in this situation, ask yourself some other questions:

- At which point would this conflict be "too intense" for you?
- When, if at all, would you intervene directly or try to get help?
- What do you think others in the train would do?

What do your answers tell you about your response to intense emotional expression?

This kind of inquiry is important for those of us who seek to help others with conflict. Many of us have significant discomfort with the expression of strong emotions. A few of us actively move toward them, whether motivated by fear or attraction to the intensity. Most of us have limited repertoires for responding; the dominant culture has taught us that emotions can be murky, swampy territory that is dangerous to dispassionate analysis and clear-minded action. Having spent our time avoiding emotions, we do not open our cupboard to find a varied wardrobe of responses when we come face-to-face with them, whether our own or those of others.

Discomfort with strong emotions is not equally present across cultures. Some cultures are more expressive, open with emotional displays, and comfortable with a wide range of emotional behavior. Arab and Latin cultures tend to condone higher levels of emotional expression, though they also have social rules about how and when displays are appropriate.[5] At the same time, there are significant variations within cultural groups. Personality preferences, environmental influences, and contextual factors exert powerful influences on the way emotions are experienced and expressed.

It is useful to be aware of cultural generalizations, if only to inform our guesses and understandings. Kochman,[6] for example, tells us that African Americans may view requests to check emotions at the door as political ways of silencing their voices. Knowing this is a possibility, a third party who is facilitating or mediating welcomes a wide range of communicative styles and modes of expression.

Can We Cultivate Emotional Intelligence?

Whatever our style of emotional expression, conflict trainers and third parties are well advised to cultivate emotional intelligence. Central to our work is the capacity to be aware of our own and others' emotions and to take them into account as valid resources informing our actions. It makes sense that we need to be comfortable with emotion before we can invite it into our processes as an asset, a resource, and a partner with thought and analysis.

We do our best work when informed by our hearts and our heads. And others respond better, too. Coming from the heart humanizes our processes and infuses them with warmth and positive regard. It affirms those parts of ourselves that, in the past, may have been pushed out of relevance through personal discomfort, social constraints, or procedural rules. It does not mean that emotions take over, making mediation a time of wallowing, wailing, singing, or hand holding.

The task is not to take the hierarchy of reason over feeling and turn it on its head. We seek the intelligent balance of the two. As we cultivate emotional intelligence in ourselves as third parties and trainers, we can help those with whom we work build their capacities, too. Because this is a process, it is never finished. But it is better to begin than to continue neglecting the alchemy that is possible when all available elements are present.

The Terrain of Emotional Intelligence

What does emotional intelligence look like? Goleman speaks of it as a meta-ability—something that determines how we can use whatever other skills we have, including raw intellect. The term *emotional intelligence* refers to how well we are able to recognize and manage our own feelings and read and deal effectively with other peoples' feelings. This idea corresponds with Howard Gardner's work on interpersonal and intrapersonal intelligence. Gardner, a psychologist at Harvard, defines *interpersonal intelligence* as "the ability to understand other people: what motivates them, how they work, how to work cooperatively with them."[7] *Intrapersonal intelligence* is simply these skills turned inward and refers to having access to our feelings, having the ability to discriminate among them, and knowing ways to draw on them in choosing our own behaviors.

Conflict trainers and third parties need both interpersonal and intrapersonal intelligence. As we become aware of our true feelings moment-by-moment, we are more sure of our decisions and less likely to be controlled by emotions we are unaware of. Because emotions are impulses to act, we can choose if and how we act on them when we are aware of their content and our emotional habits. Because emotions are potent, it is important to get familiar with our habits at a time when we feel clear and calm rather than when we are in the middle of an emotional response.

In a class I taught on diversity and conflict, participants drew on emotional intelligence to move through a conflict among them. They were engaged in heated discussion about the extent to which negotiation theory and mediation practice reflect patriarchal values. About two-thirds of the class were women. Of these, about one-third were strongly of the view that negotiation theory and mediation practice are gendered in ways that exclude and disadvantage women. Some of the men in the class argued strenuously against this view, insisting that participation is open to all and that feminist theorists have distorted the picture.

One man in particular expressed himself emotionally, displaying anger and frustration at the views of some of the women. We'll call him Greg. Greg was particularly offended by Lois, who strongly argued that women can never achieve the same level of satisfaction as men in negotiation because the table is always uneven. In his journal, Greg recounted how he "wrote Lois off" at that point, even though she had been a friendly acquaintance of his. He distanced from her by changing his seat after a break to one as far away from her as possible. He deliberately did not greet her when they passed, and he avoided her at breaks. After class, her insistence on women's disadvantages gnawed at him, and he found himself pre-occupied with building a set of reasons why she was wrong.

The next morning, Greg realized that he was still uncomfort-able. Exploring his feelings, he realized that he felt tension arising from the contradiction of being in a class on transforming conflict and his avoidant, judging behavior. Was he willing to apply a spirit of inquiry to his situation, or was the material we were learning only a body of theory that related to others? Greg's emotional intel-ligence told him that he would be less uncomfortable if he explored his feelings and understood more about Lois's feelings.

Having spent some quiet time with himself, Greg decided to try another way. When he came into class, he sought Lois out, greeting her casually and respectfully. At the break, they exchanged a few words. At lunchtime, they took a walk together, and he asked her sincerely to tell him about her experiences and how they led to her strong feelings about women's disadvantages. This was not an invitation to continue the debate of the previous day. It was an inquiry that invited emotional fluency into their exchange. Reflecting later in their journals, they each registered surprise at what had happened and feelings of caring for each other. Greg wrote, "I always thought feminists were just politicized, distorting things . . . but when I heard Lois's experience, I realized that there is more to this issue than I thought. I still don't see all of her points, but I can see how she got there."

This experience illustrates how intrapersonal intelligence and interpersonal intelligence are linked. Greg came to acknowledge his own feelings after first trying to build a case against Lois—a case that was challenged by the very processes we were studying in our course. As he got beneath his analysis to his feelings, he found a genuine curiosity about Lois's feelings and experiences that led to a more constructive relationship. The climate in the class improved, too, as Greg and Lois were no longer tense and upset.

Reflecting on this experience, I realize the importance of lead-ership in the demonstration of emotional intelligence. As a trainer, instructor, or third party, I set the tone by using feeling words alongside thinking words, asking parties not only what they think but what they feel and sense about an issue or a process choice. I invite emotional responses to issues as well as rational ones, acknowledging that each influences the other. When I hold a particular point of view, I acknowledge the feelings that support my analysis. When I have strong feelings, they shape my point of view, making some aspects of an issue seem prominent and others less important. Acknowledging these dynamics provides more complex and transparent understanding of issues and facilitates more multifaceted dialogues. This is true in many aspects of practice, not just those that we think of as obviously emotional.

The Emotional Content of Conflict

Emotions are present in any dispute that touches people's ways of making meaning and their identities or concepts of self. Whether a dispute is commercial, environmental, or international, it is probably about negotiating meanings and protecting identities if it matters to those involved. Divorce mediation is a setting where emotions can be especially intense. Our most primal selves are triggered when we find ourselves in a situation where the most important relationships in our lives are being reframed in ways we can't control.

As Celeste and Jim go through the divorce mediation process, it is clear that their emotions are significant in ways they have not acknowledged and are at a loss for how to deal with. Jim is a university professor nearing retirement; he has an impressive record of publications and an international reputation. Celeste is a nurse whose community work has been fulfilling but not nearly as lucrative as Jim's. Their children are grown. When Celeste talks about her financial needs, her voice gets louder, her breathing becomes more rapid, and the tension in the room builds. The financial settlement between them becomes more than numbers of dollars or ways of splitting retirement funds; it becomes a symbol of the resentment and frustration she has felt for the previous thirty years of being, as she says, "the wind beneath his wings."

At these moments, Celeste is aware that she is frustrated, but she has little understanding of how much emotional punch her words are conveying. She is caught up in emotion, losing her temper and launching into accusations and recriminations.

Physiologically, when strong emotions are triggered, our brain is "washed" in chemicals that Goleman calls a neural hijacking. A center in the limbic system of the brain releases hormones that heighten and focus brain activity, making the brain more alert and the body ready to act before the thinking parts of the brain have figured out what is going on and what to do about it. Like a flood, the entire brain is washed in the emotions, and actions proceed from this place. This is what happens when we "lose it," and it explains how emotions can sometimes trigger behavior that we later regret. It is also probably the reason that emotions have developed such negative associations. We do not ordinarily aspire to lose all sense of perspective and act before we have had a chance to reflect on the implications of our choices.

For her emotions to be assets in the process of decoupling, Celeste has first to become aware of them. Acting from her agitated state, she is likely to overreact and amplify her perceptions of unfairness. Only as she is able to observe her state while feeling it does she have different choices. So emotional intelligence means cultivating our inner observer as an antidote to getting swept away by a tide of raw emotion. How do we do this?

Practices for Developing Our Inner Observer

Our inner observer can be trained to become attuned to our inner feelings as they manifest physically and as they shift and change. One of the ways we can cultivate this capacity is to take the time to explore our emotional states and habits through writing or other practices. For example, I know that one of my tendencies is to amplify emotions when I feel stressed. This is not true for everyone; some of us "go cold," pushing emotions out of our awareness when we are stressed. Because I tend to amplify them, it is important for me to take time out to restore my internal balance, even if it is in the form of a long, counting-to-ten breath, before responding. When stress combines with unhealed wounds or triggers, emotions carry even more of a punch. Then it is important to be aware of emotions and work with them rather than simply from them.

One particularly helpful way for me to work with my emotions is to write about them. I use the "three-page rule"—an adaptation of Julia Cameron's ideas from her book *The Artist's Way*.[8] This means that I write whatever comes into my mind, starting with the presenting feelings, for at least three continuous pages. For me, it sometimes takes three pages to lull my conscious mind into getting out of the way. My conscious mind concerns itself with image, with trying to figure out motivations, with strategies for responding. It is often less aware of my deep feelings about an issue. As I write without concern for the form and without managing the content, my writing gradually takes on a more fluid quality and my feelings begin to write themselves onto the pages.

Often in the process of writing, clarity emerges about the feelings themselves. As the feelings are named and acknowledged in the writing, they frequently shift. Here's an example: I feel worried and upset that a friend missed a meeting we had planned and left me waiting without calling. Even after I hear her explanation and find that she is all right, I am still frustrated with her and have negative feelings about planning another time. I sit down to write three pages, beginning with writing what I feel about the situation and my friend without censoring or being concerned with her feelings. As I begin, I write about fairness and respect and indignation at having my time wasted. Continuing, I begin to list all of the other things I could have been doing at that time, and I associate the experience with other times I have felt discounted or disrespected. I name the feelings that connect these times: frustration, diminishment, a desire to strike back. I notice that some common threads connecting these experiences are imbalances in power, status differentials, and lack of mutuality and that the threads are weighted down with childhood slights and hurts.

Finding myself at the end of three pages, I notice a sense of release in my chest, and I smile to observe the wisdom in the expression, "She got it off her chest." I don't feel the same intensity of frustration at my friend. I understand more about how my own sense of being overextended amplified my frustration at the missed meeting. I remember how this is an old trigger for me and realize that I have also had unavoidable things come up at different times and had to change or alter plans without much notice. Empathy for her and a broader understanding of myself in context were both possible as I went into my feelings rather than dismissing them as unimportant or unreasonable. Writing allowed me to let go of my attachment to my feelings of justification and frustration and to move forward.

Whether emotions are explored through writing, drawing, walking, meditating quietly, talking with another, or exercising vigorously, it is useful to invite them into the open. In contrast to the emotional punch that accompanies a crisis, our feelings may be quiet, subtle, and easily missed. There are many ways to surface and attend to them, each an investment in keeping our lives and our relationships fluid, supple, and flexible.

Taking Time

To cultivate emotional intelligence is to turn our attention to the "being" part of humanness. We get so busy with "human doing" that we sometimes forget we are human beings. To borrow some wisdom from the French, cultivating emotional intelligence turns our attention to savoir-être (knowing how to be) instead of the more familiar savoir-faire (knowing how to do).

My mind turns to those early years with my children when the laundry never ended and I was running from morning until exhausted evening without getting to half of the things on my list. When my children came into the kitchen where I was preparing supper, balancing the checkbook, and on-hold with the preschool on the phone, I had little receptivity to their emotional traumas. How many times did I absent mindedly assure them that things would be better soon or suggest that they stop being so angry with each other and just get along? All those parenting books with their "I" messages and consequences for misbehavior did not materialize as white knights and help me respond with emotional intelligence. I fear that I implicitly taught them a lesson I had learned at my mother's knee: emotions interfere with efficiency, accomplishment, and desirable harmony.

My experience is less unique than we might like to believe. Sue Bender writes about her friend Helen, who said that balancing being with doing is "a constant process of asking myself what is important. . . . [Before] it was as if I was on a moving escalator . . . always racing through my life, having fun, but not really stopping to savour or distill what was important. It's all . . . there, everything . . . but I didn't see it because I was going too fast."[9]

When I arrived at my massage therapist's office one day, breathless and tense from negotiating traffic, he said he was not going to work on me any more unless I slowed down. Like Helen, I was speeding along without taking time to notice or enjoy the feelings that give cues about how I felt, what I needed to adjust, or where I needed to pay attention. In the circumstances, massage therapy was just another "to do" rather than a place to relax into awareness.

Inviting emotional intelligence into our lives is to legitimate the process of smelling the roses and to ask what that means to us. It is to invite the raw, the aesthetic, the bawdy, and the graceful into our activity-driven lives, to fill out our experience, to live more deeply, to imagine this for others. Come with me to a training session where I learned something important about this process.

Using Emotional Intelligence to Design Training and Intervention

What does an emotionally fluid training or intervention process look like? It surely gives permission for a range of styles of expression. It means that trainers and third parties attend to their language. Do my questions and statements to participants include positive references to emotional ways of knowing? Do I share my feelings about the process as it unfolds? Am I modeling attunement with my own and others' emotions, recognizing when breaks are needed, noticing feelings that are expressed but not named? Sometimes it takes a painful experience to show us where we need to make changes.

In this particular class, our topic was gender and conflict. A colleague had once suggested that I write a book about gender and conflict—a subject I have taught for several years. "It is certainly needed," I agreed. But I wasn't ready to venture into that place of impoverished language, political struggle, and multilevel tension. Many groups I have taught wrestle with the research and theory in this area. The struggles come from many perspectives, laced with emotions, fraught with the conflicts we all mediate internally. What is it to be a woman in this new century? A man? How are we to relate, to engage in conflict, to work with each other? Roles are changing rapidly, mirroring complex societal change. Generalizations break down when faced with individual examples, yet powerful social forces constrict us like current-charged invisible fences when we violate gender role expectations.

Understanding Gendered Conflict

Participants in the class were working in small groups, discussing various assigned readings. As with the earlier example of Greg and Lois, the participants had strong reactions to the suggestion Barbara Gray[10] made that conflict theory is gendered and that our ways of thinking and behaving in conflict reflect the implicit adoption of male gender norms, including rational expression and logical problem solving. Some of the men in the group felt insulted. Some of the women were surprised that these unmarked gender assumptions were so controversial. In this atmosphere, the conversation turned to how we parent.

There were wide-ranging opinions among this group of professionals, some of whom were parents. Generally, there was support for the idea that children should be raised without restrictive gender role expectations, that girls should be encouraged to play with trucks and assert themselves, that boys should be given dolls and cuddled when they cry. Having arrived at a natural stopping point, we moved into a break.

Having once more passed through the land of gender and conflict, I breathed a sigh of relief. Strong emotions had been expressed, and the continuum of views could still be felt in the room. Some of the participants had never talked about these things, at least not in this way. But there were prospects for moving through the tension, buoyed by our convergent dialogue about parenting. Then I saw her coming toward me—a woman who had participated somewhat haltingly in the conversation.

"My eight-year-old son cross-dresses," she told me tearfully. "He loves to put on his sister's ballerina suit, to wear feather boas, fishnet stockings, and sequined shawls. It is a source of terrible conflict between me and my husband. My husband says that we have to discourage him or he will get slammed by the world. Yet I want him to feel accepted for who he is. Who knows what our attempts to suppress this behavior might do to him? When we were talking just now about parenting, I don't think people realized that it is not as simple as it seems."

Did the class not realize that it was an emotionally complex subject, or were we collectively unready to acknowledge the extent of our emotions related to gender? This topic connects to our identities, our ideas about appropriateness and right order, our understandings of roles and relationships. It is about the way we make meaning of the world and our places in it.

In the vortex of swirling messages that surround us, is it any wonder that we are cautious? On one side are the glib answers that men are from Mars and women from Venus,[11] with all of the role prescriptions that flow from these supposedly different cultures. On another, there are theorists and researchers staging debates in the literature about whether men and women are all that different. If they are different, is it because of social expectations, biology, parenting, or some combination of these? And wherever the differences originate, what difference are the differences making?

Her pain stopped me. Shaken out of self-congratulation for negotiating a swampy subject, I listened to her struggles. Her story spoke for itself: gendered ways of being are not as discrete or as easy to negotiate as we might wish. We spoke about ways she could negotiate the situation and the conflict with her husband, about the supports she had available to her. She chose not to surface the issue again with the class, acknowledging her desire for privacy about this issue that was anything but academic.

Reflecting later, I wondered how we could have proceeded in ways that welcomed and legitimated more of the complex emotional aspects of this subject. This student may not have surfaced her issues with her son and husband, but she may have felt more able to contribute and less offended if the conversation had evolved differently. And everyone would have had a richer experience, understanding more of the nuances and the complex dynamics involved in gender and conflict.

To stay away from the dichotomies and categories that accompany an intellectual investigation of difficult topics, I have since grounded dialogues in personal stories and images. As we will explore later, in the chapter on stories, personal experiences open up space, inviting listeners to consider context, feelings, and dynamics relating to issues. Here are some of the questions I have used in exploring gender and conflict in an effort to invite emotional content into dialogues:

- What were your earliest experiences of gender?
- When did gender begin to mean something in your life?
- What messages were you given about gender and roles for women and men?
- How did those messages accompany you, shape you to meet new situations, change in the presence of others or through study or experience?
- What in your experience helped you make sense of how to "do" gender?
- Can you change the way you do gender at will?
- What factors limit or assist you in changing?
- Can you draw your metaphor or image for gender? For gender and conflict?
- What does your drawing show you about your relationship with gender?
- Can you imagine a genderless world?
- If so, what would you welcome? What would you miss?
- Can you imagine a world with ten different genders, twenty-five?
- What would it feel like to live in that world?

Answers to these questions are not abstract or analytic; they tend to contain significant emotional richness because they speak to our feelings about the ongoing process of composing our gendered identities.

Why are questions like these effective in bringing emotional ways of knowing into dialogues? Asking participants or parties to remember or imagine experiences evokes smells, tastes, sensations, sounds, and images. These sensory memories are recorded in our bodies in ways that connect to the feelings associated with experiences. When we bring sensory memories into our awareness, the feelings come back, too. This is why we feel sad when we hear an old song associated with a time in our life when we broke up with a partner; this is why the scent of popcorn may induce a feeling of warmth or pleasure.

Sounds, sights, and senses connect to feelings in a kind of web; they don't come back disjointed or atomized. When we communicate these feelings to each other in telling our stories or sharing our imaginings, we build empathy, trust, and relationship. From this foundation, we can apply research or theory with more awareness and with the compassion that emotional intelligence infuses into our processes.

When we ground dialogues in personal experiences, emotions do not come out of context, intense and threatening; they simply are. In the training example just given, emotions were present, arising in response to theories and claims but without a legitimate seat at the table. Having constructed expectations of a calm, rational forum, we were surprised by the vehemence of responses. When we construct a forum that welcomes more dimensions of ourselves, we have more permission to welcome and work with emotions.

Another way to express this is to say that it makes sense to begin with the people, that is, by centering processes in relationship rather than the material realm. In many cultural contexts, it is important to have tea, share a meal, or talk about families or hobbies before addressing the substance or topic. Could it be that this approach is not as much about social niceties as it is a reliable way to build emotional connection before talking about something that might be difficult or give rise to conflict? Recognizing the positive potential of emotions to connect us, we are well advised to design trainings and interventions so that emotions are part of the process.

I love the image related to me by a First Nations[12] friend of a willow basket filled with eiderdown as a container for difficult conversations. Our precious stories are the willows, woven together into a strong basket to contain our dialogue. Our capacity to listen deeply from the care we feel for each other is the eiderdown, softening judgment, muting defensiveness, cradling hurts. As we ensconce our conversations in the basket, the issues we discuss become less divisive. We may feel as differently about them at the end as we did at the beginning, but we feel less different from each other. I carry this image with me now whenever I participate in conversations about conflict and gender. I don't want to have a conversation that happens metaphorically in the middle of naked pavement in the glaring noon sun where softness and compassion are difficult to summon.

Finding a Right Place for Emotions

Although we recognize that emotions are resources, it is also important not to let them "take over" a process. Because we feel them viscerally, emotions are powerful and have a powerful impact. Emotionally fluent processes are most effective when emotions inform but do not control—when emotions are part of the atmosphere but not the whole weather system. In this section, we explore how to invite emotions as resources without losing perspective.

Think about a really moving film you have seen. How did it affect your mood, the way you felt and experienced things? I recently saw *Life Is Beautiful*—a movie full of pathos, pain, and joy. It was beautifully acted, and the cinematography was a feast for the senses. It left me wanting to hug the world, to cherish living, to treasure moments. I looked around with more gratitude, more appreciation for those people and things that surround me. I had taken on some of the emotions of the film, absorbed them, brought them into my experience with the popcorn. In this case, it felt good, because I felt more alive.

Now consider this. Have you ever come home from a mediation or facilitation session drained and spent? Have you been in the presence of intensely sad or angry or distrustful people and later found yourself acting out these feelings? This is the flip side of the experience I described with the movie. One of the ways to deal with our unconscious process of taking on others' emotional states is to engage in specific preparation and closure activities before and after mediating or facilitating.

Before meeting with parties, whether for the first time or a subsequent one, consider your state. Use visualization to cleanse your mind of thoughts. Here is one way to do that. Let thoughts and feelings pass through your awareness and find a place to rest. Focus on your breath, centering, becoming a clear channel to receive what the parties bring. Perhaps you imagine a place that is serene, secure, and welcoming for you. Is it in nature? What are the colors, the scents, the textures that surround you there? From that place, envision strength, concentration, and energy for the process. Trust that you will have what you need, whether discernment, inspiration, or clarity. Even if you feel tired, dispirited, or resistant, feelings may begin to shift as you make yourself available to the process. This availability occurs not only on the level of being mentally receptive but in being emotionally open to sensing and discerning the dynamics among the parties.

And now the session is over. The parties have departed. Some were easy for you to relate to. Others reminded you of that 5th-grade teacher you never did like. Some you did not understand. They brought their realities with them: emotions, thoughts, attributions, regrets, guilt, strategies, solutions. Some were voiced; others felt. All were present. You danced with them, you observed them, you listened. Can you feel their presence in the room, even when the people have gone?

What do you do with all of it? Later you may want to analyze, recreate, consider alternative ways of proceeding, imagine. For now, get quiet. Go again to that serene place and bring the faces of the parties to mind. Can you see them, talking as they did a few minutes ago, or receiving something that was said in silence or resistance? Surround them with goodwill, and give them back their realities. Give them back their thoughts and feelings, expressed and unspoken. Imagine that you have a sack on your back. The sack holds the contents of the session just ended. Is there anything in there that belongs to anyone else? Parties don't need you to take over their problems; they need you to help them manage, resolve, or transform them. Make sure you don't offer to carry them along the way. After a few mediations, your bag will be so heavy that you have to put it down if you do.

Some of us are more like emotional sponges than others. We find it difficult to be around someone feeling pain or sadness without experiencing it, too. When someone we care about feels something, it is even harder not to "take it on." As we feel it, we become identified with the experience. Have you ever done this, only to find that your friend has moved on, leaving you with the unwanted baggage of his or her emotions? I remember hearing of a friend's frustrations and irritations with a new partner. I listened as she spoke about her emotions. I would have said that I felt them with her. Later I realized that I had crossed a boundary from acknowledging the emotions in her atmosphere to taking them on as my weather system. Long after she and her partner were happily living together, I carried feelings of distrust and suspicion that she had discarded, based on more experience. I realized then how essential it is to be aware of emotions but not become identified with them.

Drawing Healthy Emotional Boundaries

It is all very well to say that emotions are useful, positive things and that we should welcome them. They surely point to important parts of what is going on with us and others, and they need to be attended to, consulted, and brought into conflict for a conflict to be transformed. As they are brought in, they may become assets; emotions can be not only negative and divisive but positive and connective. Love, affection, trust, and respect are feeling parts of the relationships we hold most dear.

Before opening our arms to emotions, it is important to look at some of the reasons we may feel apprehensive. Emotions are potent and powerful. Negative ones can bring enormous destruction to feelings, relationships, property—even human life. Yet pushing them away doesn't make them go away any more than denying the existence of a loss obliterates it. It may pack them with more intensity so that if and when we lose control, the result is even more destructive.

We live in an age when we get all kinds of messages about managing our feelings. Emotions take on the image of a fierce beast living inside of us. Either it is not to be let out at all, or perhaps it can be taken for short walks but only on a lead. So in our conflict processes, we suggest that parties should vent, express their anger. The assumption is that doing this will help get it out of the way. But does this work? Is it not possible that venting leads to reinforcement of the angry feelings for the speaker and more pain for the listener?

I observed a therapist in training who noticed that one member of the couple he was counseling had a great deal of anger toward her partner. After a few sessions, he proposed that they devote a session to her feelings. She was to express these feelings; her partner was to communicate understanding but no argument or contradiction. As she expressed her anger, it intensified. The therapist coached her to express it even more, to "really get in touch with it." Her partner listened as instructed, not contradicting or countering. After twenty minutes or so, the speaker stopped and the couple sat in silence. It was clear from the listener's face that the experience had been devastating. I wondered how much of what was said had really been heard. At some point, we shut off to avoid more pain.

This experience left me questioning the so-called wisdom that expressing negative emotions will exorcise them, leaving them dumped in a heap where they can't do anyone any more harm. Did the woman speaking feel lighter? To me, she appeared anxious, guilty about the hurt she had inflicted on her partner, worried about the efficacy of what had happened. Even if the experience was cathartic for her, the damage to her partner may have outweighed the gain.

We know from neurological studies that anger triggers a flight-or-fight response in the brain. This has two powerful effects: a quick rush of energy (to make either fight or flight possible) and a general action-readiness, which stays around for hours or days, much longer than the initial rush. This action-readiness means that there is a general level of emotional excitement. If another trigger is pushed that might ordinarily elicit no response, the entire cycle may be reactivated. When triggered in this way, we may feel an illusion of power and invulnerability. This may lead to aggression and will certainly severely strain our capacity for self-observation.

Venting anger often works to prolong the angry state rather than calm it. As we give our feelings expression, we pump up our brain's arousal and get more angry, not less so. Goleman quotes a Tibetan teacher, Chogyam Trungpa, who advised this when asked how to deal with anger: "Don't suppress it. But don't act on it."[13]

So expressing negative emotions in conflict is not a complete prescription. It may not release them in the owner, and it risks significantly damaging the receiver and the relationship. At the same time, unacknowledged negative emotions can freeze the process, arresting its development and the potential to move forward. How much emotion to invite, how to invite it, and when, all depend on the context. What are the parties' levels of comfort with emotion?

What is your comfort as a third party? You can be sure your attitudes and comfort with emotion will influence ways you intervene. You may see danger and escalation where parties perceive little; you may miss danger and intensity where they are implicit. Part of competence as a third party is knowing your own emotional blind spots and Achilles heels when it comes to working with emotions.

It is also important to remember that emotions are received and expressed differently by men and women and in different cultural contexts. Some researchers suggest that women tend to experience both positive and negative emotions with more intensity. Whether or not this is true, there is surely a wide range in the degree of acceptance for emotionality expressed by men and women. Those of us who are very vigilant about what might happen or who tend to pay close attention to the surrounding dynamics are more likely to experience intense emotions. Our earlier example of Alice's and José's responses to losing their pens emphasizes the possible range of emotional intensity. Our challenge as practitioners is to develop awareness of this range and fluency in dealing with it.

How Can We Enhance Emotional Fluency?

A process centered in relationship nurtures relationships; this is self evident. Central to relationships are the experience and expression of emotions. Competent trainers and third parties examine the ways they convene processes, engage parties, reflect on their work, and care for themselves for degrees of emotional fluency. Here are some of the ways this can be done.

Extending

We extend our hands to each other in greeting. We extend an invitation to friends for dinner. *Extending* means offering a part of ourselves to another. In our courses and interventions, we extend an offer of a respectful environment—one that welcomes a range of feelings not acceptable in a courtroom and not appreciated in many social settings. One of the most powerful ways that we extend this offer is through the language we choose.

Emotionally fluent third parties and facilitators extend a welcome to feelings, positive and negative, through modeling emotional expression. Imagine a boring presentation. What was the delivery like? For me, a presentation without much expressiveness comes to mind, perhaps someone reading a paper, reciting facts or statistics without context or commentary. Mindful of this, I engage parties with emotionally expressive language and nonverbal communication. My goal is to communicate interest, positive regard, and an invitation to construct, with me, a container that will provide safety and respect appropriate to their needs. When I talk about the kind of process I envision, I pay attention to using some feeling words such as *hopeful, optimistic, concerned,* and *apprehensive.* Using words with both positive and negative associations can normalize varied expression for parties without casting a negative shadow on the entire process.

Another aspect of extending involves building a process that is not entirely problem-focused. A positive climate for dialogue can be nurtured by extending an invitation to participants to share memories that are positive and precious, as well as problems and traumas.

Emotionally fluent third parties and facilitators balance negative expressions by anchoring the process in positive visions from the past and imagined visions of the future. Before identifying issues or solving problems, I invite the parties to share images of the past that are precious (in the case of family mediation), places or experiences of community collaboration that stand out (in the case of public policy processes), or things they are proud of about their school or workplace (in educational or organizational processes). This may be resisted as unproductive, but it truly sets a different emotional tone for the process and helps the hard parts unfold with more lubrication. Asking participants where they want to be in the future with each other, in their community, or in their lives can also be very powerful.

Appreciative inquiry is one approach that engages participants in detailed descriptions of their desired future state, coming from the view that you won't know when you've arrived if you weren't sure where you were going. The sensory, emotional aspects of these future visions are important anchors for a process that transits rough water on the way from here to there. Participants can hang on to the positive feelings, the relief, and the hope that are generated as part of the visioning process.

In a recent public policy process, this way of beginning transformed what promised to be a protracted process into a single, successful meeting. The siting of an access road to a school had been the subject of several rounds of litigation, political appeals, and entrenched community conflict. Parties, including representatives of local and state government, the school board, the developer, and community members, met to try for a consensus outcome. They were surprised when they were asked to introduce themselves by talking about what they valued as unique and precious about their area. They were proud when the state representatives spoke of its magnificent beauty and competition in the state office to do field visits. They were moved when the facilitator recounted his first visit to that state and his experience of falling in love with the nearby mountains. Beginning in this way disturbed their patterns of conflicting with each other, extending the invitation to center their discussions in what they shared: a commitment to the community and the safety of the children who were its heirs. Brought into constructive relationship with each other, they were able to find solutions to the material issues that had divided them for years.

Engaging

One of the reasons the introductions worked so well to set an appreciative climate was that they invited authentic engagement. When we are sincere, or authentic with each other, trust is developed and commitments are reliable. Carl Rogers[14] based his successful career as a psychotherapist on this foundation—that it is powerful to create relationships characterized by genuineness and transparency, in which real feelings are welcomed and explored rather than pushed away.

Emotionally fluent third parties and facilitators show authentic feelings in relationships with parties, with co-trainers or cofacilitators, and with their material. We may be strategic in our interactions with parties, but we also need to be authentic. If we are not, then the lack of

congruence between what we profess and what we do may ultimately undermine the process. It is simple to see this. If a parent,
teacher, or other person in authority asked you to do something
that they were not willing to do themselves, did it make you more
or less willing to do it? The story of Gandhi, recounted in Chapter
One, is instructive. When asked to tell a young boy not to eat sugar,
he replied, "Go away and come back to ask me in two weeks."
When the mother brought her son back, Gandhi admonished him
not to eat sugar. When she asked why he had asked her to return
in two weeks, he gently said, "I had to stop eating sugar myself
first." Gandhi understood the importance of congruence, of doing
what he asked others to do.

In our relationships with co-trainers and cofacilitators, authenticity is also essential. Co-training gives us a powerful way of demonstrating the capacities and approaches we are advocating. As we
respect and acknowledge our colleagues, we create a positive climate for participants. If we have unresolved conflicts with our colleagues, these may play out in our work or at least undermine its
effectiveness. Many evaluation forms in my teaching and intervention have included appreciative comments about the genuine
regard my colleagues and I demonstrate for each other.

It is also important that we are genuine in our relationship to
the material we teach. If I am teaching something old or stale, I
ask myself how I can shift or change it until it feels new. If I don't,
my lack of authentic enthusiasm will be communicated to participants, and their experience will be less compelling. If I am unsure
about an aspect of my material, I find it useful to acknowledge my
questions and feelings. Doing so invites participants into more
complex engagement with the material. As participants engage
emotionally with the material and each other, we are challenged
to guide the engagement in constructive ways.

We have said that it is neither productive to bathe ourselves in
emotions like a weather system nor to vent them as though they
were a finite collection of waste. At the same time, it is important
that they be expressed so that the process is not frozen by their
unnamed presence.

*Emotionally fluent third parties and facilitators teach participants about
a state of "witness," in which it is possible to hear emotions and not take*

them on. They teach them about how to attain this state and how to maintain it in the face of difficult interactions. What is a state of witness? *Witness* is the description I use for a particular quality of listening and talking. It means to prepare myself by adopting a spirit of genuine inquiry and curiosity, letting go of judgment in advance. I also cultivate openness to outcome, knowing that I do not know what either the dialogue or the closure will look like. It is to let go of control, let go of responding, justifying, defending, or contradicting. It is to create a space for words to be spoken and feelings to be expressed that may be raw or unformed. Paradoxically, it is to be exquisitely present and emotionally observant at the same time. It is to step away from the trigger of emotional reactions, choosing to act as a witness to what is disclosed. It is to let go of fixing, resolving, undoing, explaining. It is a decision to "be" not to "do," to ask rather than to know, that is adopted by two or more people for a fixed period of time to address a particular subject.

In engaging a witness state, the role of silence cannot be overemphasized. Because this state is different from our usual habits, we need time to transition. A few minutes of silent preparation to still the mind and prepare for openly listening the other into speech is very useful. The communication that follows is not active listening involving paraphrasing and feeding back. The receiver tends to be quiet, inviting the other with stillness and nonverbal encouragement to continue. From this quiet place, distractions are minimized and exquisite attention is paid to the speaker. This gives the speaker unusual permission to explore and express feelings, perhaps becoming aware of them in new ways.

When I have worked with parties who adopt a "witness place" for an agreed-on period of time, I have heard many poignant and authentic disclosures. Sometimes anger and contention cover up a hurt or sad voice that wants to speak. When it is no longer resisted, the voice expresses itself with eloquence and deep acknowledgment of self and other. Witness places are places of inquiry, from where we can ask, What does this really mean to me? What is really important to me? What does it really mean to you? What is important to you? What do I really want for you, for me?

A witness state is a state apart from usual time. In this sense, it is like a ritual. It is an agreement to let in and surface the sensations and feelings associated with a particular exchange while suspending judgment, reaction, and response. Although it will not solve conflicts, it may shift the emotional tone to make problem solving possible. A witness state is an agreement to suspend usual patterns of interaction. It is like standing in the eye of a storm. There it is calm, and it is possible to see the storm swirling all around, to recognize its power and its intensity. Knowing that boundaries are present to keep the storm from engulfing you in its fury, curiosity is possible about how the storm works, what constitutes its patterns, even how it is beautiful. Having had this experience, you may perceive the storm differently as you encounter and navigate it.

Listening from a witness place helps free emotional expression without becoming completely identified with it. Those expressing emotions also need discipline; there are times we all need help to express emotions while preserving relationship.

Emotionally fluent third parties and facilitators use ways of helping parties express emotions while maintaining respect, positive regard, and relationship. One way of helping parties express emotion safely and respectfully yet genuinely is to help them learn about the state of witness. Modeling measured emotional expression yourself that is both strong and respectful is another. Capturing positive visions for the future or scenes from the past as pictures or placing lists of feeling or sensing words on the wall is another way of normalizing emotional expression. Listen and watch for the ways the parties express emotions. Try to catch them doing it respectfully but clearly. Then point it out, encouraging them to do more of what they already know how to do.

No matter how effective our processes, people who are engaged in deep conflict with each other will have unaddressed feelings.

Emotionally fluent third parties and facilitators promote additional ways for parties to address the full range of their emotions. Some of these ways may involve activity within processes; others relate to outside activities. It is impractical to think that parties can or should deal with the whole range and extent of their emotions with each other in conflict resolution sessions. Working with emotions outside of sessions is ideal, though it cannot be prescribed or necessarily suggested. Family mediators have an easier platform for suggesting that parties attend to their overall well-being than commercial or public-policy third parties. This is because there is societal understanding that divorce is a life-changing, unsettling process that people may need different kinds of support to get through.

Yet any experienced public policy mediator or facilitator will acknowledge that emotions run high in these settings as well. Although the conflicts may be less unsettling personally, they still involve clashes over meaning and threats to identity. Respecting people's privacy and their capacity to take care of their emotional well-being, it may still be possible to create opportunities for everyone to cultivate emotional fluency.

A friend led a group of senior government managers through a short yoga session before mediating their dispute. They were surprised but found themselves more relaxed and ready to tackle their issues after the yoga was over. Short, energizing activities that draw on feeling components, movement breaks between intense times of talking or negotiating, and modeling language that accords emotions validity are all helpful.

Within organizations or during long-term processes, higher levels of activity are possible. Organizational development consultants use hiking, white-water rafting, cooking, and rope climbing to engage teams in self-observation, both collectively and individually. From these observations and experiences, they are better able to develop ways of working together. These activities provide emotional and physical releases that create a better climate for joint work, as well as a deeper sense of connection among participants.

Movement or physical exercise is well known as an antidote to emotional stress. Practicing yoga, tai chi, qi gong, or the martial arts may help; meditating or journal writing are other possibilities, depending on personal preference. Visualization or creative writing may be useful ways to uncover and acknowledge feelings. Therapy of various kinds may also be a useful adjunct to processes. The appropriate vehicle may change over time and with practice, but we have only begun to realize the importance of cultivating emotional fluency in our lives and our conflict processes.

Reflecting

As emotional fluency informs our work as practitioners, we need to develop vocabulary and tools to assess our progress.

Emotionally fluent third parties and facilitators consider questions of emotional fluency, as well as measures of substantive progress when reflecting on teaching or intervention, individually or with colleagues. Samples of the kind of questions that might be asked include

- How comfortable were the participants?
- What range of emotional expressions did you invite in setting up the process?
- Did you use a number of modalities to reinforce a wide range of emotional and sensory expression?
- Did you engage participants in using a witness state when the moment was ripe?
- Did you suggest other ways that participants might experience and express their emotions, both in and outside the session?
- Did you monitor the ways your comfort with emotional expression affected the parties?

Emotional fluency as a category for reflection and self-evaluation opens many doors. You might also consider whether you modeled emotional language in your speech, whether the questions you asked acknowledged emotions as valid ways of knowing, and how you experienced emotional expressions by parties. Did you help provide safe, respectful ways for emotions to be expressed while not foreclosing opportunities? Did you take time for silence in the process, during which parties could reflect and come into contact with their feelings? Did you encourage parties to explore emotional dimensions of issues, without getting mired in them? Using imagery and ritual may also help parties make emotional transitions. Ways to do this will be explored in Chapters Six and Eight.

Another aspect of reflection relates to the emotional fluency of our processes.

Emotionally fluent third parties and facilitators consider the elements of the processes they use and those they teach. Are they based primarily in reason or feeling? Are there additional ways to balance them so that both reason and feeling are welcome? Our field has been pervasively influenced by an admonition by Fisher, Ury, and Patton to "separate the people from the problem."[15] From many cultural perspectives, this notion does not serve us well. I remember clearly a Vietnamese woman who patiently explained to me that relations are her life, her water in the desert of existence. Conflicts involve people and need to be worked out by drawing on the relational glue that connects people.

A friend has worked extensively with American expatriate managers in Asia. In talking with employees reporting to them, he found that they were perceived as cold, mechanical, and uncaring. They tended to focus on problems and solutions without engaging their employees on a personal basis. As a consultant, he worked with these managers to engage the person first in an authentic way before inquiring about or handling a problem. During and after handling the problem, he reminded them to ground their interaction in human connection and caring. As they experienced the benefits of this approach, the managers recast their ideas of efficiency and effectiveness in the context of a workplace where strong relationships made everything else work well.

Even if it were possible to separate people from problems, we risk losing what is precious when we seek to screen out what we see as negative or problematic. Emotions are not clearly divisible into those that help and those that hinder. Anger may cover sadness, and sadness may unlock empathy or compassion. Frustration may lead to determination to change—an energy that will animate and advance a conflict process.

As our theory and practice evolve beyond the prescription to separate people and problems, we are better advised to cultivate creative caring. From a foundation of caring, things are possible that seem out of the question in the cold, harsh light of historical wounds and the emotional scars that accompany them. The Dalai Lama reminds us that "it's important to recognize that if human conflicts are created by misuse of human intelligence, we can also utilize our intelligence to find ways and means to overcome these conflicts. When human intelligence and human goodness or affection are used together, all human actions become more constructive."[16]

Our actions can be more constructive when we invite emotions in as assets in our processes. Consider the training or intervention processes you use. When stories are shared, how much space do you make for emotional dimensions? Is there a balance between problem solving and exploration? What do you do in your processes to encourage and model a spirit of inquiry and openness to outcome? How do you create the space and conditions for parties or participants to experience connection with each other and with you? When do you use a witness state, and how do you communicate its importance to parties? What other ways do you use to engage emotional intelligence?

In training or teaching, using many modalities for instruction is a way to cultivate emotional fluency. Working with real-life experiences, storytelling, giving demonstrations, showing videotapes, engaging in perspective-taking exercises, writing, drawing, sculpting, imagining—all are ways to engage and validate emotions. Be sure to include questions that relate to emotional fluency in your debriefing. Also consider how the skills you are teaching relate to emotional fluency. Are you teaching empathy, ways to elicit and validate emotional dimensions of issues, symbolic skills that help with emotional transitions, ways of being in touch with feelings as third parties? What other skills and capacities would you add to this list?

Self-Care

Just as we cannot separate conflict from the relationships in which it develops and is addressed, so we cannot separate our own issues with emotions from the way we do our work.

Emotionally fluent third parties and facilitators cultivate emotional fluency. They find ways to increase their repertoire of emotional expression and awareness of emotional dynamics internally and externally. They practice. In the dominant culture of North America, women are given more opportunities to develop emotional fluency and more latitude to express it. By this I don't mean that women are more emotional but that they are less likely to be judged negatively for having and expressing feelings. Of course, because feelings are not considered legitimate ways of knowing in many professional settings, women's views are also discounted when expressed in emotional registers. Women are encouraged from infancy to display emotions and to care for others who do. Of course, not all women are comfortable with emotional expression. And many men have gone beyond their social conditioning and developed broad emotional repertoires.

Take stock of your emotional fluency by asking these questions:

- Do I generally know what I am feeling about a particular person or situation?
- Do I spend quiet or contemplative time every day when I let feelings come into my awareness and then pass through?
- Do I have practices that help me name and deal with, then shift difficult or painful feelings?
- Am I learning more about ways to do this in my life?
- Do I have a wide repertoire of choices when I feel strong emotions?
- How can I broaden these choices?
- Do I have comfortable ways to respond to emotional intensity from others?
- Am I learning about my emotional blind spots and ways that I may limit myself emotionally?
- Am I applying what I've learned in my practice?

There are some wonderful resources available to help with this exploration. One of the best is Jeanne Segal's book *Raising Your Emotional Intelligence*.[17]

As you become aware of emotional fluency, you will find yourself reading, encountering new resources, and expanding your choices. As you do this, you will increase your capacity for effectiveness as a third party.

Emotionally fluent third parties and facilitators know their emotional limits. They do not try to feed their processes from an empty well. If you are feeling depleted, find ways to nurture yourself. Tend to your whole self, including feelings. As one who believed that feelings got in the way of efficiency, I sometimes failed to see my limits. I would push myself to do one more course, one more consultation, one more article, until I was exhausted and drawing from a dry bucket of energy. Usually, I was able to carry on through the days of training at the end of such a streak of demanding tasks. But during the evenings and after the training, I would find it difficult to do anything. Many people who want to help others do get themselves into situations like this, finding it difficult to set boundaries and to stop long enough to listen to their own feelings. If this sounds like you, use this as a reminder to slow down and listen. As Margaret Atwood reminds us in her books, it is important to pay attention. We can continue only so long on autopilot.

As you cultivate emotional fluency, you will be an inspiration to others. Then your job is simply to continue. What have you read in the last month that speaks to your spirit, to the part of you that makes meaning? Where have you taken yourself that is a feast for your senses, where you feel more alive, inspired? What gifts have you given yourself of friendship, quiet time with loved ones, unplanned hours alone? These are not meant to be prescriptions but suggestions in the spirit of honoring our need for attunement. As we do, we will have more to offer as a trainer and third party.

In addition to nurturing ourselves, the process of cultivating awareness continues.

Emotionally fluent third parties and facilitators know their emotional hot spots. Do you find intense anger frightening? Know your strategies for dealing with triggers. Do an inventory of emotions you find difficult. Some of us find accepting love and praise more difficult than criticism. Others find it hard to be in the presence of jibes and insults, even when they are not directed at us. If you are not sure what your hot spots are, try to remember stories from earlier in your life when you were uncomfortable. What was happening emotionally at those times for others and for you? As you identify your hot spots, note them down. Choose one at a time and focus on it.

For the next few days, attend to any situations, whether real or on television or in movies, where situations like this occur. What do you notice about your gut-level, first response? What other choices do you have at your disposal? How can you find ways to increase your comfort with this kind of expression? If it is not the kind of expression you want to use in your life (frequent criticism of a partner, for example), think about how you will handle it the next time a similar behavior arises in mediation. You may find that your views about particular forms of emotional expression do not change but that your ability to let others experience what they need expands as you come to know your own triggers.

Emotionally fluent third parties and facilitators learn and use a process for centering and letting go of the emotional intensity of processes. Develop relationships with colleagues where you can talk about these approaches and get support for what you are doing. As you bring the idea of emotional fluency into your collegial relationships, you will find that you develop new ways to cultivate it. Colleagues are a rich resource for coaching and honest exploration of processes, training approaches, and personal progress. As more and more of us speak in this register, we will discover new ways to develop emotional fluency, both individually and collectively.

Continuing Development

Anais Nin[18] writes that the richest source of creation is feeling, followed by a vision of its meaning. As we invite emotions into our processes, it may seem strange or soft or limiting or cloudy. It is this way with anything that is unfamiliar and outside the realm of what we have evolved as orthodoxy or accepted practice. Yet emotions more often derail conflict processes than we might like to think. Consider what you have heard about the Israeli-Palestinian conflict or any other protracted situation. Each side speaks emotionally, conveying feelings about "the other" that include distrust, enmity, contempt, and blame. If we leave these feelings out of negotiation, focusing on the issues via rational analysis alone, we have missed a significant dimension of the problem.

Much work remains to be done on ways we can bring emotions into our processes that honors their wisdom without obscuring clarity. This work will be advanced as emotional fluency becomes acknowledged as important for trainers and third parties. It will be complemented by the development of capacities on the sensory, imaginative, and spiritual levels. These levels are examined in the chapters that follow.

CHAPTER THREE

Somatic Ways of Knowing
Enacting Change

They were quite good friends, the two of them. But on this particular day, it seemed as though they couldn't do anything harmoniously. Old wounds were nudged when one made a careless remark. A misunderstanding arose from a shorthand phrase. Although they were in a beautiful place hiking, they both felt on edge, on guard. Little things escalated, as they sometimes can. After attempts to clarify that seemed to make things worse, conversation ceased. Their feelings were raw, and it was difficult to enjoy the scenery.

They were both surprised when they came upon a deserted recreation area along the way in a clearing. There they found a Ping-Pong table and two paddles, complete with a couple of balls. Without speaking, they picked them up and began to play a game. They played intensely, volleying back and forth, hitting the ball first to one corner and then to another. Their faces were pictures of concentration, and their hands gripped the paddles intently. After an hour, they put the paddles down and met near the net, giving each other hugs of relief.

What happened? Conflict, like a moribund appliance, had been grumbling between them as they had hiked. Talking about it had not helped. Silence did not make it disappear. The Ping-Pong table, appearing as if by magic, gave them a chance to enact their feelings so they were able to shift them. What can we generalize from this experience? It points us to our bodies as assets in addressing, preventing, and transforming conflicts. Yet most of our processes are designed to function from the neck up. Have we brought limiting assumptions about our bodies to the conflict field, thus missing important opportunities?

A quick search under "physical" in a few leading conflict textbooks yields information about physical settings, table shapes, room configurations, and the prevention of physical aggression, but nothing about the positive effects of physical movement or about the body as a source of knowing. Although some training programs address the importance of physical movement in dealing with impasse or team building, few are concerned with developing body awareness or using body-based techniques with disputants. There are exceptions, but too much of our theory and practice misses the opportunities available via our physical selves.

In this chapter, we explore the capacities of our bodies for emotional and sensory awareness and examine how our bodies assist us in negotiating change. We survey some of the physical practices currently in use in the conflict resolution field and suggest ways that physical activities and awareness can be integrated into practice and theory.

The Importance of Bodies

The importance of our bodies is often underestimated until we experience illness or injury. Only when my foot is injured do I become aware of how much I treasure my ability to walk. Only when my stomach is upset do I reflect on the miracle of digestion—how my body daily turns nutrients into energy. Absent physical problems, we tend to import our values of efficiency and management into our attitudes toward our bodies.

Seeing our bodies as inconvenient or as impediments to higher consciousness, we focus on disciplining them, building them, managing them. This relationship of control and minimization distances us from our bodies and pervades our conflict processes. Artificially maintaining a distinction between our minds and hearts, between our bodies and our spirits, we fail to acknowledge the body at the center of our lives, our possibilities, our instinctive knowing about how to navigate conflict.

It is not surprising that we take bodies for granted, associating them with the prosaic and the inconvenient. Bodies are dominated by needs for food, drink, shelter, sleep, sex. They become ill and deteriorate; they slow down thought; they smell and make noise; they both transport us and limit us. Bodies are constantly engaged in "everyday reality." They mechanically perform repetitive actions like getting dressed or driving a car.

Our tendency to underestimate the multidimensional gifts available through the body is illustrated in a story told by Gabrielle Roth.[1] She met a rabbi who had just buried his father, who was also a rabbi. He had asked his father on his deathbed, "What was the most important thing in your life, the Torah?" And the old man had answered, "My body." "I was stunned," reported the rabbi. "I had always thought my body was just a vehicle for my mind; feed it, clothe it, send it to Harvard."

The dying rabbi knew that the body is a pathway to emotional and spiritual wisdom—a precious gift that he was losing. Yet his son had followed the time-honored tradition of seeing the body as incidental. Indeed, the son's spiritual values may have reinforced the idea of the body as an impediment to spiritual evolution, believing in the need to leave behind the ballast of matter to rise through the vast dimensions of the spirit.

What would the old rabbi tell us about the importance of our bodies if he still walked among us? We cannot know, but we can use his insight as an impetus to explore what our bodies know, what they have to offer us when we consider them more than vehicles for task accomplishment. Bodies, after all, see, hear, taste, sense, vocalize, touch, feel, think, and receive. Bodies also bridge, connect, dance, play, create, and discover. Our bodies' intelligence is a rich resource in times of conflict.

Body Wisdom

It is a truism that we cannot extricate ourselves from the conflicts we have gotten into through logic and analysis alone. Emotions are an important guide—important to helping us know what we want and also important for their role in animating and deepening relationships. In discussing emotions, we noted that emotions are made known to us through our bodies.

Emotional experience is body-centered, not intellectual. The constant interplay between our bodies and our emotions is almost a cliché. Consider these common expressions:

- My heart is broken.
- She keeps a stiff upper lip.
- This boy had such a chip on his shoulder that he was really a pain to be around.
- I knew it in my gut.

Emotions, as we have seen, fire the nervous system, which triggers the release of the hormones that affect and produce emotions. Adrenalin, which accompanies fear or anger, enables us to flee or attack with more power. Hate turns inward and makes us sick. Given these physiological reactions, the possibility of being able to shift our feelings through physical channels opens up to us. It is possible, for example, to change feelings through breathing exercises.

Feelings do change through movement, as anyone who has done aerobic exercise knows. Athletes report experiencing states of intense well-being and freedom, having altered perceptions of size and field, floating, flying, having exceptional energy. I started running after years of gentler exercise, partly to find a way to process anger and frustration. Psychologists prescribe vigorous exercise for people who are depressed. More than drugs that mask or manipulate symptoms, exercise works to shift mood and state of mind. Once our mood is shifted, our thoughts become lighter and more optimistic. We can see possibilities that were obscured to us previously.

Movement, whether through vigorous exercise, dance, yoga, or a Sunday afternoon walk, is useful not only for its positive effect on mood and state of mind but because it brings us into contact with our bodies, heightens our awareness of the resources our bodies hold. Bodies are more than receptacles of pain and instruments of pleasure. They are more than vehicles that we have to keep in shape so they will last throughout our lives. Bodies are also wise.

Nietzsche advised that it is important to learn to think with the body. What would it be like to do this? Consider when you have thought with your body. Many of us can recall moments of panic or crisis in which our body responded while our mind was in shock. Stories of mothers lifting cars off their trapped children come to mind, as well as other Herculean feats where bodies take over, leaving the mind to try later to reconstruct what happened. Aside from these extraordinary examples, let's consider what thinking with the body might look like in everyday life.

Perhaps thinking with the body is what Rollo May had in mind when he wrote his classic book *The Courage to Create*. He wrote:

> We need a new kind of courage that will neither run rampant in violence nor require our assertion of egocentric power *over* other people. I propose a new form of courage of the body: the use of the body . . . for the cultivation of sensitivity. This will mean the development of the capacity to listen with the body. It will be a valuing of the body as a means of empathy with others, as expression of the self as a thing of beauty and as a rich source of pleasure.[2]

Listening, thinking, and feeling with the body—all of these are possible when bodies are tuned, both discerning and communicating at many levels at once. We do use our bodies these ways and acknowledge our body's versatility and sensitivity with our language, without realizing it. With our eyes, we reveal ourselves to each other, looking for understanding and connection. So we say, "I saw into him" or "I let her see inside." We say we have "reached out" when we make an overture of understanding; we say we have "shut down" when our bodies cannot take in any more information.

Our bodies engage in dynamic and subliminal exchange with others in ways that connect or distance, mediated by the release of hormones and nonverbal signals. Take the experience of going for a walk with a friend. Our bodies adjust their movements to move at the same pace. Our breathing may synchronize. There is a cadence and a rhythm to our conversation related to the pace our bodies are moving. We may pick up feelings or knowings in our bodies that speak to the state of mind or heart of our friend.

As my friend speaks of her recent visit with her parents, I feel pervasive sadness, though she has not named this. When I ask about it, she unfolds a new level of the visit—one beneath the apparent conviviality, where concerns about her father's drinking cast a shadow over the love and connection they feel. How did I know the sadness existed? I sensed it, felt it physically as a kind of heaviness around my diaphragm. We don't have a very well-developed vocabulary for expressing our bodies' knowing, yet most of us can identify a time when we have experienced it.

When we are together in a group, communication occurs constantly, systemically, and physically. When we are facilitating or mediating, our bodies serve as barometers of the group climate and dynamics. By paying attention to our bodily sensations, we are cued to dynamics in the group. At times, I feel the sudden onset of fatigue, an almost overwhelming desire to curl up in a corner and go to sleep. Because of the suddenness of the feeling, I am quite sure that it is not just fatigue but something heavy in me or in the group. Something needs to shift, to move, to unlock, so that the work of the group can proceed.

At other times, I feel a quickening, a sense of lightness, an opening. It is as though a sun ray angles into my heart, illuminating and creating space. As I experience this physical sensation, I pose the internal questions: What is possible now? What needs to happen? Sometimes it is appropriate to pose the questions to the group. The answers come, manifesting in a new discovery, an agreement on an issue, or an insight for one or more of the participants. The body sensed it before the mind could explain or even apprehend what was happening.

As I mentally scan for examples of times when my body wisdom helped me as a third party or trainer, I remember small inklings more than dramatic discoveries. Many times the process was internal rather than overt or obvious. The bodily sensations were subtle and could be explained away as "something I ate" or with the admonition to the self to get more sleep. Yet when I did not explain my body wisdom away but consciously paid attention, I was more attuned to my body's messages. The messages came in the form of general discomfort or tightness in my chest. I wriggled in my chair, knowing that the conversation needed to shift. I walked around the room as I lectured and found myself stepping toward a topic I had not planned to address. Recognizing that my body has intelligence that helps reveal, shift, and inform, I tie theoretical presentations to physical and sensory experience as often as possible.

Physical Dimensions of Encountering Difference

In a recent class, I was giving a lecture about levels of conflict and how it involves issues, communication, and symbolic cultural meanings (see Chapter One, Figure 1.1). I had drawn a chart of the levels and was going through them in sequential order. I was careful to explain that the dimensions are not linear, that most conflicts involve all of them, though they can be centered in any one of them. This theoretical framework is helpful for understanding the complexity of conflict, but it remains theoretical and abstract until it is directly experienced.

It is easy to see that most conflicts have a symbolic dimension, touching us where we make meaning and where we hold our pictures of ourselves or our identities. Because our identities and ways of making meaning are so close to us, we react defensively when they are challenged. It is a very short leap from noticing that someone has a radically different way of being in the world to making negative attributions about that person. This is true, even if we are not in conflict over any material item; it arises from the discomfort we feel when confronted with fundamental difference.

An exercise called Alphaville helps participants in my classes experience the physical and emotional dimensions of symbolic differences. Students who have been studying intercultural conflict are asked to meet in groups of six. From their groups, they select two people who will act as cultural "consultants," traveling to Alphaville to investigate the beliefs and behaviors of Alphavillians to help an industrial client decide whether to site a facility there.

While the consultants are out of the room planning their strategies, I instruct the class that the communication norms in Alphaville are simple. In communicating with strangers, residents of Alphaville say only yes or no. It is impolite to expand in any way and would cause any Alphavillian who did so to be an outcast. How do they decide whether to say yes or no to a specific question? If the questioner is smiling, they answer yes. If the questioner is not smiling, they answer no.

I then meet with the consultants and inform them that Alphavillians will only answer questions from outsiders with yes or no. I invite the consultants in, and they begin their quest to learn about the culture in Alphaville. Some consultants are very earnest and serious in their quest and receive repeated "no" answers. Others are relaxed and playful and receive many "yes" answers. Sometimes pairs of consultants are opposite; they begin to think that Alphavillians give different answers, depending on who asks the question.

Although it seems a simple activity, very few consultants ever figure out the nonverbal cues that dictate the answers given. Even when I tell them that there is a nonverbal cue involved and send them back to work on it, it is rare that they come to identify it. This is probably because they are acting from within their way of making meaning—a way that ascribes literal meaning to *yes* and *no* as affirmative and negative. Because these terms mean something else when used by Alphavillians, it is difficult for consultants to understand how they are being triggered and what they mean.

But the most interesting part of this exercise happens after the simulation is over. Before debriefing, I ask each consultant duo to report their findings about Alphaville to the group. Most of the time, they suggest that Alphaville is not a suitable place to locate any facility. They report diverse and rather incredible findings, describing Alphavillians as friendly but difficult to come to know or understand, contradictory, unwilling to work, members of a peculiar religious cult, childless, confused, and slow-witted. All of this when Alphavillians said only yes or no in answer to questions!

The exercise shows everyone how assumptions and preconceived ideas infiltrate our understanding of others. Because it is physically enacted, the lesson is viscerally remembered by participants long after other class activities have faded from memory. The exercise demonstrates powerfully the thinness of the line between not understanding someone who is different and diminishing them, seeing them as less than ourselves. When our meaning systems are different, negative images are associated with "the other," and some sort of bridge is needed.

Talking about meaning systems will not persuade "the other" that his or her system needs to change. Meaning making is a deeply personal, cultural, iterative process and not one easily amenable to negotiation. What can help build a bridge are activities that rehumanize the other, engaging people in doing something together. This is one reason that the physical realm is so useful and important. As we work on a project together, we come to see ways we are similar. As we accomplish a task, we share a sense of accomplishment. As we physically touch, we come into irrefutable contact with each other's humanity. In ongoing relationships, physical awareness and shared activities are important resources for shifting old patterns.

Physical Activity to Create Shifts

Encountering conflict in relationship, I may play old patterns out over and over again through repeated interactions. If someone is proposing a very different way of looking at the world, my way of making meaning may feel threatened, and I may project my discomfort onto the other, seeing her or him as unwise or unworthy. Internal physical tension is a cue that something is stuck or blocked. I will probably experience this tension in a way that is familiar to me because it arises from the physical habits I have internalized related to my ways of seeing and being in the world.

Our bodies are meaning-making beings; through them we discern and communicate the patterns of meaning we have made. We tend to reenact these patterns again and again. In integrated body psychotherapy, this is called the primary scenario.[3] According to this approach, our early years give us our roles and imprint those roles into our bodies. We become the "good son," the "fussy one," the "easy-going child," depending on our interactions with caregivers. We experience ourselves as excluded, celebrated, silenced, or shamed. As adults, these experiences inform our favorite strategies for addressing conflicts. These strategies have physical referents associated with them.

If I have an internalized relational pattern of feeling discounted or excluded, I will be more likely to interpret interactions as involving exclusion or minimization. They will manifest in my body as a sense of being covered up, silenced, or held back from the center of things. I may experience shallow breathing, constraint in my chest, or the sense that my voice is muffled. Because the feelings and physical sensations are internalized, I may not recognize when I am reenacting that pattern. If I recognize the body sensation associated with feeling covered up, I can then make different choices about how to respond.

It makes sense that bodies learn and then act from their learning in patterned ways. Recent discoveries have made the interconnected, learning capacities of our bodies even more clear. In 1994, Robert Ader showed that the immune system, like the brain and central nervous system, learns.[4] Ader found that when he gave animals a chemical that depressed their t-cell count in a certain liquid, the t-cell count was depressed whenever the animals were given the same liquid, even if it did not contain the chemical. It turns out that there are many pathways by which the immune system and the brain communicate—biological pathways that make the mind, the emotions, and the body completely connected and intertwined, not separate.

Applying this understanding to behavior, we internalize behavioral patterns that become a certain shorthand, that inform our interpretations, expectations, and attributions that are accompanied by patterned physical experiences. An external stimulus starts a habitual response, and we engage in a dance our bodies know well, leading us into familiar situations and, sometimes, cul de sacs.

The dance can be interrupted if we realize it is unfolding and make a choice to step out of habit and into awareness. We can use our bodies to enact change or experiment with what change might feel like. When we feel covered up or held back, we can explore ways to throw off the cover or move into the center of a conversation. Feeling discounted or pushed away, we can engage the physical feeling of rejection and use it like an aikido practitioner to reengage in the interaction. If our chest feels tight, we can send breath to release it. If our voice sounds muffled, we can make a different choice, summoning a voice that is strong and commanding. As internalized patterns are interrupted, we access more ways to shift how we hold ourselves and our ideas. In turn, this leads to shifts in relationships.

Bodies and Shifts in Relationship

Intervenors can draw on the awareness of physical patterns without necessarily naming them. Because physical patterns are not only individual but relational, it is useful to assess the physical dimensions of group behavior. How do members position themselves with respect to each other? Are they distant, close, receptive, imposing? Where do they choose to sit, and what do their collective actions reveal about their positions? How do these patterns serve the group or hold it back? Posing these questions to himself, a mediator was able to shift the relational climate between two adversarial councils over a zoning dispute.

The meeting seemed to go on forever. The councilors and mayors from both sides had been involved in the dispute for years, and this first meeting with the mediator was not diffusing the tension in the room. Although they adopted a set of procedures with relative politeness, the mediator's invitation to develop an agenda launched them back into their familiar dance of distrust. They disagreed about the issues and the order in which issues would be discussed. They descended into repetitive patterns of negative interaction. The atmosphere was drawn and tense.

At the break, the mediator reflected on the physical arrangements in the room. The two contingents of councilors were seated across from each other at a long board table, defining and accentuating the two sides and communicating formality. They lobbed arguments and justifications at each other from across the table, just as they might debate during council meetings. It was clear that something had to shift for anything productive to come out of the meeting.

Following the break, the mediator produced blank index cards and asked them to meet in dyads, one person from each council. Their task was to listen to each other as each identified her or his three priority issues and for the listener to record these on index cards in a way that was satisfactory to the speaker. These were then posted, clustered, and used as a way to formulate the agenda. Sitting and working together provided a positive way of moving forward, and everyone felt relief that the meeting had been, after all, productive.

The importance of physical movement in shifting out of stuck places is not a new discovery. We have long known that one way to deal with impasse is to "go to the balcony," from which we may return with different perspectives or at least more oxygen. Third parties and trainers also know that asking parties or participants to work together into small groups or dyads builds relationship and empathy. But this empathy is built not only through the feelings evoked in the sharing. It is also built symbolically and physically, as people seek to reduce dissonance and act in socially appropriate ways.

When the councilors came together in groups of two, it was harder to maintain enmity. Away from the insulation of the large group, they behaved with less indifference and negative judgment and with more interest and openness. Through semistructured speaking and listening, and from a desire to "do the task right," they found a way to listen to each other differently than they had in the large group. The table was no longer a physical buffer, defining "sides." Sitting close together, they related with more intimacy and less posturing than they had in the large group.

Subsequent meetings went much more smoothly, built on the foundation of this one departure from "business as usual." The physical arrangement of parties in dyads built their capacity for partnership as they collaborated over a noncontroversial task of listening and recording. This brought them into a constructive experience of relationship, emphasized and reinforced by their physical proximity. It opened a previously closed door to the experience of empathy and curiosity that improved relationships and outcomes.

Bodies and Connections

To value the body as a means of empathy with others is to explore nonverbal dimensions of relationship. It is to enter a terrain that we know anecdotally more than scientifically. Indeed, our science has sometimes kept us from knowing, as in the story of two premature infants. When the two babies were born, they were very small and the weaker one was not expected to survive. They lay in their isolettes, connected to life support equipment to enhance their chances of developing normally. Contact with caregivers was limited, and they had no contact with each other. A nurse in the hospital argued against hospital policy that prohibited putting the babies together in an incubator. She succeeded in getting permission. As they lay side by side, the stronger twin put his arm around his weaker sibling. In the next two days, the weaker twin's respiration and heart rates reached normal ranges, and both went home a few weeks later.

Coincidence? Perhaps. Yet there is much from our experience that supports the idea that we get strength from each other, that our bodies are channels of knowing that we do not fully comprehend. When I teach listening in conflict resolution sessions, I frequently begin by asking participants to tell each other a short, true story from their lives. Each has about four minutes to relate the story, and the listener is asked to receive it in silence, only asking questions if absolutely necessary for clarification. The unusual thing is that I ask them to sit exactly back-to-back, whether in chairs or on the floor.

Deprived of the usual visual cues, the partners frequently sit so that their backs and heads are touching, straining to find a way to connect besides through words. Once each has told a story to the other, they face each other for debriefing and finally come together again in the large group. Even though they often report frustration as a part of this experience, they also reflect surprise. They are surprised that empathy felt so present. Many observe that empathy was communicated by touching backs or heads or shoulders.

They are becoming more aware of the body's instinctive ways of connecting and communicating. By screening out the ways they usually communicate empathy (head nodding, maintaining eye contact, saying uh-huh), their bodies found a way to connect, even when they felt themselves to be in an unnatural listening position. Ironically, the position actually fosters concentration because it makes hearing more difficult and the listener is less likely to be distracted by her or his own thoughts.

When two individuals are in conflict, the last thing they want to do is to touch, whether back-to-back or hand-to-hand. Touch involves acknowledgment physically, relationally, and symbolically. How often we have referred to the handshake between Chairman Arafat and Prime Minister Netanyahu on the White House lawn after the peace brokered by President Clinton. The handshake signaled acknowledgment and progress in a more powerful way than thousands of words.

A story from South Africa emphasizes that touch between those in conflict changes relationships and, therefore, the course of conflicts. In 1991, South African businessman Sidney Frankel invited two families from opposite sides of the political spectrum to his remote vacation cottage. They were Cyril Ramaphosa, a prominent black leader in the African National Congress, and Roelf Meyer, a white leader in the then-ruling Nationalist Party government. Just as their guests arrived, Frankel and his family had to leave suddenly because Frankel's daughter had fallen and broken her arm.

This left the Ramaphosa and Meyer families unexpectedly and awkwardly present with each other, without the host who had invited them, to smooth out the time. When Meyer's two young sons wanted to go fishing, Ramaphosa volunteered to go along and instruct them. Meyer, a novice, got a fishhook deeply lodged in his finger. Ramaphosa's wife is a nurse, and she tried to get it out but could not. After an hour, as Meyer was getting fatigued by the pain, Ramaphosa pulled it out with a pair of pliers.

The experience became a bonding one, as Ramaphosa acknowledged, "I've always wanted to hurt you Nats (National Party members), but never as much as this."[5] Over the course of the next several years, the friendship between Ramaphosa and Meyer played an essential stabilizing role in the negotiations that led to democratic government in South Africa. Relationship stood in the face of all the possible ways the process could have gotten off-track, cemented by physical interaction and physical assistance.

The Body as a Resource in Conflict

How do third parties and trainers use the body as a resource in their work? Neal Milner, writing in *When Talk Works,* observes that in most mediations, "[t]he process is typically quite *civilized* (italics mine). The disputants stay on their chairs or get up at mutually agreed-on times."[6] It is probably also true that third parties do not take advantage of a wide range of body-referenced language in their assessments or interventions.

Incorporating body-referenced language into our practice requires mindfulness and attention. We can do this by using words that refer to physical or sensory ways of knowing, inviting participants to pay attention to their sensations, and designing physical activities into training sessions and interventions. Hawaiian mediator Linda Colburn asks potentially violent disputants questions that relate to their physical selves: "What do you notice when you start getting upset? What do you feel? What goes on in your body when you notice that you are starting to get upset?"[7]

Colburn also refers to her own physical center as a source of wisdom. She explains, "I think there is a sort of Zen, if you will, to dealing with violent conflict, and it has to do with getting back to your own center and quickly determining what really matters."[8]

Invoking our physical wisdom in our practices and our training requires that we develop the ability to "get back to our centers." It requires ongoing attention, activities to build awareness and facility with listening to and acting from the body, and practice. Over the centuries, practices aimed at developing physical capacities and awareness have emerged. A variety of traditions teach about the body, its architecture, its functioning, and its relationship to our personal stories. In Hindu, Hopi, and Sufi traditions, the body is seen as having distinct energy centers. Hindus call these energy centers chakras. Keeping the centers open facilitates optimum functioning. This openness can be achieved and maintained through breathing, yoga, and meditative practices. Postures and breathing techniques enable the body to be more than the incarnate summary of our histories and our weaknesses, our triumphs and failures. They enable us to shift through conflict, using the body as an instrument of change.

Development of Sensitivity

What is needed to cultivate the body awareness so necessary to shifting conflict? Martha Graham, the American pioneer of modern dance, once stated in a lecture that to achieve the mastery of the body necessary to become a dancer, a long period of training is required. At the end of the period, something beautiful happens:

> You will know the wonders of the human body, because there is nothing more wonderful. The next time you look into the mirror, just look at the way the ears rest next to your head; look at the way the hairline grows; think of the little bones in your wrist; think of the magic of that foot, comparatively small, upon which your whole weight rests. It's a miracle. And the dance in all those areas is a celebration of that miracle.[9]

What can we learn from this? We who are neither dancers nor yogis nor spiritual aspirants, who feel out of breath after climbing the stairs? We can learn that our bodies are not just matter but are states of consciousness: ways of feeling heavy, alienated, or bitter. We also learn that it is possible to reconcile ourselves with our bodies, that we can give them a rhythm and a discipline. It is possible to learn to live in our bodies, to use them as a means of expression in the world, to perceive them as a source of lightness and energy. Then our bodies are no longer enemies but allies and friends, exquisitely tuned receivers and transmitters, simultaneously doing both.

Roth teaches us that movement is not only meditation; it's also medicine that heals the split between our minds and hearts, bodies and souls. Bodies help us move through our inner wilderness, however blocked it may be with the remains of emotional and psychic struggles. They help us negotiate relationships, however associated they may be with pain, hatred, and suffering.

Addressing conflict through movement is to experience the edge between matter and spirit, masculine and feminine, darkness and light, leader and follower, stillness and motion. Physical practices help us know and soften our armor—the network of muscular tensions that reflect our emotional history. Each body is a constellation of memories and tensions—an individually and socially defined emblem. Bodies hold memories. This is why we experience nostalgia, the giddiness of childhood, a lightness of being when we unexpectedly come into contact with the smell of cotton candy first experienced at a county fair years before. A special song from ten years ago brings us back into contact with a whole range of feelings, images, and sensations associated with that time. Someone touches us in a particular way, and it evokes a memory that is not thought but felt; it is not simple but the aggregate of all the times we were touched in that way and how they made us feel.

As we engage in the discipline, pain, and pleasure of physical practices, we become more aware of the way our bodies store memories. We notice where we warehouse tension and find ways to release it. Not until it is released do we realize we have carried it, sometimes for years. As we seek to keep our physical channels clear, strong, and responsive, we are better equipped to help bridge conflicts.

Use of Somatic Intelligence in Practice

Physical dimensions of our processes have been acknowledged for a long time. Yet we would be well advised to do a fresh inventory of our work from the perspective of somatic intelligence. This need was reinforced for me at a recent gathering of conflict resolution practitioners and scholars. At the meeting, we were asked to choose a theme to focus our dialogue in small groups, later forming the basis for a presentation. I chose to participate in the group on creativity. We spent some very exciting hours exploring ideas about creativity and what it means for practice. We ran into difficulty when we had to devise a presentation reflecting the work of our group. True to our group theme, we generated many ideas, some of them quite unusual. But getting consensus on one idea was much harder.

In the end, we came back to an idea that had fascinated us as a group throughout our dialogue. The question of how physical space and arrangements affect interpersonal dynamics in conflict intrigued us and engaged our creative imaginations. After all, how did we know that it is best to use a round table, best to seat the parties so that they can see each other, best to sit down to talk through problems at all?

Experimenting, we tried having an ongoing simulated dispute while changing the physical arrangement of the chairs every three minutes. We talked with our chairs facing each other directly, with the chairs placed back-to-back, with the chairs placed side-by-side, with the chairs angled toward each other at 90 degrees, with chairs angled away from each other at 90 degrees, with the chairs separated by round and square tables.

As role players, we watched for changes in the climate of the conversation, for emotional shifts, for breakthroughs in the substance of the issue. The others in the group observed, also watching for subtle changes. To our surprise, the two disputants felt most comfortable expressing themselves when they were not in each other's direct line of vision. Others noticed, too, that when the chairs were placed back-to-back or at angles away from each other, there was less emotional intensity and more of a sense of space in which each could speak freely.

We wondered whether the assumption that it is best for disputants to face each other across a round table arises from the needs of the third party to monitor nonverbal communication rather than from an assessment of what might work best for the parties in any given conflict. It may be that different physical arrangements work best in different situations. Perhaps varying physical arrangements would help facilitate communication and resolution at different stages of conflict. Just as some third parties recognize that parties may not feel comfortable directly addressing each other initially, so it may be that parties would feel more comfortable if they were not seated confrontationally at first.

There are many possibilities related to the issue of creative physical arrangements. What is clear is that changing physical orientation does have an effect on communication and interpersonal dynamics. Although any prescription about this would be necessarily flawed, it is useful to question accepted practice, generating appropriate configurations as situations require. In some aspects of our work, we do this as a matter of course. Conflict resolution trainers are notorious for rearranging furniture. We know it is essential to create a physical atmosphere that emphasizes openness and participation as much as possible. Yet in our interventions, we tend toward a mean of habit, not always exploring the way different physical arrangements or physical movement might help shift conflict dynamics. As we investigate all aspects of our processes for ways they do and do not welcome somatic intelligence, we will find many other resources for bridging conflict.

Somatic Strategies

Physical and sensory resources are already used in many teaching and conflict process environments to engage parties or participants in somatic experiences related to the conflict or learning goals. These experiences serve multiple purposes. They facilitate group development and trust building, giving insight into individual and group dynamics. They also provide concrete experiences that make theories and ideas come alive. As ideas and theories come alive, new perspectives, choices, and ways of orienting to ideas become visible.

Many examples illustrate this. Untying human knots teaches about interdependence and creative strategies. Practicing aikido gives a dynamic experience of power. A classic way of introducing adversarial and collaborative approaches to conflict is through an assignment to arm wrestle, asking pairs to see how many times they can get their partner's arm to the table. When they notice that they can accrue a larger total by cooperating rather than competing, learners take away understandings that are reinforced by physical experience.

The circumstances and goals of training or interventions dictate different somatic approaches. Sometimes physical images can be evoked as a way of getting acquainted, recalling positive aspects of relationship or taking a break from intense problem solving. Some questions that invite sensory exploration include

- Name a favorite smell. Why do you like it?
- What color would your name be, if it were colored, and why?
- In the times we have shared together, the one that had the best taste was the one when we [fill in the blank]. To me, it tasted like [fill in the blank].
- A sound that reminds me of a peaceful and beautiful place is the sound of [fill in the blank]. I like it because [fill in the blank].
- Where does this conflict live in your body? What does it feel like? What animal is it like? How does it move?

One somatic excercise involves partners taking turns closing their eyes and taking each other around a room or outdoors. The partner with open eyes identifies three things, the texture of which conveys something of her or his associations with conflict, guiding the partner with closed eyes to touch them. Then they switch roles. Returning to their seats, partners discuss their responses to each other's choices, insights, and discoveries.

Another way to invite all the senses into the room is to use music. In a recent residential retreat for an organization, I asked participants to bring music to share with the group that had meaning for them. We played it at breaks, during nonverbal activities, at lunch, and before and after sessions. It became a way for people to know each other better, a source of surprise, enjoyment, and an anchor for connection. It set a tone of energy, of celebration of diversity; it marked the time as being apart from the usual.

One of the evenings of the retreat, I went into the conference room where the retreat was being held to get some things I needed to prepare for the next day. I found several members of the group in the room, lights dimmed, playing each other songs, dancing with socks off or sitting next to each other quietly. Others walked in and out of the room, staying for a few minutes and then leaving again. The music was a way for them to communicate with each other things that they had no words to express. It was a way to play, share, and bond that enhanced intimacy and understanding.

There are countless untapped ways to incorporate somatic ways of knowing in our practices and teaching. From the foundation of our own physical practices, we move to consciously incorporate sensory language in our processes and training sessions to engage participants' physical ways of knowing. Our ongoing challenge is to develop increasingly effective experiential, somatic dimensions of our work as third parties and teachers, connecting theory to practice in ways both memorable and powerful. This is important not only because it helps parties and participants integrate and connect ideas but because sensory images are central to imaginative and intuitive ways of knowing, as we will see in the next chapter.

CHAPTER FOUR

Imaginative and Intuitive Ways of Knowing
Seeing with Both Eyes

We are "so both and oneful"
E. E. CUMMINGS[1]

The atmosphere in the room is electric. There is anger, and darts of dislike are moving between eyes that scrutinize, appraise, and challenge. Accusations, threats, and ultimatums pepper the discussion. Some of the people are uncomfortable. Others are oblivious to discomfort, animated by adrenalin and energy. Everyone is aware of strong convictions about the issues and each other; at the moment, few of them are constructive. Conflict is in full flower, and the actions of those in the room only serve to feed it.

Is this a scene from a war-torn country, a hostile corporate takeover, a meeting of rival militias? Not at all. It is a scene from a faculty meeting in a department where all the faculty members teach peace studies. Although there is no reason to expect these faculty members to be immune from conflict, it is surprising to see them behave in apparent forgetfulness of the theories and practices they spend their days professing. This scene reminds us that conflict is not an intellectual event.

Conflict disturbs our equilibrium. It can play havoc with appetite, sleep patterns, and mood. It leads to preoccupation and distracting thoughts, feelings, and sensations. Conflict gets a grip on us, creeping its fingers into our guts and tugging this way, then that. It puts a stranglehold around our hearts, so that sometimes the thing we are most aware of is a strong desire to commit an anti-social act. Conflict is the knot that we can't untie; it just gets tighter the more we try. Stuck in its clutches, we realize at last that we have to try something we have not tried before. We come to innovation from desperation. Arriving breathless and tense at the station of frustration, we feel the need to design a new kind of conveyance to carry us to a different destination. In this enterprise, imagination and intuition are our most important allies.

Imagination is the ability to create. Surpassing the known, we generate new forms and envision new ways forward. Leaving stereotypes, preconceptions, and assumptions by the old railroad tracks, imagination liberates our minds to conceive new ways of transportation.

Imagination is complemented by intuition. Intuition helps us know what to do in the moment we need to know. It is there on our shoulder, helping us choose from imagined alternatives. At any choice point, dozens or even hundreds of options confront us. Intuition is our sieve, sifting through them at lightning speed, yielding an answer that feels congruent and right in the moment. When intuition and imagination work together, what was daunting becomes doable and what was formidable becomes just a little bit friendlier.

The late Danaan Parry understood imagination and intuition very well. Before his untimely death in 1996, he had worked in countries around the world helping people connect across divides of war and ethnic enmity. Those fortunate to have known him remember an intuitive, bold man with an expansive imagination and unstoppable determination. His friend Reverend Richard Levy quoted Danaan as saying, "Let's take on something big like saving the planet, and let the ordinary stuff work itself out." Daring to imagine a transformed world, he brought teenagers from conflicted cultures together to reforest the earth and develop friendships at the same time. Concerned to further reconciliation after the Vietnam War, he initiated a landmine-clearing program in Vietnam, then engaged international citizens to work side-by-side with Vietnamese citizens planting trees on the reclaimed land.

Danaan was fond of telling this story.[2] A woman was having a terrible nightmare in which she was being pursued by a menacing monster. Wherever she went, the monster was on her heels, breathing his disgusting breath down her back. Terrified, she ran across meadows and plains, hills and deserts. Finally, she could run no more. She found herself trapped in a box canyon, with cliff walls all around her, rising hundreds of feet in the air. The monster had followed, and she could feel his imposing presence immediately behind her. In desperation, she turned around and faced the monster. Haltingly, she asked him what he was going to do with her. The fearsome monster of her dream looked down at her and said, "Hell, lady, I don't know. This is *your* dream."

In this chapter, we consider our waking dreams and the power they have in our lives. Imagination is the fuel of these waking dreams; it orients, animates, and engages us in the process of becoming who we are in our families, workplaces, and communities. For third parties and teachers of conflict resolution, imagination is an amazing resource. Little in our literature addresses ways we can make intentional use of it, yet it toils away, unacknowledged, to vitalize our work and enliven our efforts. At the same time, the dark side of imagination amplifies threats and escalates conflicts, making our jobs harder.

With its partner, intuition, imagination shapes our choices and the range of possibilities we see, whether narrow or broad. Because conflict resolution is ultimately about change, developing creative and generative possibilities is of central importance. Imagination and intuition are the bridges from rigid to fluid, from knotted to relaxed.

Imagination

My seventy-eight-year-old friend Jessica is fond of reminding me to be careful what I dream because it may come true. Make the picture as specific as possible, she says, and think through it carefully to be sure it is the picture that you want to manifest. Why does this admonition speak to us? It can only have currency if our waking dreams actually can and do come true. Increasingly, we have evidence that our capacity to imagine another future is a powerful step in creating that future. Future search conferences, creative imagery workshops, and countless books draw on this truth: that when we can see something in our mind's eye, we can manifest it.

If we cannot picture it, it is much harder to be agents of creation in our own lives.

The painter Gauguin related imagination to the essence of something: "Imagination simplifies what the eye sees, rejecting all nonessential details."[3] Rather than try to faithfully reproduce a scene, he sought to convey its essence. As conflict resolvers, we are also on a quest for essence—for the essence of a conflict, uncovering its heart as source and resource for engagement and transformation. We have developed detailed assessment instruments to help us analyze and map conflicts. And although they are useful, it is important that we do not get so preoccupied with trees that we miss the essence of the forest. What would happen if, in addition to our multidimensional analyses, we asked a single question: What is at the heart of this conflict?

As third parties entering an organization or community in conflict, we first encounter confusion and discomfort. Dynamics swirl around; people posture, and different theories about what should be done abound. A small nonprofit organization found itself embroiled in multiple conflicts relating to communication, authority, exclusion, and control. In dialogue with staff and management, I heard many details about dysfunctional communication, double messages from management, racially based exclusion, ineffective performance, and lack of trust. I filled a notebook, mapping the conflict as it played out through issues, miscommunications, and organizational structures. I also considered the symbolic dimension, asking how meaning and identity were a part of the picture. Later I sat alone with one blank page in front of me and asked the question, What is at the heart of this conflict?

A surprising image came into my mind. I saw a group of chickens scrambling around in the corner of a pen, competing over scarce food; the fence at the other end of the pen was broken open, leaving clear passage to a variety of food sources. Having grown and changed its mission and leadership structure, the organization was busy scrambling to catch up. But it was doing this within the confines of the old chicken pen rather than taking advantage of the resources available to it through growth and expansion. What was at the heart of this conflict? At its heart was a poverty of imagination. The organization had no template for imagining itself into the future. Without a template or shared vision, all kinds of conflicts had arisen, contributing to schisms, acrimony, and ineffectiveness.

Attempting to resolve these conflicts without having the big picture in mind would not have been effective. Without the heart of the conflict being addressed, new conflicts would have arisen, symptomatic of the core issue. Ironically, as effort is made in tending new conflicts, the heart of the issue may become more deeply buried and even less accessible. This is especially true if progress is being made on these new issues. In the relief that accompanies the engagement of troublesome issues, it's tempting to leave the heart of the matter to another day. To create meaningful change, we had to address the imagination gap as well as attend to specific issues.

Over time, we worked together on structural and organizational issues, strategic planning, and team building. As incremental progress was made, relationship was built, and that foundation made it possible to begin to engage individual and group imaginations. In one staff meeting, we helped participants imagine private places where they felt safe and were surrounded with things that pleased their senses. Moving into dyads, they shared these spaces, taking each other on a sensory tour of their smells, tastes, visual images, sounds, and textures. Before leaving their partner's imagined place, they could ask for something, whether a scent, texture, flower, or memento. Their partner was free to refuse to give something precious, but in all cases, they gave gifts to each other from their imagined spaces.

This assignment to imagine brought the textured, vibrant world of sensory experience into the flat, dry atmosphere of the workplace. Finding themselves on uncertain sands, imaginations had run for cover while workers kept their heads down and did their best not to attract attention. In the parched desert of conflict, new ideas withered on the vine, foreclosed from voice before harvesting by unpredictability and ubiquitous tension. This imaginative experience gave the meta-message that something new was being invited into the workplace. Combined with progress on identified issues, it strengthened the playful spirit and appreciative atmosphere that had begun to take root.

The experience also deepened relationships and turned the staff's attention to the synchronicity that operates unseen in a group working together toward a goal. Although there had been no previous discussion or planning, some pairs found they had imagined similar landscapes. In one dyad, both partners found themselves on the seaside; in another, each person imagined a heron. In another pair, each described interior places—cozy refuges where they could curl up in a corner and read near a fireplace. Although not all their imagined places were similar, enough common themes surfaced for one participant to reflect aloud on the amount of communication that takes place nonverbally, completely outside our conscious awareness. What we intuitively know about each other can serve us as we imagine new ways into being.

Fast-forward a few weeks beyond this experience. Building on it, staff members were able to create new, shared images of their organization in the future. They imagined features of their workplace, including a collaborative atmosphere and increased productivity. Many used images from nature to describe these future scenes, including wide-open skies, powerful tides, and mountaintop views. Their imagined spaces, shared weeks before, informed their choice of metaphors. At the end of our work, one of the participants observed that the process had taken her from running in circles in front of a gray concrete wall to drawing a door in the wall and walking through it with her co-workers. Their imaginations gave them the sensory detail that kept the images alive, even when daily tasks and difficult issues weighed heavily.

These uses of imagination not only helped participants imagine their shared futures but gave implicit permission for more imaginative interactions in the present. As new ideas were accepted and a spirit of inquiry crept in to replace tension and vigilance, the workplace became a more comfortable place. Returning to my original image: the chickens had moved beyond the pen, no longer confined by outgrown ideas of who they were or could be.

Imagining also engaged participants in two aspects of life that are universal yet often ignored by conflict practitioners: play and aesthetic pleasure. It is our ability to play, to be light with each other, that is strongly helpful when we are frozen in the grips of conflict. It is our love for aesthetic pleasure that inspires us to create workplaces, communities, and families that feed our needs for connection, beauty, and harmony. An essential step in manifesting these visions is bringing them into being via imagination. Doing so engages our memories as well as our capacities to imagine.

Imagination and Memory

Physicist David Bohm calls imagination "the power to display the activity of the mind as a whole through mental images."[4] To imagine is to create a new picture of what we had not seen before that comes from deep inside ourselves. Breaking the bonds of the known, the mind generates new forms, ideas or images, music or prose, mathematical insights or mechanical inventions. Our capacity to resolve conflict depends on our ability to imagine a different order of things: reconfigured relationships, new structures, unwound enmities. As third parties, we inspire others to imagine new ways of being and doing that will produce something other than competition and destructive conflict. In this we have two main tasks. First, we create and hold a space where something new is possible, knowing that we do not know what it is, yet trusting that it will emerge. Second, we work with groups to build relationships and processes that may yield imaginative outcomes.

As we consider how to do this, it is important to recognize the role of memory. We do not come fresh to our conflicts; we come with baggage from life experiences and with a series of images of the other side. These images of who the other party is and ideas of what is possible both limit and shape what we see. Memory is a function that selects and recreates experience. We remember neither every detail of our lives nor every part of our interactions with members of a group we are in conflict with. We remember what Vamik Volkan[5] calls chosen traumas. Those acts that symbolize our experience of "the other" are often those that hold the kernel of meaning we have assigned to the conflict. Tending to hold a consistent picture, we nurture these meanings and the memories that ensconce them and support our bias—our chosen point of view.

To test this, it is only necessary to go as far as the daily newspaper. Read the comments of political leaders and community members on either side of a conflict. Descriptions of "the other" will read as though they were painted with one brush. Seldom will we find nuanced, balanced descriptions acknowledging that everyone, even the other, can be either monk or maniac, Cinderella or wicked stepmother. The more extreme the harm done by "them" to "us," the more stark the images of right-wrong, good-evil, just-unjust. Psychologists tell us that this preserves our self-esteem. As we project negativity onto the other, we are spared from seeing our own flaws, fissures, or failings. Although this may help us feel better about ourselves, it escalates conflicts and ultimately contributes to undermining our collective possibilities of living peacefully together.

This projection is seen most clearly in times of escalating conflict. The ubiquitous pairing of the word "Muslim" with the label "terrorist" crowds out awareness that terrorists come from many religions and ethnicities and that Muslims are as diverse as any other group. During World War II, Emperor Hirohito was portrayed as a symbol of evil, his negative image so powerful that it spilled over onto Japanese Americans in the United States.

Recognizing the ways memory works to select nuances, obscuring complexity and contradictions, our task of creating space for those in conflict becomes more challenging. When identities are wrapped up with these memories and the subsequent limited view of our conflict, flexibility and spaciousness are diminished. If we resolve an issue ensconced in layers of memory on the material level, we will see similar social and symbolic dynamics surfacing through other issues. If we aim our work at the social level, we will meet resistance. Who among us wants to risk the approbation of our group to make friends with "the other"? Who among us wants to break ranks with those we love, those who have been hurt by "them," to do the unpopular thing, even if it is only as simple as trying to understand the other in context? Who among us has the clarity and the courage to go in a different direction than our collective memory points?

Resolving conflict asks us for this clarity and courage. As long as we remember selectively, drawing from limited and preselected recollections, conflicts will remain static or escalate, fueled by concentric circles of self-fulfilling reinforcement. To break this pattern, we have to change the memories we access, expanding our pools of recollections, allowing them to become tempered and deepened through dialogue. In dialogue, conflict parties become aware of how they have kept their old experiences of physical and emotional damage alive through memory. These memories and warehoused conflict stories limit the field of imaginative possibility from which the future is created. They act like a deep freeze, keeping views static and frozen, away from the sunlight of contact with others.

Dialogue processes invite participants to set their well-worn stories aside, making room for new stories reflecting multiple perspectives. As we access more complete and balanced memories of the past, we come to imagine new futures.

What makes this kind of dialogue possible? When are parties to conflict ready to relinquish their attachment to their stories—stories that have become precious symbols to them, laced with identity and meaning? In many instances, they may be unready. At other times, a window of opportunity cracks open, pushed by pain, frustration, or other experiences leading to an acknowledgment that the status quo is not working. Faced with the insecurity of proceeding with business as usual in an escalating conflict, parties summon the courage to listen with new ears to each other, reexamining the memories that have kept them apart. This process is not linear, nor does it proceed in comfortingly regular increments. It proceeds by fits and starts.

A colleague tells a story of two groups of youths from a divided society who had met over some weeks for dialogue. They had shared stories, making some progress toward unfreezing their views of each other. But memories, individually held and collectively influenced, still permeated the room. Everyone knew that outside the safety of its walls, one of the participants wearing a uniform might one day shoot at a participant from the other side. The tension of the ongoing conflict acted on their memories, keeping them semifrozen and intact, even as they earnestly listened to each other. This had the effect of limiting the progress beyond the first levels of expanded awareness that were achieved in the initial days of the dialogue.

As they returned from a break, one of the youths suggested that they play a game of "spin the bottle." In this game, a bottle is set in the middle of the circle and spun around. When it comes to rest, the person at whom it points follows the instructions of the group. Group members can ask the person a question that might not be asked in usual conversation. They may ask the person to do something, disclose something, or describe something. In the ritual of the game, the usual bounds on what can be asked and what can be shared are relaxed. After all, it's only a game.

The facilitators watched, intrigued, as the game worked to elicit memories that had not been shared in the more formal dialogue process. Some were trivial or humorous; others were serious and vulnerable. Sharing them gave implicit permission for all participants to loosen their grip on their memories. There were stories of childhood traumas, moments of realization, and times of confusion. Playing with memories in this way both filled out their pictures of each other and opened the possibility that the ways their memories caused them to see each other were skewed. After this experience, deeper dialogue ensued, made possible by the way their frozen images of each other had been disturbed by sharing memories that were untinged with chosen traumas.

Imagination, too, had been loosed in the circle. Imagination lives in our stories. Without meaning to, we reveal more than the events we are recounting in storytelling. We invite others to imagine themselves in our shoes. We show, if only briefly, our vulnerability and uncertainty when faced with hard choices. From this place, there is space to imagine shared futures—alternatives to the trajectories from the frozen memories we nurture without thinking.

Memory as a Constructive Tool

Before we find an opening inside ourselves to share our stories with others and receive theirs, we have to imagine that it is possible. We have to locate a seed of willingness to do so, imagine a different way of relating than has characterized the past. We need, in the words of Danaan Parry, to "give birth to the Mother Teresa that is in each of our beings."[6] To heal conflict, we need her qualities of intensity and clarity of focus. We need to know the answers to some important questions, such as

- What quality of community are we trying to create?
- Which aspects of relationship are we trying to build?
- What are the features of the picture we see of the future?
- What hope can we find within ourselves to sustain this image of the future?

The more clear our questions and answers, the more we are able to harness the power of memory and intelligence of the body in positive ways.

Imagination as Preparation

When we are doing something we feel uncertain about or something we are unfamiliar with, we rehearse both physically and mentally. We prepare by imagining ourselves in the situation. When I played piano concerts, I would see myself on the stage in front of a full auditorium. I imagined details of how I would walk onto the stage, the moment I would take to breathe deeply after sitting down, placing my hands on the keyboard in position before sounding a single note. I imagined playing passionately, flawlessly, in a way that invited the audience into dialogue with the music, within themselves. Imagining this scene, playing out the concert from my simple living room as though it were a grand concert hall, I created memories that helped me in the actual performance. Memory selects and recreates experience. To imagine in this way is to use the selecting function of memory to open possibilities for the future.

Professional athletes know the value of imagination; research shows that imaging is an important accompaniment to physical training for exceptional performance. David Hemery in *The Pursuit of Sporting Excellence*[7] maintains that 80 percent of athletes habitually visualize their performance. By imagining with vivid precision the details of all that they want to accomplish, athletes familiarize themselves with their practice; they mobilize the body's psychophysical energies and prepare the nervous system. As they come to believe that what they want to do is possible, they can perfect their performance.

Why is this so effective? The body, suggests Bernie Siegel,[8] does not distinguish between a vivid mental experience and an actual physical experience; thus learning occurs during imagined actions just as it does during actual activity. In Eastern Europe, athletes lie down and listen to Baroque music with a strong, regular bass line of about sixty beats per minute. As the listeners' heart rates become synchronized with the music, deep relaxation is produced. Guided by a facilitator, the athletes then envision, in full color and complete detail, a winning performance. They repeat this experience, alternating between visualization and actual practice until the physical act is a duplication of the mental act that has already been successfully visualized. Research shows that athletes who spend a proportion of their time in such mental training do better than those with only physical training.

By harnessing the power of the mind, impressive feats are possible on the field, the ice, the track. It is possible to use the same power to invoke a different future in our organizations, communities, and schools. What if we knew that imagining specific, detailed images of the future was as important as problem solving, action planning, and conflict analysis? What if we believed that mental rehearsals of peaceful interaction were potent allies in achieving it? What if we found that positive projections generated in relaxed states helped shift negative images of "the other"? Our processes might look different indeed. This leads us to examine the role of visualization in achieving change.

Visualization and Change

Some of the greatest creators known to us used visualization extensively. For the artist Georgia O'Keefe, it was a basic tool. O'Keefe was thrilled when she realized that she could freely invent whatever she wanted with her painting and did not need to imitate something she had perceived with her senses. This realization made it possible for her to create worlds never before seen. During the days when inspiration came to her, she thought she would go mad. "I know what I am going to do before I begin, and if there's nothing in my head, I do nothing," she is reported to have said.[9]

Visualization is not just the province of the artist. In the field of science, visualization is also fundamentally important. Einstein engaged in what he called thought experiments—creating imaginary situations to draw on for theoretical work. He said that he arrived at the happiest thought of his life when he imagined a person in free fall from a roof of a house; from this, he derived his theory of relativity. Heinrich Schliemann, the archeologist who discovered the ancient city of Troy, visualized people and activities as they must have been centuries before while he looked at the ruins and used these visualizations to help him in his exploration.

Probably the most creative and imaginative work of scientists has been the development of theories, especially those so deeply explanatory that they apply to a wide range of phenomena or important questions. The word *theory* derives from the Greek *theoria*, which has the same root as *theatre*, in a verb meaning "to view" or "to make a spectacle." This suggests that to theorize is to look at the world through the mind rather to generate immutable knowledge. Looking at the world through the mind, we harness the power of visualization to imagine change. Bringing our hearts into the process, we match conviction and action with image, creating the change.

Visualizing is powerful in creating results in the world. Cancer survivors use it to enter states that enable their bodies to perform, like those of athletes, at levels beyond the ordinary. People in pain use it to control and manage discomfort. Nicolas Hall, a physician at the George Washington Medical Center, found that patients using visualization increased their number of circulating white blood cells and also levels of a hormone important to the auxiliary white cells. He found that visualization worked best when patients chose their own images and were able to see them as clearly as if looking with their physical eyes. A child with cancer successfully imagined it as a big, dumb, gray lump that he repeatedly "shot" with a rocket ship. Within a year he was cured.[10]

Appreciative Inquiry

Visualization is part of appreciative inquiry—a process widely used to address organizational conflicts. Appreciative inquiry builds on the work of some influential thinkers in the conflict resolution field, including Kenneth Boulding,[11] who maintained that the image determines the current or direction of behavior in any organization. Image acts as a field; members of the organization gravitate toward the most highly valued part of the field. Given this tendency, the appreciative inquiry process seeks to bring those factors that give vitality and life to the organization to the center of participants' awareness. Building on these positive anchors, they move to envision what might be. According to David Cooperrider, originator of appreciative inquiry, "valuing the best of what is leads [naturally] to envisioning what might be. Envisioning involves 'passionate thinking'—it means allowing yourself to be inspired by what you see. It means creating a positive image of a desired and preferred future."[12] All of this emphasis on seeing works well for those who are visual thinkers—who prefer seeing as a mode of taking in information, processing information, and relating to the future. Others prefer auditory or kinesthetic modes of experience. Actually, visualization involves all of these. It is not only to see but to imagine scenes, hear sounds, and feel as though we have touched things in our mind's eye. Doing this engages our creativity, our intuition, and our collective wisdom about the future. There is no particular talent needed to do it, just a willingness to still the busy mind long enough to create a space for seeing. When visualizing involves going in a different direction than the one in which our minds are pointed by habit, stilling the mind also means finding an opening, even a slim one, where the possibility of a different unfolding can be entertained.

Visualization for Improving Test Scores

It is not always easy to intercept the mind's trajectory with a new visualization. This is especially true when we attach a lot of significance to an event or when we feel pressured or afraid. A fluid, fertile imagination may be foreclosed by stress and tension, producing the negative results we most fear. I saw this as I taught preparatory classes for those planning to take the Law School Admissions Test and similar standardized exams.

Research showed that candidates could improve their scores by practice with specific question types and familiarity with the exam format. Experience showed me that psychological factors were at least as important, perhaps even more important, as predictors of success. When a candidate took the test with a sense that her or his entire future rested on the results, the stress was extreme. My job was not to convince them to change their visions of the future but to hold those visions more lightly. To help with this, we used guided visualization to see the test situation differently.

Before candidates could visualize any positive experiences of test taking, they had to quiet their minds. An imagined picture needs room—a space in which to be viewed—or it can become buried in the clutter that permeates so much of our thoughts day-to-day. So we began by focusing on the breath, imagining a chalkboard eraser, clearing the mind of other thoughts and ideas.

Participants found this deceptively simple. A moment or two focusing on the breath, and they were looking around, impatient for the next instruction. Gradually they learned to quiet their minds.

With quiet minds, participants entered the picture I painted for them. I suggested to them that they would approach the test calmly and efficiently, with access to remembered information and positive expectations for success. The pretest anxiety they had felt would be replaced with confidence and clarity. Their memories of this imagined scene would be with them on the actual test day, supplanting jitters with self-assurance. They would focus on applying their skills to the test in the present moment, pacing themselves effectively through the questions. When thoughts of the test results or the future arose, they would set them aside for another time.

With the felt experience of walking with calm confidence through the projected test scene, the participants' confidence in the terrain increased, and their sense of risk was reduced. They were able to see that risk had inflated itself beyond likely or reasonable levels. Many reported that these experiences with positive imagining helped them approach the actual test with less anxiety and better outcomes.

Visualization helped these test takers prepare to take an active and constructive role in their future. Assisted by these sensory, somatic experiences, they created new templates for success. They learned that visualization is not a passive experience. This reality is confirmed, not only through Western scientific thought but by a variety of spiritual traditions. In Tibetan Buddhist thought, visualization is a living entity with a psychospiritual force of its own. Everything the mind creates comes to life. This fits with the accounts of some novelists and playwrights who say that their characters, once developed, talk to them, saying, "Make me like this; make me like that." As we take an active role in imagining ourselves into new pictures, the pictures take on lives of their own, speaking to us of possibilities we have not seen.

Imagination Used Retrospectively

Knowing the power of visualization, the wise third party builds opportunities into conflict resolution processes for explorations "out of real time." Joseph Montville[13] writes of taking parties on a walk through history—a walk in which their parallel stories of the same events become the subject of dialogue. The dialogue eventually leads to the construction of a new, shared story that honors what is important to each side, framing events in ways that integrate perspectives while acknowledging trauma, loss, and pain.

This retrospective use of imagination and memory need not be confined to the negative and the painful. In any long relationship, there are times of harmony that may not fit into the picture of conflict. Winslade and Monk[14] suggest asking questions like these:

- Have there been times when this dispute has let up and allowed you to cooperate more, even for brief periods?
- Have you experienced any lulls in the dispute when things have gone better for a time?

Such questions bring the complexities of ongoing relationships to mind. They emphasize that conflict is not simply negative; it is a tension between contrary impulses, whether freedom and belonging or mobility and rootedness. Questions such as these can balance the process of walking through the past, easing conflict, and opening possibilities for the future.

Visualization and the Boundaries of Time

As our visualizing of the past prepares the way for future-focused uses of imagination and memory, we must resist seeking facile solutions. Visualization can help us develop shared pictures of relationship, material cooperation, and autonomous meanings that abide beside each other, even as conflict continues. We know, in the words of M. C. Richards, that "in the intricate mesh of our mutual involvement, we befall each other constantly."[15] Befalling each other constantly, we are challenged to imagine and re-imagine ourselves in relation to each other and in relation to what we hold precious. One of the ways we can meet this challenge is to relax our boundaries around time.

Typically, we use visualization to invite parties to imagine their organization or community two, three, or five years into the future. Strategic planning and appreciative inquiry processes include this kind of future projection, grounded in what is precious and hopeful for the group. These visualizations yield specific, helpful pictures to anchor planning, shape initiatives, and sharpen focus.

Yet when conflict is deep-rooted, we hear, "This cannot be resolved in our lifetimes." In a conflict that has taken generations to develop, quick extinguishing may not be possible. Faced with the formidable complexities of identity-based conflict, we may be tempted to resign ourselves to the status quo or to nibble around the edges of issues, without any real expectation of progress. Of course we are limited by our lifespan expectations. Visualizing five or ten years into the future seems fraught enough with difficulties, factors beyond our ability to control or predict, and shades of hubris.

Just as politicians may have trouble making controversial long-term decisions when they have only another year in office, so we have trouble seeing our roles as change agents in a longer continuum of time that survives us. Invoking expansiveness of time helps us live in the boundary between now and the future, between us and those who will succeed us. "At the boundary, life blossoms,"[16] James Gleick reminds.

What if parties to a conflict were to visualize a hundred years into the future? What if they planned not a few months or years ahead for a world that they would like to inhabit but took themselves out of the picture completely? What if they asked,

- What legacies am I setting in motion with my actions?
- What stories will unfold from the stories I am co-creating with members of my community, my organization, my family?

Could they have conversations with great-granddaughters unborn, sharing their struggles and dilemmas, asking what they most need to have begun now? Could they listen to the answers?

Expanding the boundaries of time is only one variation on ways visualization may be used. It is a tool ripe for exploration and application in conflict resolution processes. Though the use of visualization is not unknown, there are many ways it could serve us that we have not yet invented. We have not yet invented them because we have not seen its powerful potential for creating change, its legitimacy as an approach that draws on our senses, emotions, and cognitive insights in the service of invention.

Using visualization to see within, we may find the seed of change that has eluded us. For Henry James, invention comes from a seed:

> Most of the stories straining to shape under my hand have sprung from a single small seed, a seed as minute and wind-blown as that casual hint . . . a mere floating particle. . . . Its virtue in all its needlelike quality, the power to penetrate as finely as possible, reduced to its mere fruitful essence.[17]

Visualization is powerful because it connects us to the essence of a new way forward. We do not yet see it in all of its aspects or experience the barriers that may challenge us along the way there. But we welcome the essence, however subtle or transitory it may seem, to point our way forward.

Imagination as Empowerment

John Dewey[18] said that imagination is a gateway through which meanings derived from past experiences find their way into the present. It is the conscious adjustment of the new with the old. This adjustment process may not always be lovely or easy. When we have experienced trauma, it may take months or years of sorting out memories to clear the way forward. One of my students put her practice of law on hold while memories of childhood abuse flooded back during therapy. She wrote stories in the voice of the little girl in the yellow dress about what she saw and how she felt. The little girl needed her attention to the memories before she could be integrated into her adult life.

One of the ways that the little girl in the yellow dress found healing was through her imagination. In her imagination, she took walks to places she loved, places of calm and pastoral beauty. While there, she chose objects that spoke to her. At first, they were quickly turned to vehicles for her anger. Rocks on the beach became missiles to hit her abuser in the head. Branches became tools to poke him and make him go away. Used in her imagination, they became tools for her to take back her power, owning and transforming her memories.

Gradually, she came to imagine the beach as a place of refuge—a place where the rocks and the branches gave color and texture to her enjoyment of the scene. It took a long time, but she reported enormous relief as it happened. Imagination can bring cathartic relief to parties in conflict for whom direct confrontation is not possible or desirable. Perhaps the perpetrator has died; sometimes power dynamics or strategic considerations preclude engagement. Rather than carry the burdens of the past in a metaphoric sack on their backs, parties can let their imagination provide a way to release them. As this is done, conflict dynamics shift, and movement is possible where before things were static.

The Dark Face of Imagination

But imagination, like anything, is not only a source of positive power and virtue. Imagination can also be a doorway into self-deception or self-reinforcement. The capacity to imagine can be either harmony producing or conflict enhancing. Perhaps this is why Samuel Johnson panned the imagination as a "licentious and vagrant faculty."[19] We have only to recall a frightening dream to know the power of negative and emotionally potent images of dark forces and difficult places. Whether from dreams or wakeful reveries, negative images of "the other" harbored in our minds give rise to projections of what the other might do in the future, matching negative expectations with past experience. Sometimes our imaginations do not focus on the other but enliven the shadow part of ourselves.

A friend who struggles with self-confidence finds that the shadow in her imagination has a habit of undermining her, setting her up for difficulties at work. During off hours, she analyzes work dynamics, personal frustrations, and the unfair workload she has been given. Into these scenes, she projects future difficulties and hears ominous warnings about ever-increasing burdens. Her spiraling frustration is accompanied by feelings of hopelessness and free-floating anger as she goes over these scenes. Arriving at work on Monday morning, she is not free to invent herself anew. She exudes the tension and apprehension she has lived with in her imagination over the weekend. Thus unfolds the proverbial self-fulfilling prophecy. Within a limiting structure, she compounds the problems fueled by her imaginings.

As she has become aware of the negative effects of her shadow imaginings, she has worked to change her images. But insight is not always sufficient to create change. Our shadows are our teachers and are not supplanted neatly and easily with new, appealing images simply because we wish for them. The shadow comes from those parts of ourselves we suppress because they are not nice, not welcome in polite company. But the shadow also reveals. Rather than moving immediately to replace her shadow images, my friend has found it useful to voice them to herself. Tracing their stories, she sees how they have arisen as protective mechanisms. Looking beyond their strident tone, she has seen fears, outworn strategies, and old "tapes" once set up to guard a powerless child against difficult to resist requirements and difficult-to-meet expectations. Once they are named, she can be in dialogue with them and choose, as an adult, to acknowledge the kernels of wisdom they carry.

As exploring even negative imaginings is helpful in intrapersonal conflict, it is also potentially useful in interpersonal situations. When fears, withholdings, and pain are given reciprocal voice, they may unseat the guard at the gates of impasse. Sometimes what is said is not as important as the process of saying it. In a conflict between a mother and her nineteen-year-old son, the son expresses dissatisfaction about their communication. He indicates that the mother's indirect way of making requests of him ("You wouldn't mind driving, would you?") feels manipulative and dishonest to him because it masks a directive behind an apparent inquiry into feelings. He prefers that she ask directly, "Please drive today." He says that he has been stockpiling resentment for the many times he has felt pressured to say yes when asked indirectly. He carries an internal library of complaints, catalogued by date and type, that fuel his dissatisfaction with his mother and create ongoing discomfort.

A friend who has listened asks him to imagine the effect of carrying these into the future rather than trying to reframe or challenge the negative memories. "We'll grow further and further apart," the son predicts. He will avoid contact with her, living his life in increasingly discrete circles. Imagining this picture, he feels both the relief of frustration removed and the loss of an important relationship sidetracked. Invited into this picture, his mother feels the tension between his increasing need for autonomy and his desire to be respected and connected to her. Imagining a possible logical consequence of their current trajectory helped both mother and son see where they did not want to go. From this place, they were both motivated to talk about the kind of relationship they wanted to move toward as he negotiates his independence and they invent new ways to relate adult-to-adult.

How difficult it can be to negotiate these changes in roles and relationships. Too often, we prefer unspoken simmering to the risks of surfacing our discomfort. We hold on to the picture as we believe it is rather than venture into the unknown terrain of naming discouragement, confronting pain, and inviting exploration. Then conflict grows in potency and rootedness, eventually strangling the tiny green shoots of new life that tried to spring from truthful words. Eric Williams quotes W. H. Auden:

> We would rather be ruined than changed;
> We would rather die in our dread
> Than climb the cross of the moment
> And let our illusions die.[20]

Discipline and Imagination

Because our imagination makes everything real, fears as well as possibilities, we have to employ discipline and discernment in its use. Lauren Artress[21] traces a pervasive modern fear of the imagination to the split between reason and mysticism that grew out of the Reformation. If we continue to shy away from imaginative, intuitive ways of knowing, we are left without their grace, spark, and inspiration. At the same time, we are wise to guard against breathing life into the shadow side of our memories. Our memories, loosed in imagined spaces, can become vehicles of torture. We wallow in regret, resentment, or nostalgia related to negative and positive representations of the past, both the battlefields and the Camelots.

Memories held rigidly become cognitive frames that define and limit future events. The present is seen in terms of past experiences; the future is also a reflection of the past. Paradoxically, though life is being lived in constant interplay with the past, memories are empty of the life that might animate them. They become like dusty, messy objects piled into a forgotten cupboard, devoid of living relationship. Like old museum objects, they can be named and recited, but the link of vitality is missing. Divorced from feelings of a past held rigidly, the person becomes blocked from the transformation of memory stories, unable to mine them for contributions to fertile intuitions.

When this kind of calcification of memory occurs, resolving conflict is very difficult. Sometimes this happens only in one area of life; other times it is more generalized. Serious trauma can lead to an emotional shut-down accompanying the rigid memories. I am reminded of a woman who suffered terrible teasing as a child, as well as humiliation in church. She left both the place where she was raised and the church as an adult. Years later, when the subject of the church was mentioned, she spoke in dismissive and derogatory ways. But her affect was strangely disconnected from the words she was speaking. Like a part from a play rehearsed too many times, the bridge between authentic feeling and the present was broken. Had members of the church sought reconciliation for the hurts so many years before, they would have found someone who could not offer an authentic channel into the past. Resolution between them would have been very difficult to achieve.

It is understandable that we sometimes construct a shell around painful memories to protect us. Experiences that bring pain are hardly enticing; we seek to move from them rather than vitalize them, even with the work of healing and regeneration. At the extreme edge, the construction of these shells leads to automatic behavior, to going through the motions of interaction without really investing, without authentic engagement. T. S. Eliot[22] observed that it is not the pastness of the past that is important but the continuing presence of the past. The past lives in us in the traumas and the wounds we have experienced. Those we experienced as children can be particularly potent. They operate autonomously within us when we are not conscious of them, even when they are no longer happening in real time. A person may continue to feel persecuted by an abusive parent, even after the parent dies.

We live simultaneously in the world of the senses and the world of invisibility peopled by spectral presences psychologists call complexes or projections. They are present in our choices, part of our sense of self, influential in our relationships and powerful in our conflicts. Becoming aware of the way we hold memories gives us new choices. Sometimes an event that rearranges us inside unlocks a way we have held things for a long time. The event may be happy or sad; it may seem dramatic or trivial. In some way, it poses for us the opportunity to tell a different story about our life. Telling a different story, the spectral imaginings of the past no longer influence us to live out old scripts. As we choose new scripts, the course of our interpersonal conflicts is changed; dams are dismantled, and water flows freely. Patterns of relating that may have landed us in repetitively painful situations need no longer be repeated.

A friend has always believed that she was abandoned as a child. Her mother was sickly, self-absorbed, and prone to ferocious, unpredictable temper outbursts. Her father absented himself in work. She felt oddly old at age five, caring for a younger brother and flying strategically beneath the radar of her mother. For years afterward, she carried resentment and a sense of loss for what she had not known. It took her years to realize that she was recreating, in her adult relationships, this story of abandonment.

One day she was sitting in a class on health psychology. "How many friends does a person need to be psychologically healthy?" asked the professor. He let the students offer answers, then he detailed research showing that one good friend can make the difference between despair and hope, between alienation and a sense of connection to life. Sitting there, she saw the face of her grandmother—the one who was always there, the one at whose knee she heard stories, who patiently taught her to fold origami. And she realized that she had carried the specter of abandonment into adulthood, not realizing that the strength of her grandmother's devotion had taught her about the reliability of love and about her own lovability. The story of abandonment had crowded out this story of loyal connection, and this had played out in destructive, painful relationship patterns. Seeing this for the first time, she took the risk, in W. H. Auden's words, to climb the cross of the moment and let her illusions of abandonment die.

Confronting patterned stories held in place by memory is an important part of change. Anais Nin[23] suggests that we do this when the risk to remain tight in a bud is more painful than the risk it takes to blossom. Recognizing the patterns in her stories, this friend realized that the theme of abandonment had caused pain in more than her intimate relationships. She found herself marginalized at work, outside social groups she wanted to join, looking in as though through a glass wall that kept her always on the perimeter of things. She saw that her habit of expecting abandonment kept her withdrawn and disconnected from others. Choosing to challenge the dark face of her imagination, she at last moved through her dread of abandonment that kept her insulated from others into the spaciousness of new ways of seeing her past and her present.

Creative Play with Imagination

Making transitions like this in our personal and interpersonal stories asks lightness of us. We take ourselves so seriously—doubly so in conflict, earnestly maintaining our perspectives even as we tenaciously try to unwind our differences. When we see that our perspectives are rooted in stories from the past, maintained by imagination, we see that transforming conflict is an inside job as well as an interpersonal one. When we are literally at odds with ourselves and with others, we may be pulling in two directions at once. In the process of unwinding old stories held in place by imagination, we need more than our intellects to move forward. We need imagination, intuition, and the willingness to play.

Creative minds play with the objects they love. As we let illusions die, we come to new stories and new relationships to old ones. We find energy in new ways of seeing that show us ways forward we could not think of from old ways of being—ways encumbered by illusions and limiting stories about self and other. Carl Jung[24] wrote that the creation of something new is not accomplished by the intellect but by the willingness to play with inner and outer experience "borne on the stream of time." Play may seem remote when we are in the throes of negotiating stuck conflict, but this may be the time we need it the most.

A spirit of play inspired a colleague to invite board members in a conflicted meeting to climb onto their boardroom table in stocking feet. "What do you see from up there?" she asked them as they tentatively climbed up onto the table in the formal, wood-paneled room. Several were surprised to focus on a large photograph of the

Himalayas that had been hanging at the end of the boardroom for years. It seemed to yawn into infinity, inviting them to enlarge their vision, to step into the magnificence that exists alongside the tunnel of conflict. The whole character of their dialogue changed once they climbed down, their imaginations primed by a playful moment.

When we enlarge our perspective, we see that imagination is not easily pigeonholed into dark and light sides. Complex and rich, images from imagination contribute texture, vitality, and beauty to our interior lives. We all inhabit a deeply imagined world that exists alongside the real physical one. As harsh as life may seem, it would feel much harsher without the imagination. Imagination lends poetry to our psyches. It helps us soften hardness, order chaos, relate familiar things, and create mental cushions. Imagination gifts us with a poetic version of life. In the everyday ways we tell stories is the elemental poetry of imagination that either maintains or solves problems. It is our challenge to let it flow free at times, leading us to undiscovered places, and to control it at others when it forecloses our ability to be present to the moment.

Imagination and Intuition

We know intuitively that there is always more to experience and more in our experience than we can cognitively track or name. Putting our imagination into practice, we are guided by intuition. Through imagination, we loose the bounds of old memories, seeing new possibilities. Through intuition, we discern ways of enacting these possibilities as we live into the new. In the margins between old ways we release and new ways we adopt, intuitive feelings we may not have understood when they surfaced reveal themselves as enormously helpful.

Intuition

Intuition may come in answer to a question; more often it comes unbidden, like a bag of diamonds offered to us with no forewarning. But they are diamonds in the rough, raw and unpolished by social niceties; they come as a gut feeling or a current that stands the hairs on the back of our neck straight up. To intuit is to know without knowing exactly the process by which the knowing has arrived. To intuit is to sense strongly—feelings that are from a deeper or different place than emotions. Trusting our intuition, we pay attention, accepting that knowing is enough.

The Nature of Intuition

On the surface, intuition may be difficult to see in action. Because we experience it as a surprise, we are unaware of its route. Intuition calls us to attention more by its arrival than its progress. Yet this does not mean that there is no progress until the arrival.

The Irish poet William Butler Yeats[25] captured this phenomenon in a poem about a fisherman. The fisherman apparently casts his line into the river and waits in tranquility. He seems not to be doing much of anything. Yet to those knowledgeable in the art of fishing, there is much more happening. The subtle movements of the fisherman's wrist belie a world of activity beneath the surface, where fish engage in a drama of survival as they vie for the bait. When a fish emerges from the water, our minds register action. But action has been in process all along. Similarly, intuition is a process quite outside our usual ways of paying attention, seeming to emerge suddenly but actually developing internally as we pay careful attention.

Intuition is sometimes called our sixth sense. Some say it comes from deeply ingrained emotional, cognitive, and relational skills. Others say it comes from experience. Surely our intuition, like our imagination, arises in part from memories. Our memories are working tools, assembled data banks to which we turn. Goethe said that our experiences are taken in and woven into our hearts. Then they live in us as memories, forming and reforming our identities, perpetually creating us. One of the creative forms they inspire may be what we call intuition.

In this way of thinking, intuition flows from memories held within, fertile and flexible, for informing novel situations. Our past serves us as we contemplate, study, elaborate, enjoy, and assimilate it into our present. In moments of surprise or surrender when we don't know what to do, intuition emerges with an answer that does not come from nowhere. It comes from the somewhere of our experiences, deepened in the fire of reflection and gently held memories.

But this explanation of intuition is incomplete. Theorists attempt to break intuitive moments down, analyzing them according to their origins in experience, memory, and internalized patterns. Yet intuitive moments come not only from these places. Children, after all, can be very intuitive. They sense motives and nuances that we adults, trained to observe more methodically, may miss. Intuition arises not only from experience but from innocence—the innocence of believing that it really is possible to receive information through channels outside our five senses and the usual routes of our cognition. Intuitive intelligence is an art— the art of perception through the mind. The deep source of this intelligence is not only the mind but the unknown and indefinable totality from which all perception originates.

All of us have felt it—the intuition to turn down a particular road in an area we have never visited and have no way of knowing. Sometimes we delight to find a pot of gold at the end of it; sometimes we encounter a dead end. Intuition does not generally proffer an exhaustive explanation. We are thrown back to our imaginations to consider the meaning of the diversion, never knowing for sure what would have happened if we made a different choice.

The Language of Intuition

In conflict resolution, we ask a question that presents itself to be asked for reasons we cannot identify. Or we suppress the intuition to ask the question. Whichever choice we make, we cannot know what would have happened if we had proceeded differently. Sometimes we get to the pot of gold, sometimes not. It serves us not to become too identified with our capacity to intuit; by definition, it is beyond our conscious control. Still, we can ask questions of it. And we receive answers, though sometimes the answers come cloaked in symbolic robes that stretch our ability to understand.

The potter M. C. Richards writes about a dream that gave her insight into how to write a piece about conflict for a book on the future. The dream increased her intuitive understanding of "a kind of peace that includes the freedom to conflict."[26] From her long experience as a potter, she knew that paradox is a central part of art. Working the clay, there is both surrender and concentrated attention. In conflict, she believed the same to be true. But how does one reconcile the destructive image of conflict with the lovelier image of peace? How do connection and separation work together to create richness and balance in life?

As she pondered these questions, she remembered a dream. In it, she saw a tremendous fire rapidly burning across the full length of the horizon toward her house. She and a woman neighbor packed bags and ran away. One person remained behind. He was a friend of hers, the director of a craft school where she sometimes taught. Seeing this, she felt fear. But though the fire coursed through the house, the pottery vessels, and even through him, nothing was consumed. When she returned after the fire, he observed, "Everything is still here. Only the color is deepened."[27]

The intuitive wisdom of her dream helped her find words to express the paradoxical nature of conflict. She wrote, "As vessels, we are deepened by our capacities for darkness and for light,"[28] going on to suggest that knowledge and openness to both of these capacities is critical to navigating conflict. Using symbols she knew well, the dream had presented her a way to express her intuitive understanding that both conflict and harmony are to be welcomed as agents of deepening in our lives. If we seek only harmony, pushing away our shadow selves, we find them manifesting "everywhere, sleeping and waking."[29]

As M. C. Richards discovered through her dream, intuition speaks our language. It seems exquisitely tailored to fit into our ways of sense-making, to get our attention, even when we are preoccupied with other things. It is a bridge across communication styles that does not break into units of micro-skills but somehow swallows and mirrors a gestalt. Intuition arises not only from data taken in with our senses but from seeing with the eye of the mind, feeling with the heart, and learning to listen to wisdom from outside our habitual channels of knowing. Intuition shows us images we did not know we possessed—contours of strange landscapes that we don't remember traversing.

Psychologist Robert Johnson tells a compelling story of intuition about his first meeting with his mentor Carl G. Jung, then seventy-three years old. Jung had summoned the twenty-six-year-old

Johnson to his home after learning of Johnson's archetypal dream that he believed called Johnson to a life of the spirit. "If you will remain loyal to the inner world," he told him, "it will take care of you. This is what you are good for in this life. I must tell you at the outset that you should never join anything."[30]

Johnson was surprised but felt compelled to listen. As Jung spoke with him, he was amazed at the sense of being known. In interpreting Johnson's dream, Jung used language that fit with Johnson's personality and his affinity for feelings. Only much later did Johnson learn that Jung tended to speak intellectually and that he had masterfully adjusted his communication to a style that matched Johnson's, even though they had not met before.

Intuition helps us know without conscious data how to adjust our communication style to others. It leads us to ask the unusual or exactly pertinent question that acts to unfreeze a conflict. Intuition is much-trusted yet difficult to empirically unpack. Few conflict resolution textbooks address intuition at all; it is not a capacity that is covered in training. Yet practitioners speak of it when they describe their work, using phrases like, "I just knew it," and "It came in a flash." Here is the way one mediator describes it.

Milner quotes Linda Colburn, a community mediator from Hawaii, as saying, "I think that a rule for me is to pay homage to my intuition. If I sense that one party has a reservation about discussing the matter fully or lacks confidence in his or her position, then nine times out of ten that is one of the first things I try to surface in caucus."[31] Colburn describes intuition as the ability to "read the bubbles above a person's head" as if related to a character on a comic strip. Intuition, Colburn maintains, means using nonverbal, psychological, and spiritual cues to decide whether a style of peacemaking is appropriate. It helps her choose a language that will reach the parties in conflict.

Linda Colburn is one of the few mediators to speak in print about the way she uses intuition. With little in the way of catalogued knowledge to guide us about intuition, third parties may ask what can be done to cultivate this capacity. Is it a zero-sum attribute, either present or not, given to some and not to others? Can it be trained, improved, or honed? If it can, how is it used? How can we listen to the symbolic language of our intuition and correctly, quickly decipher a path to action that will serve others?

Can it be wrong? If so, how do we develop the discernment to tell the "pot of gold" roads from the dead ends?

Intuition in Conflict Resolution

As third parties, we use intuition in a wide range of ways in conflict resolution. When intuition taps us on the shoulder, we notice conscious or unconscious omissions in parties' stories, behavioral inconsistencies, and moments pregnant with unspoken words. We evaluate our responses to the needs and idiosyncrasies of particular parties and diverge from our agendas in light of intuitive "hits" we receive. Many of our uses of intuition may pass below our radar screen, barely breaking our conscious awareness, even as they inform our decision making. This is especially true when we are new in practice.

Newly trained mediators and facilitators face the difficult task of entertaining several levels of attention at once. They track the substance of what is being said, measuring it against consistencies with nonverbal communication, previous indications, and stated goals. They monitor the process, considering timing, emotional tone, and boundaries. They assess the comfort of parties and their openness to each other. Through it all, they track themselves, attending to their bodies and emotional intelligences for information about impasses and opportunities.

Whether or not we admit it to ourselves, as third parties we bring agendas to conflict processes. Though we have no substantive stake in the outcome, we often have a stake in reaching one, with party satisfaction and even our continued employment contingent on it. We respond to parties differently, finding one person easy to relate to and another a challenge. Though we try to set our biases aside, they are with us no matter how impartially we strive to behave. If we are to use intuition in the service of effective intervention, awareness of these dynamics is a minimum. Otherwise, as we attend to these many levels, we may miss the insistent tap of intuition.

Even as we attend to intuition, it is important to acknowledge that we are not flawless channels. Our biases and judgments may cloud or shape it. Our agendas may obscure it or reframe it into a self-reinforcing message. Recognizing, cultivating, and applying intuition as conflict practitioners is a project of awareness, intention, and sensitivity. Because intuitive moments are not planned or programmed, they require attention followed by curious engagement. Cultivating intuition is a bit like focusing on letting go; the more we try to do it, the more elusive it becomes. It works better to catch ourselves in the motions and then follow the tributaries back to the river from where they sprang.

Intuition is enhanced by concentrating less on the particulars of situations and the agendas we have for them and more on the present moment. Intuition is less about interpreting body language or expressed ideas as facts, and more about sensing them at the symbolic level, listening for the language that speaks directly to our symbolic receptors. The good news is that we do this all the time. We enhance our intuitive capacity as we increase our attention to the levels at which we take in information, sharpen our discernment of the information we receive, and recognize the riches our intuition carries.

One of the helpful gifts of intuition for third parties relates to predicting behavior. I may have a sense after working with a couple in family mediation for a few sessions that the husband will not show up for the next meeting. He has not failed to keep our appointments in the past, but I sense that he may not show up this time, when our goal is to come to closure about several of the issues we have been discussing. When this prediction comes true, I am able to trace back through the meetings we have had and see the pattern: as closure is approached, he absents himself. Sometimes this has taken the form of losing concentration, absenting himself mentally and emotionally from the process. In his marriage, it took the form of various trips—"geographic cures"—when they were on the verge of separating.

Looked at in this way, his failure to show up for the session flows naturally from his pattern of behavior throughout the marriage and the mediation process. My intuition was the result of an integrative process, bringing together contextual cues, emotional fluency, logical reasoning, and memory with that "I-know-but-can't-put-my-finger-on-it" sixth sense. Informed by my intuition about what his behavior may mean, I turn my attention to ways that closure may be eased for him to facilitate both parties getting on with their lives.

This predictive capacity is one of the more startling manifestations of intuition. Other elements of intuition include mindful receptivity, empathy, and deep listening. These elements are not exhaustive; they are not even all present in every instance of intuition. But they do run reliably through experiences of conflict intervention as practitioners speak about it. As such, they are worth exploring and cultivating.

Mindful Receptivity

Mindful receptivity means to respond to a situation with openness and a spirit of curiosity. Judgment is not consistent with this state; neither is the expression of a stereotypical emotional reaction out of habit or knee-jerk response. As we maintain a calm demeanor, matched by an inner state of stillness, we are a more ready canvas on which the parties may paint their conflict. One person at the table makes a statement that outrages another. If we also respond with anger, we are aligning ourselves and losing our effectiveness. Responding with curiosity and calm, we open the possibility of finding out more about what lies behind the statement.

Mindful receptivity is challenging, not only because of complex relational dynamics in the room but because of the cacophony in our heads. As Robert Grudin writes, "Looking for self, I found many selves, a noisy parliament of voices, a variety of components, some familiar and some strange, some conscious and some unconscious, some controllable and some uncontrollable."[32] To be mindfully receptive, we need to have some sense of our multiplicity of selves, as well as a way to quiet all of the voices. For this reason, meditative or focusing practices are helpful in developing the capacity for mindful receptivity.

The range of meditative or focusing practices that work is very wide. Just as we have an internal multiplicity of selves, we differ from each other in ways of stilling our minds and focusing. For some, writing on a blank page is a way to come clear. For others, it may be running, walking, driving, sitting quietly, or listening to music. In meetings or conflict resolution sessions, mindful receptivity can be renewed by taking a break or changing physical arrangements or positions. There are no set prescriptions for what works, and sometimes what works best is simply a change of mode or scene or focus, thus creating space for new ideas and perspectives to surface.

Moments of mindful receptivity find us available, not distracted with our own agendas or later plans. They are often marked by a memorable quality because the state of mindful receptivity is not how most of us spend our lives. We can cultivate them by using techniques to still our minds before meeting with parties and taking time out when needed. Mindful receptivity, when modeled for parties, is a powerful teaching tool for those who have received each other only through the small apertures their conflicts have allowed.

Cultivating mindful receptivity means paying attention to the cues our body sends us about the dynamics in the room. Our stomach feels tight: what about the process needs to relax? Our entire self starts to feel tired: what about the process needs to shift? Our breathing becomes labored: what about the process needs to be released? It also means holding a soft but clear focus on the process and maintaining a level of engagement that is active yet allows for flexibility, space, and change.

This focus on the body as a sensing instrument begs the question of whether intuition talks to all of us through the same channels. Just as we hold tension in different parts of our bodies, we have an individual lexicon of body language that informs us, moment-to-moment, about what we have absorbed but not named. Enhancing our intuition requires studying our pattern of physical language, asking questions like

- Which part of me hurts when there is pain in a group? Where do I first feel it when things are stuck?
- When I get that creeping pain in my forehead, what kind of situation tends to be happening?

The patterns we identify have physiological referents as well as meaning interpretations. Practitioners of a process called Brain Gym teach a series of physical movements that stimulate thought, relaxation, and receptivity using pathways in the body. Neurolinguistic programming practitioners have catalogued physical movements and their correlates of meaning. As we learn from these approaches and explore our individual responses, we become more able to listen to our bodies as intuitive channels and more adept at maintaining receptivity. We may ultimately be helpful to parties in conflict as we share our knowledge with them.

What does mindful receptivity do for intuition? It is a fertile place for its emergence, a state from which we are more likely to attend to it. From a place of calm, we are more able to assess intuition's veracity when it does emerge. As a process is convened, taking time for silence and acknowledging the goal of receptivity is also convergent with mindfulness.

Empathy

Empathy is an important way of relating to others; it is a bridge across which our heart travels to enter another's path. As we suspend judgment and engage mindful receptivity, we increase our ability to understand another in context. We find ourselves understanding not only the words but the feelings expressed and unexpressed by the speaker. We find ourselves understanding meanings not expressed at all. Empathy draws on imagination and intuition at once, as described by philosopher Martin Buber:

> [Empathy] rests on a capacity possessed to some extent by everyone, which may be described as "imagining" the real; I mean the capacity to hold before one's soul a reality arising at this moment but not able to be directly experienced. Applied to intercourse between men, "imagining" the real means that I imagine to myself what another man is at this very moment wishing, feeling, perceiving, thinking, and not as a detached content but in his very reality, that is, as a living process in this man.[33]

In an example given by Warren Zeigler in his book *Ways of Enspiriting,* a male participant in a weekend dialogue was assigned to listen to a story from a female participant. Afterward he said,

> I listened. I caught your words, was silent, gave attention. I heard her speak her thoughts, her concerns, her images. But I got more. I received a great sense of pain. You didn't speak it. But I got it. I got a sense of great turmoil in you, wrenching and pulling and tearing. It hurts. I don't mean *you hurt.* I mean *I hurt.* I don't mean *I hurt for you.* I mean, I hurt.[34]

This man, who apparently had little in common with his partner, had joined in empathy with her. She acknowledged it, saying, "You felt me. I said nothing about what's going on inside. Yet you caught it. You were there. You were me, just for those moments."

This is empathy. Through his receptivity and willingness to enter into his partner's reality, the man was able to intuitively understand his partner's state (we explore more about how to cultivate empathy in later chapters). As we develop our innate capacities to relate to others, opening ourselves to the full range of their feelings and the strange yet traceable ways they attach meaning to experiences, we receive information we cannot trace. We listen not only with our ears but with our hearts and our bodies. And that is the essence of the final element of intuition we will consider: deep listening.

Deep Listening

Deep listening goes hand-in-hand with mindful receptivity and empathy. It provides a focus for receptivity—a focus on words and what is unspoken, on what is said, felt, and meant. Listening is as powerful an act as speaking; it has been astutely observed that there are no true speakers who are not also listeners. Deep listening combines the stillness of receptivity with the emotional fluency that makes empathy possible. We pay another a high compliment when we listen to them with our full attention. Conflict resolution sessions attended by this kind of listening are compelling and powerful.

In deep listening, we pay exquisite attention to those with whom we work. We are really willing to put ourselves out, stepping out of self-absorption into a liminal space where our agenda is clarity of mind and heart. A classic Zen story is revealing:

> One day, a man of the people said to Zen Master Ikkyu: "Master will you please write me the maxims of highest wisdom?" Ikkyu immediately took his brush and wrote the word, "Attention." "Is that all?" asked the man. "Will you not add something more?" Ikkyu then wrote twice running: "Attention. Attention." "Well, remarked the man rather irritably. "I really don't see much depth or subtlety in what you have just written." Then Ikkyu wrote the same word three times running: "Attention. Attention. Attention." Half angered, the

man demanded: "What does the word attention mean anyway?"
And Ikkyu answered gently: "Attention means ATTENTION."[35]

As we pay attention, we develop greater capacities to do so.
Paying attention to our intuition, in addition to the more prosaic
fruits of our senses' labors, we become more effective interveners
in conflict.

Of course, not all practitioners have developed their intuitive
capacities. Guided by their experience, the experiences of peers,
and what I hope will be an emerging literature in this area, they
can. Thus it is not an all-or-nothing phenomenon but a capacity
that can grow just like emotional fluency or the ability to listen to
the messages of the body. Indeed, each of these compliments the
other as they are developed. In every case, it is important to recognize that none of us are clear channels all the time. To engage
in the most ethical practice we can, we must remember that even
when we have confidence in our intuitive "take" on something, we
may be wrong.

The Possibility of Being Wrong

One question remains: Given that intuition is difficult to evaluate
using empirical methods, how do we account for the possibility
that we may be wrong? Because intuition arises with a strong
impact, we may be inclined to trust it and act from it. This is one
thing in our own lives; it is something else again when we are intervening in others' lives. Can you think of a time when you had an
intuitive "hit" that was later not borne out? It is also important to
exercise caution; psychologists tell us that when we make a judgment about someone, we tend to hold to it rather tenaciously, even
in the presence of evidence to the contrary.

To keep in mind the sense that we may be wrong is important,
not only with intuition but with all aspects of our work. There is
no fail-safe way to know whether our knowing is correct in every
moment. Perhaps it helps us more to ask whether our knowing is
helpful or whether it stands in the way of progress. Because we
may be wrong, it is important to cultivate our capacity for self-
observation, noting somatic and emotional cues that corroborate
or disconfirm our intuitive sense.

Because we may be wrong, it is useful to have a repertoire of ways to check ourselves when possible. First, the humility to know that we never know all is important. We can also check ourselves by asking

- Am I intuiting that someone has a selfish motive because they remind me of a diabolical character earlier in my life or because the combination of factors I am synthesizing leads me to know it?
- Am I checking out this intuition in other channels when possible rather than acting impulsively from it?
- Am I taking time to sit with my intuitive take on a situation, noticing whether it "checks out" with my somatic and emotional ways of knowing? In other words, how does it feel in my body?
- What do my feelings tell me about my certainty or doubt about this intuition?
- How can I check this out with the parties to get confirmation of my intuition?
- Am I communicating with co-interveners about my intuition and eliciting their feedback to help me reflect on my intuitions?
- Am I noticing cues in the room from others, including what they are communicating nonverbally?

Asking these questions will not guarantee accuracy but will provide an internal review process that improves our odds. Of course, the other component of this review process is ongoing self-evaluation. When fellow practitioners are available to work with us in reflecting on our work, the experience is even richer. But this is not a substitute for time spent reviewing the cases we have done, the choice points, the judgments made, whether informed by intuition or analysis. As we do this, we hone our ability to be of service and to draw on connected ways of knowing, the subject of the next chapter.

CHAPTER FIVE

Connected Ways of Knowing
Energizing Change, Emphasizing Relationship

Members of two groups in conflict had been through three days
of dialogue. They were tired. Participants were sitting on the floor
of the great room in the grand country house that had been their
temporary home during the process. There was a fire in the fireplace and a mixture of feelings in the air. The next day, they would
pack up and return to their daily lives. They felt regret and relief
to be leaving; they felt guarded hope, yet fear, about what would
follow. Could the insights they had experienced guide them
through the questions and suspicions that members of their home
groups would harbor? Could the nascent relationships they had
formed withstand the tests that would follow as their two peoples
continued to struggle with each other? Would the larger conflict
mute and swallow the steps toward imagining a different future
they had taken there?

The questions hung in the air, mostly unspoken. The formal
activities were over. Evening was beginning. Into the dusky silence
came the voice of one of the women, humming a shred of a song.
The melody belonged to a folk song known to members of both
groups. Its images were pastoral and peaceful, powerfully invoking
the strength of the mountains that were loved by members of both
groups. Another group member moved to the piano and began to
play the song. Everyone gathered around the piano, some singing,
some humming, some using spoons or hands to keep the rhythm.
The questions that had troubled them were calmed as their sense
of connection played out through the music.

Later someone asked the woman who sang the original fragment why she had done so—what had reminded her of the song?
No singing had taken place during their time together at all. If
someone had suggested singing, it would probably have been
rejected in the atmosphere of tension and frustration that accompanied much of their dialogue. She said she had no idea where the
tune came from. If asked to sing a folk song, she would not have
been able to think of one. It simply came into her mind so strongly
that she began to hum it without being aware she was doing so.
And it engaged everyone present in a way that all the thousands of
words they had spoken in the preceding days had not.

The song became a ritual—a way for everyone present to join
together in awareness of the caring they felt for each other and for
their land. Its simple melody focused attention on ways they were
connected and what they shared, away from the challenges ahead
and the pain of the past. After the singing, the atmosphere
changed. There was laughter and playfulness, quiet conversations
and reflection. Surprising the participants out of their fear and
analyses of what lay before them, the song invited connected ways
of knowing that were both powerful and generative.

Our Desire to Make Meaning

In this chapter, we explore such connected ways of knowing—ways
often unacknowledged yet as vital as the food we eat. Together,
emotional, physical, imaginative, and connected ways of knowing
are facets of creativity essential to resolving conflict. The heart,
body, and imagination in dialogue with the head provide us reliable ways through conflict into resolution. Connected ways of
knowing are the hub of the wheel, inviting us to center our
processes in what we and others care about as sources of inspiration and energy for the way forward.

From Meaning to Understanding

Connected ways of knowing, centered in relationship, remind us
that conflicts are part of relational systems. The ways we construct
our identities and relate to each other are informed by our ways of
making meaning. It is also true that through composing identities

and relating, we make meaning; we come to know ourselves through relationships and the stories we co-create. Only by making the invisible visible, by naming and exploring meanings related to conflicts, can we address issues connected to who we believe we are and how we see the world. Conflicts that matter, that may be difficult to resolve, always involve this meaning-making level.

On a Hollywood movie lot, a film set in Japan was being made. The floors were covered with tatami mats, common in traditional Japanese temples and homes. In Japan, removing shoes before walking on the fragrant, revered tatami is a must. For American members of the crew on the film set, it seemed less practical. Crew members were requested to remove their shoes before walking on the tatami, but as they were frequently walking on and off the set, they did not consistently do so. Their failure to remove shoes was offensive to the Japanese actors and producers.

On the material level, this conflict was about shoes and tatami. Because the tatami did not have to last for a generation, as it might in Japan, the American crew members had a hard time understanding why there was so much concern. On the social level, there was a desire to get along and cooperate in making the movie. This led to increased attention to shoe removal, but as pace picked up and pressure built, the tatami was again walked on by shoed crew members.

Only when the Japanese and Americans sat down and talked on the symbolic, meaning level was the matter resolved. The Japanese explained that removing shoes when walking on tatami was not a purely practical norm aimed at preservation or cleanliness of the tatami. Tatami is considered sacred; it is revered and respected. The Americans understood this better when the Japanese used an analogy. "Would you walk on the floor with your shoes on if it were covered not with tatami but with an American flag?" The reference to the flag was meaningful to the Americans, who were then able to understand the meaning of the tatami to the Japanese in a new light. There was no more walking on the tatami floors with shoes on. Conflict resolved.

Not all conflicts are resolved so simply. Yet this illustrates how useful it is to think about conflict resolution as a meaning-making activity. We are meaning-making creatures. With threads of information, we create stories. With hints and guesses, we create theories. In the richness of silence, we make sense of our choices. In dialogue, we share the sense we have made. Viktor Frankl wrote that our basic motivation is a "will to meaning."[1] We seek tasks that add meaning to our existence. In our quests for meaning, we move beyond necessities into the realm of possibilities. In achieving the dreams we imagine, we draw on connected ways of knowing.

From Meaning to Relationship

Connected ways of knowing arise from the invisible threads that link us to those we know—those whose ideas have affected us, those we love, and those we conflict with. They arise from acknowledging the relational systems that ensconce us and extend us. Seeing this, we note that an action of ours may have an impact on someone a world away or on the fate of our natural environment. We cannot dispose of conflict in an us-them way, because we are all part of a relational score, interdependent in a global village.

This insight has been explored by chaos and complexity theorists: we are connected in multiple webs of relationship and meaning that truly bring a new immediacy to John Donne's line, "No man is an island." Connected ways of knowing function to give us a wide range of tools for navigating these relationships, drawing on our capacities for making meaning.

Our desire to make meaning extends to all parts of our lives and our relationships. Listen to someone telling a story about her or his life. Even though the events related may have seemed disjointed at the time, in the telling the story becomes coherent; it flows. We seek and create stories to give meaning to our lives; we find it disquieting when events happen that we cannot explain, that we cannot "story" because the motivations or the coherence seem to be missing. Extreme acts of violence and natural disasters challenge us because it is difficult for us to tell a story that situates the events in a way that makes sense to us. In the aftermath of such events, people come together to grieve and assist each other in ways that make their connections more visible and more precious. Thus we reconstruct meanings and become more aware of the importance of our human connections in the face of attack or suffering.

When we see conflict resolution as a vehicle for making meaning, we draw on this human capacity to tell stories that give meaning to events. We acknowledge that people make sense differently, depending on their cultural, personal, and experiential ways of being. Conflict resolution becomes a forum in which different ways of making meaning are explored in the service of finding joint ways to story the future. Conflict resolution becomes a container in which people's meanings—their values, deep beliefs, convictions, and passions—become important components of new, shared stories. We will explore ways that meaning making is accessed through stories, metaphors, and rituals in the next chapters. For now, we explore how connected ways of knowing help to form and deepen relationships, even across histories of intractable conflict.

The Spaciousness of Connected Ways of Knowing

Connected ways of knowing are evoked in relationship, whether within ourselves or with others; they reference something more expansive than our personalities. This expansiveness may be manifest in a variety of forms. We may expand our awareness, our sensitivity to the meanings that inform a conflict, our intuition about how to proceed. Expansiveness may operate on a practical level as we embody an attitude of service and compassion, acknowledging our connection to others.

Connected ways of knowing are not only about our relationships with each other. The foundation of these ways of knowing is our relationship with ourselves—with our purposes for being and ways of making meaning. As connected ways of knowing are about expansiveness, they refer not only to an external sense of spaciousness but to our internal experience. J. Krishnamurti, a wise Indian teacher, is said to have put it this way: "The distance to the stars is nothing compared to the distance within ourselves. We are infinitely more than we think." Thus connected ways of knowing connect inner processes of discerning with outward appeals to creative, shared wisdom or collective intelligence, however we perceive these to operate around and within us.

Connection and Community

Connected ways of knowing emphasize connection rather than distance, convergence rather than conflict. They draw connections among disparate ideas, and so are creative. They strengthen us as we act from our deep beliefs and convictions, and so are powerful. Connected ways of knowing remind us to center our processes in our sources of meaning, in those things and awarenesses that take us outside the boundaries of our egos. They remind us to keep human connection at the center of our approaches rather than believe that theories and formulas work somehow as abstractions or disembodied tools.

These ideas are not new, least of all in the conflict resolution field. Decades ago, Mary Parker Follett wrote about connection as a deeper reality than individual separateness and community as the crucible from which all lasting resolutions are forged. She concluded, "It is now evident that self and others are merely different points of view of one and the same experience, two aspects of one thought. Neither of these partial aspects can hold us, we seek always that which includes self and others. To recognize the community principle in everything we do should be our aim, never to work with individuals as individuals."[2]

Connected ways of knowing inform us in ways we cannot fully analyze or unpack. They animate us, leading toward possibilities we may not have envisioned. Connected ways of knowing link us to the expansive, bigger picture. This bigger picture may relate to the purposes that inform and breathe life into what we and negotiating parties are doing; it may be a sense of perspective that takes the meager picture we hold of the possible and shows us whole other sets of ways forward. Connected ways of knowing remind us to make room for the things we know but cannot name, places we go but cannot touch, the other we have learned to hate yet must join in co-creation of a new story despite the discomfort it gives us.

Connection and Mystery

Connected ways of knowing are neither impenetrable nor magical, though sometimes they may seem so. Relying on them, it is possible to achieve unanticipated results, to experience unexpected progress. Although we may be tempted to attribute these results to genius, luck, or even mystical forces, much of the value of connected ways of knowing arises from expanding our awareness. Because we have built thought-walls around what is possible, we are surprised when something else emerges. The revelation of connected ways of knowing is that the walls were never impermeable or there was a way around them we failed to see.

The resources available to us to find our way through or around walls are not only personal ones. Connected ways of knowing remind us that when we commit to an intention (for example, to shift a stuck conflict), then "providence moves too."[3] Von Goethe reminds us that all sorts of things occur to help us once we are bold enough to step outside habits of narrowing our awareness when faced with conflict. He suggests that the commitment to initiate or create brings "[a]ll sorts of things . . . to help one that would otherwise never have occurred. A whole stream of events issues from the decision, raising in one's favor all manner of unforeseen incidents and meetings and material assistance which no man could have dreamt would have come his way."[4]

Connected ways of knowing draw on our capacity to absorb things without being aware of them. As I sit writing this chapter, I get a clear image of a friend. Pausing, I phone her only to find that she is sad, depressed, and needs to talk. How did I know? Not in the conventional ways we think of knowing but because there is some channel of communication between us less tangible than the telephone. Similarly, a mediator may get a gut feeling to do or say something during a session that unfreezes the conflict. It is the turning point to which everyone aspired but had no map to find. How did the mediator get the gut feeling? She or he may have absorbed or sensed the information that led to the inspiration without being aware of it.

As I talk with practitioners, I hear these kinds of stories over and over again. Seasoned, successful practitioners may use quite different procedures and have vastly different personas, yet they are helpful in facilitating shifts. What do they have in common? A honed, connected way of knowing guides them moment-by-moment about what might help, when to stay silent, and what might underlie a particular hardness displayed by a party. These practitioners are not unlike experts from a diverse range of fields.

We know that experts arrive at solutions to problems by channels they sometimes cannot describe in a step-by-step manner. They take shortcuts, perform mental leaps, make connections that get them to the right answer faster and easier than the untrained. When the expert is a mathematician, it may be possible to go back and trace the series of formulas that explain the answer that is derived. When the expert is a conflict resolution practitioner, her or his analysis of parts may not be sufficient to explain the whole. We have, even in retrospect, only hints about what works well—only guesses about how timing, context, choice, and creative ideas moved through a crack in the wall of conflict to achieve a breakthrough.

The Use of Connection

This chapter poses questions for conflict practitioners and teachers about accessing connected ways of knowing in our work. How do we draw on the parts of ourselves that lend expansiveness to our training and intervention? How do we connect to others in ways that tap into shared reservoirs of spaciousness? How do we situate our processes so that participants feel invited to access and share connected ways of knowing, as anchors to steady themselves and bridges to others?

The answers we explore will not be exhaustive; they are beginnings. Although many conflict practitioners draw on inner resources and a sense of connection to that which is bigger than themselves, there has been little written about how these connections are made outside of faith-based contexts. It is a challenge to find a vocabulary that speaks to connected ways of knowing that does not relegate them to the realm of the impenetrably mysterious or the impossibly intangible. Yet it is important to begin if we are to draw on this capacity in our work. And our work is enriched when we do.

As we go forward, a reminder: a common tendency when exploring underused capacities is to see our own deficits. We may imagine ways our practice would be transformed through increasing our use of connected ways of knowing, or using them with more awareness. Yet all successful third parties use them regularly. We rely on connected ways of knowing in day-to-day life. Whether inside or outside a conflict resolution session, we make millions of micro decisions drawing from our perceptual skills, experience banks, intuitive abilities, inspiration, or some combination of these. All of them contribute expansiveness to our work, accessing, building, and strengthening the resources available to us in relationships within ourselves and with others. Mindful of how these ways of knowing serve us daily, let's investigate how they can be cultivated, intentionally accessed, and amplified in our work.

As practitioners, we invite parties to access connected ways of knowing in building relationships and imagining new stories for their futures. Let's look in on a group in the jungle to see one way this is being done. As we do so, we will uncover key dimensions of connected ways of knowing.

Connection Across Borders

Another day dawns in the jungle. The night noises have subsided; delicate morning light penetrates the dense green. A group of young men and women set off on the muddy track. Their shoes are dirty and still damp from the day before, tightly laced in a futile attempt to keep the leeches out. Beside them, the river is thick with sable silt; around them, the air is already heavy with building heat. Few words are spoken, yet there is a palpable sense of camaraderie, even affinity, among the trekkers.

This sense of affinity is surprising; they grew up on either side of a divided society, never meeting someone from the other side. They speak different first languages, look to different mother countries for their heritage. Each of their governments denies the legitimacy of the other. There are no telephone lines connecting their communities; even the Internet has not broken through the line between them. And yet they are together in the jungle, relying on each other, learning about each other and themselves, away from the tension of their homelands.

But they are away from more than their homelands. They are away from their habits, from their ordinary ways of being, and their usual patterns of doing. In this place far from familiar ground, the usual rules do not apply. Their physical selves are strained, challenged, and wide-eyed awake. Their feeling selves are engaged and called to new experiences. Their imaginal selves are living into

surprising possibilities. And their habitual ways of knowing are suspended, replaced by more spacious, connected ways of knowing.
Expansiveness abounds, as time, boundaries of the self, and awareness defy old presumptions.

In the middle of the jungle, people rely on each other and
come into contact with the spaciousness and magnificence of
nature. They connect across barriers that would previously have
separated them, whether barriers of identity, status, or history.
Faced with the intricate miracle of nature, they share awe. Awe
opens the way to gratitude. Gratitude, as we will see, is one of the
hallmarks of connected ways of being and knowing.

Organizers may not call this jungle experience an opportunity
to share connected ways of knowing, but it fits in many ways. Connected ways of knowing are

- *Expanding,* stretching boundaries of time and space, self and
  ego, understanding and awareness
- *Animating,* quickening the senses and awakening vitality and
  creativity
- *Connecting,* building relationship with others and the self, reinforcing convictions about what is deeply valued, and reminding us that our theories come alive when centered in human
  connection
- *Informing,* arising from listening within ourselves and to others
  in ways that bring new and rich information
- *Inspiring,* nudging and whispering us into action arising from
  our convictions and our sense of connection with others
- *Spiraling,* taking us out of linear thought and action into possibilities for rapid transitions and lasting shifts
- *Surprising,* providing us with unexpected, often-elegant experiences of creativity in action
- *Changing,* deepening our capacity for fluidity and flexibility as
  we move out of the stuck places of conflict
- *Mindful,* bringing us exquisitely present with ourselves, each
  other, and a sense of awe and wonder

We'll explore each of these dimensions as they relate to conflict practice in the next few pages. It is not necessary to be in the
jungle to experience connected ways of knowing. The jungle is sim-

ply a shortcut, stripping away familiarity and habits to bring us into closer touch with others and ourselves.

The Dimensions of Connected Ways of Knowing

Connected ways of knowing, like wind on the water, are easiest to understand by their effects. The dimensions of connected ways of knowing run like a seam of coal in a mountain: rich and abundant, generating energy. In discussing them, I draw examples from teaching and intervention; connected ways of knowing are integral to both. I also share stories that bring the ideas to life—stories of ordinary and extraordinary people just living their lives. For it is in the day-to-day of our life compositions that we learn richly about connected ways of knowing. We begin with the heart of our definition: expanding.

Expanding

Connected ways of knowing are expanding, stretching boundaries of time and space, self and ego, understanding and awareness. Conflict is frequently about feeling trapped, frozen, or limited. No clear options for change exist; there is a sense of being stuck. If not for this, conflict would not be so difficult. It would be possible to move fluidly and flexibly through, maneuvering here and there, weaving in and out of trouble spots. In many cases, we do just that. Conflict resolution is needed for the times we get stuck, trapped by the burrs of our identity catching on someone else's way of being.

A look at our teaching and practice reveals awareness of the importance of expansiveness. We speak of expanding the pie, inventing new options, recasting the issues in so-called win-win terms. All of these ideas relate to the material part of conflict, to those things that can be manipulated or seen differently in the service of an integrative solution. We need to apply this thinking also to the social and symbolic levels.

As we do this, new questions surface. At the social level, we ask,

- What will I not let myself know about me or our relationship that keeps me stuck?

- What do I envision as possible in our relationship?
- How can we create both spaciousness and constructive connection in our relationship, given our differences?
- What creative changes in social or organizational structures would be helpful in addressing this conflict and in preventing future conflicts?

And at the symbolic, meaning-making level, we ask,

- Who am I in this situation, and how are my ways of being blocking progress?
- How are the ways I am making sense of these issues keeping us in the same dance?
- How is my identity connected to maintaining this conflict?
- How are my ways of perceiving issues and others rigid; how are they flexible?

When we are stuck for a long time, our identities shape themselves around the conflict, and there are no quick ways to extricate ourselves. Deep-rooted conflicts are addressed constructively as we make new meanings of who we are, who we are in relation to others, and how the "we" of our relationship can find a form spacious enough for both parties to pursue what matters to them deeply without violating the other.

Expansiveness is strongly evoked when people on either side of divisive issues come together for dialogue. In the Common Ground dialogues on abortion, which are described more fully in later chapters, participants had acrimonious relational histories, negative images and expectations of each other, and high levels of emotionality about the way the conflict has played out. As they met in communities around the United States and Canada, sharing their personal stories rather than their official positions, they came to see each other in new ways.

Their relationships—and through their relationships the conflict itself—expanded from being held as a narrow passageway in the dark to a place of light and possibility. Out of their willingness to sit down and quietly talk came a rich set of initiatives, including joint papers on adoption and acceptable activities outside clinics, and joint initiatives to support women and children living in poverty. The abortion issue, twisted and contorted by media, advocates, and pressured politicians, came to be seen as something linked to many shared concerns, including the prevention of teen pregnancies and more support for single mothers. This expansiveness came through dialogue, through willingness to set aside stereotypes, fears, and fighting long enough to see what else might be possible.

I often think that creating space for parties is my chief job in conflict intervention—space for them to situate themselves in new ways, space for them to move away from established patterns and face-compromising precipices. In doing this, I have to remind myself and the parties that we seek neither perfection nor an ideal outcome. Win-win is too polished and ideal an aspiration. Rather, we seek a way that is mostly OK–mostly OK. It's not as flashy as win-win, but it is much closer to the kinds of outcomes I have encountered in practice. Naming it lets parties into the secret early that they will have to find ways to be more spacious with each other if they are to find a way through the conflict between them.

Creating this space where new ways of thinking may lead to new thoughts is challenging. But it is also very powerful. It may be that the very cracks in our carefully fashioned plans are the places where the light comes in. A fishhook extracted from the finger of a former adversary can bring closeness; a pause in a tightly constructed agenda makes way for inspiration. What would happen if we imagined our practice as finding the cracks and helping people notice how they let in light? Would we worry less about control, managing strong emotions, or keeping our processes tidy and orderly? Could we find those times in our lives when we felt as though windows were thrown open to fresh breezes—windows that had been hung with the heavy crimson drapes of our limiting assumptions, fears, and images of the other? Could we use these times as reference points in helping others navigate toward spaciousness and a willingness to relax their sense of what is immutable long enough to notice the cracks where the light comes in? And could we then help parties grab onto the window frame, stepping out into the daylight where more expansive perspectives present themselves?

Animating

As we notice places where light is shed on us and our conflicts, we remember physical sensations that accompany mental or emotional shifts. Sensations of energy, of vitality, are felt as a rush or a tingle or even a quiet sense of relief that the boulder in the path has been moved. Connected ways of knowing are animating. They quicken the senses, awakening creativity. This happens frequently during the course of a class.

Several of the classes I teach take place over a four- or five-day period of intensive contact. In this condensed format, it is easier to see the ebbs and flows of energy that take place in almost every class. Sometimes time seems to drag; at the end of the third or fourth day, engaging enthusiasm feels as possible as dragging a two-hundred-pound weight up a very steep hill. Then there are moments when a discussion takes off, an activity captures imaginations, a lecture sparks passionate controversy, or someone says something vulnerable or poignant or expressive that powerfully reaches everyone in the room. At these moments, connected ways of knowing are coming into play.

Inviting connected ways of knowing into the room is not an all-or-nothing activity. Most of us experience them sometimes; there are a few highlights in my teaching career when most of the class time was infused with them. Later in the chapter, we explore ways to invite more rather than fewer of these moments so infused with the energy of connected ways of knowing. For now, let me invite you to a final session of one such class.

Connected ways of knowing have been present in this class; we know because people are animated and reluctant to leave. The atmosphere has been nurturing and respectful. Participants have felt the safety to reveal and reexamine their assumptions and have grown into the expansiveness offered by that willingness. They have learned from each other. They have experienced a range of strong feelings, positive and negative. They have been surprised. When they speak, you can hear their hearts. Some say that it will take them some time to reflect on and assimilate all that happened. Some use words to describe the energy that attended us, including *exhilarating, invigorating, inspiring.* They express desire to maintain the connections because the relationships have become precious.

This leads us to another of the dimensions of connected ways of knowing.

Connecting

Connected ways of knowing build relationship with others and ourselves, reinforcing our sense of being part of something bigger than ourselves. Because we think we cannot—and do not want to—build close relationships with those we classify as "the other," whether members of a different ethnic group, class, or society, we foreclose opportunities for connection. How many friends do you have across social, ethnic, political, racial, differently able, differently educated groups? We so often gravitate to those we perceive to be like us and so may be less likely to form relationships with those we define as "different."

It is also true that there are structural, social, historical, and perceptual boundaries that make connecting difficult. If you are a member of a group that oppressed another group, how can you transition to becoming an ally or a friend? Can you do effective work as a conflict intervenor or trainer with members of groups with whom your group has a troubled past? There are examples that show us this is possible, but it is not easy.

Yet connecting across difference is central to our work as conflict resolution practitioners. From South Africa, we are gifted with the idea of *ubuntu:* I am a person through you. Our humanity derives from each other; we are the two grasses needed to tie a knot, the two eyes needed to perceive depth. Through persistence and the willingness to stretch, we come into closer relationship. And this makes breakthroughs and peace settlements possible that once seemed out of reach. It also makes it possible to begin to make tracks across barriers that are massive and troubled with a history of confrontation.

Knowing and trusting *ubuntu,* no one sees themselves as elevated over anyone else, regardless of the power dynamics surrounding them. Far from a plea to ignore power or treat it naively, the acknowledgment of *ubuntu* makes it possible to engage genuinely, even when there are vast power differences between parties. Acknowledging and respecting each other's humanity, we find ways forward.

What would happen if you introduced *ubuntu* into the next conflict you encountered? Would it help those involved become allies and friends with each other? Sometimes we do not know what to do or how to build the relational bridges we need and want. Watchful, we may find an opening where we don't expect it. Sometimes our understanding of interconnectedness is most poignant after times of struggle or loss.

On the first flight into Dulles Airport from Denver after the September 11 tragedy, the pilot and flight staff spoke to passengers about connection.[5] The pilot said,

> First I want to thank you for being brave enough to fly today. The doors are now closed, and we have no help from the outside for any problems that might occur inside this plane. As you could tell when you checked in, the government has made some changes to increase security in the airports. They have not, however, made any rules about what happens after those doors close. Until they do that, we have made our own rules and I want to share them with you.
>
> Once those doors close, we only have each other. The security has taken care of a threat like guns with increased scanning. The threats that are left are things like plastics, wood, and knives that can be used as weapons. Here is our plan and our rules. If someone or several people stand up and say they are hijacking this plane, I want you all to stand up together. Then take whatever you have available to you and throw it at them. Throw it at their faces and heads so they will have to raise their hands to protect themselves. The very best protection you have against knives are the pillows and blankets. Whoever is close to these people should then try to get a blanket over their head so they won't be able to see. Once that is done, get them down and keep them there. Do not let them up. I will then land the plane at the closest place, and we will take care of them. After all, there are usually only a few of them and we are more than two hundred strong! We will not allow them to take over this plane. I find it interesting that the U.S. Constitution begins with the words "We, the people." That's who we are—the people—and we will not be defeated.

People had tears in their eyes, and everyone applauded while the plane taxied toward the runway.

The flight attendant then began the safety speech. She observed that everyone lives busy, fast-paced lives. We do not have the time or take the time to know each other. She then asked that everyone turn to their neighbors on either side and introduce themselves, tell each other something about their families and children, perhaps show pictures. She said, "For today, we consider you family. We will treat you as such and ask that you do the same with us."

On this first flight for crew and passengers since the September 11 tragedies, everyone leaned on each other and together everyone felt stronger through acknowledging their connections. Connected ways of knowing are built on this foundation of interdependence. As we acknowledge our connections with each other, we receive more information than if we are tuned only to one band on the radio.

Informing

Connected ways of knowing means remembering it is possible to tune into many frequencies at once. Although we may consciously be limited in our abilities to multitask, other channels are available all the time. Connected ways of knowing ask us to listen to those channels both within ourselves and within others. As we do this, we receive new perspectives, questions, ideas, inspirations, and insights. We are also open to ways of knowing that we don't know we can access.

A precious story from my grandparents' lives illustrates being informed in ways outside our conscious awareness. My grandparents were married for over half a century. Theirs was a fiery and nontraditional marriage, passionate and vibrant. Toward the end of my grandmother's life, she was confined to a long-term care hospital for several months. My grandfather was at home, cared for by his son and his son's wife, Gloria. Grandfather could no longer drive due to poor health.

One evening, my grandfather and Gloria were sitting in the garden around sunset, enjoying the summer evening. When she went into the house for a few minutes, my grandfather disappeared. Gloria searched around the garden and then in the neighborhood, mystified as to where he had gone. Then she noticed the rose bush. This rose bush had been in the garden for years but had never borne a bloom. Finally, this year, it had yielded one crimson rose. She and my grandfather had remarked earlier on its beauty. Gloria noticed that the rose was missing.

My grandfather had picked the rose and boarded a bus to the hospital where my grandmother lay, suddenly close to death. He arrived just in time to give it to her before she died. These were the days before cell phones and instant messaging. But he got the message just as surely as our in-boxes tell us, "You've got mail!"

We may not receive such vital messages in each of our conflict processes, but we will receive additional information when we open ourselves to ways of knowing outside our conscious awareness and ask for what we need. When I am feeling stuck as a third party or a teacher, I ask silently or aloud, "What needs to happen here?" Rather than push blindly through, doing more of what is not working, I invite my inner intuitive guidance or the wisdom of the group to cast more light. Sometimes something needs to be named that is not being said but is ricocheting under the table. Sometimes the conversation needs to shift or deepen. Sometimes a new question needs to be posed. More information comes in when it is invited. It is not necessary to know the answer in advance, only to have the presence of mind to ask the question. Or to recognize the answer when it comes, even when we have not consciously asked.

Spiraling

When we ask questions, we do not necessarily experience answers in the form we expect. Sometimes connected ways of knowing spiral, taking us out of linear thought and action into possibilities for rapid transitions and lasting shifts. This is not to take away from the reality that change is often accomplished incrementally through tenacity and hard work. But there are also moments when change occurs in a twinkling.

We can understand this kind of spiraling by remembering conversations that mark turning points in our lives. Can you bring one to mind now—an exchange with someone that stands out? Maybe it was a comment that unlocked something inside you, interrupted an assumption you had carried for a long time, or surprised you into a new insight. If it occurred during conflict, it may have marked a shift—a time when new possibilities presented themselves.

I recall a conversation among members of a staff going through a leadership transition. Some of them were focused on productivity, concerned that turning attention to the feelings evoked by the transition was bogging everyone down. Others were upset at the way the transition had taken place; they needed to express feelings before turning to action. Several members of the staff indicated that they did not feel as excited about coming to work as they once did; for them, the circle of connection was becoming unraveled.

The conversation seemed to inch along, one step at a time. After everyone had spoken, we turned to silence to discern a way forward. Everyone let specific images of their future in the organization come into their awareness. Some drew them; some made notes; some simply explored images with interior senses—seeing, hearing, and listening themselves into the organization five years in the future. Their ensuing dialogue addressed how to "live life backwards," unfolding the process of getting to their individual and collective visions.

As this happened, the climate of the meeting shifted, spiraling from its original linear course to exchanges marked by energy and initiative. It became clear that realizing their visions involved maintaining close connections to each other and the organization's mission. Shared commitment to an ongoing process for negotiating the leadership transition emerged that included informal "connecting" time—time for airing feelings, strategic planning, and trouble shooting. From the vantage point of the future, feelings and tasks were no longer disconnected, dichotomous units over which conflict could play out. They were part of the bigger picture that connected staff members to what they cared about: each other and the organization's mission.

Did the process proceed smoothly from there? Struggles and tensions still played out, yet there was an anchor in place to keep them from straying too far from course. The anchor was their shared vision of the future, cloaked in the energy that the spiraling dialogue had bequeathed them. It remained present among them, a source of inspiration and connection when challenges arose.

Inspiring

Connected ways of knowing are inspiring. Because we feel linked to a bigger picture, we move out of narrow ways of perceiving into the realm of possibilities. Once when I was feeling discouraged, a friend asked me to try something. "Walk outside for a few minutes," she suggested, "and look only at the ground." Because I was feeling down, this was easy to do. When I returned, she continued, "Now, go out again and walk, looking up at the sky. Notice the difference in how you feel." When I looked at the sky, I felt spaciousness and breathed more deeply. It was a very simple intervention, yet a powerful one.

So, in our conflict resolution teaching and intervention, we invite the possibility of inspiration. Sharing the process with participants, we know that inspiration may come collectively; each of us has a piece of what is needed to make the final quilt. As I write about this, I remember a wonderful leader in our field, Jim Laue. Jim died too soon, but one of the marks of his genius was his receptivity to inspiration. Inspired to work with Martin Luther King Jr. in the civil rights struggle, he put himself in the path of danger. Applying his passion for conflict resolution to a series of projects later in life from leaky tank farms adjacent to residential areas to problem-solving workshops on the Palestinian-Israeli conflict, he brought reverence for relationship and an insistent optimism that led to transformative results.

Surprising

Connected ways of knowing may surprise us with unexpected, often-elegant experiences of creativity in action. Because the pathways of connected ways of knowing are largely outside our conscious awareness, we often cannot predict what they will yield. As we set our intention for an intervention or a class, we invoke connected ways of knowing to assist us in realizing our vision. It is all right that we may not be able to clearly see the way from where we are to realizing our intention. Connected ways of knowing help us get there.

This becomes clear in a story of a well-educated white Canadian woman who was asked to work with some difficult issues on a First Nations reserve. Her job was to investigate claims of widespread community damage arising from the forcible removal of children from their homes, placement in residential schools, and sexual abuse in those schools over several decades. We'll call her Marjorie. Marjorie is well dressed, bright, and articulate. She is a direct communicator and a powerful advocate with an impressive record of achievements.

In the native community, she entered an environment where these achievements took on different meanings. They marked her as a part of a system that has oppressed in the past and continues oppressive policies in the present. Indeed, she is a leader in the dominant system—one of its stars. It hardly helps that she has used her positions in the system to try to make change, to create more equitable ways of dividing resources. To the First Nations people on the reserve, she is one of "them."

If she is to be effective, she needs to get inside the stories of community members. She needs to gain their trust. Yet already she is disadvantaged in that aim. Her clothing, her way of speaking, her manner—all mark her as separate. Her strangeness, to them, is a fence that no one wants to be the first to climb over. How does an opening to create shared meaning arise in such a case? Surely there are many examples where no opening is found, where an official flies in and flies out, returning to the city to write a report that speaks little to the experience of the people. Countless times, we simply miss what we have come to find through cultural, historical, and perceptual barriers.

She arranges to rent a car, but when she flies into the area, community elders delegate another community member to drive it so that she can ride with them. They tell her not to worry, the car will be parked in front of the community center with the keys in it; she can use it later. It seems that cars and keys and rental contracts are viewed differently here than in the city. On the way to the reserve, they remind her to be subdued, receptive, and informal in her interactions with community members.

A day of meetings takes place. Questions and suggestions and ways forward are shared. People come to the meetings and talk about the process she will lead. Through it all, she is being assessed through eyes that have seen abuse. Trust is reserved.

As night falls, she realizes that she must drive back to town to her hotel before it is completely dark. She is tired and concerned that she will get lost in this unfamiliar place. She walks outside the community center, jumps into the car that someone has parked there for her, and takes off. She notices a purse on the front seat and makes a mental note to check tomorrow with the person who drove the car for her from the airport. He can return it to its rightful owner. A young man has given her directions: take the ring road until you see the sign to the town. Then, just follow the sun.

She misses the sign to town as she drives around the ring road. She finds herself driving back, circling past the community center. People are still inside. They notice her driving past and wave. She is embarrassed and gives a half-hearted wave in return. Surely this time she will find the turn-off. Continuing around the ring road, she misses the turn again. Soon she will drive past the community center once more, and everyone will witness her poor navigational skills. This time people are gathered outside, waving to her, motioning for her to stop.

More embarrassed, she imagines that they want to give her more specific directions. But she thinks she can find it this time. She gives a semi-smile and a tentative wave and doggedly keeps driving. To her chagrin, it eventually becomes clear to her that she has missed the turn-off to town again. She is coming up on the community center for the third time. This time, there are people in the middle of the road. She will not be able to drive past without stopping. She thinks to herself that it is just as well; perhaps more specific directions are needed after all.

She is shocked to stop the car in front of the community center and get out to the voice of a man yelling, "Stop! You have stolen my car!"

It turns out that her rental car was on the other side of the building. Not realizing that everyone leaves their keys in their cars on the reserve, she had assumed that the car in front with the keys in it was hers. Terribly embarrassed, she got the directions clarified and headed into town in her rental car for a much-needed sleep.

In the morning, she returned to the reserve. As she entered the local coffee shop, she heard people start to warn each other. "Hide your purses! Here comes that lady who steals things." There was laughter and openness to her that had not been present the day before. She had become vulnerable to them, her image cracked open. And through the opening, there was a place where connection could be built.

In this case, the surprise of her mistake and the humor that followed it was a bridge to connection. Whoever she was, she was someone who was human, someone fallible. This took away some of the mystique and the distrust and revealed a person who had feelings, who was making her way in life just as they were. Whatever the process she had conceived to work with these people, an organic process was emerging. It would be a process built on relationship and connection, a process that arose from what was there rather than from theories or prescriptions.

Changing

Connected ways of knowing change us, deepening our capacity for fluidity and flexibility as we move out of the stuck places of conflict. Sometimes we resist change with all of our strength, especially if others ask of us things that feel impossible or damaging to our identity or our autonomy. I remember the story a man told of how he came to change and embrace connected ways of knowing. He married, had children, and provided well for his family.

Still, to his surprise, his wife wanted more. She wanted him to be emotionally responsive to her and the children. She wanted him to be more closely engaged with their lives. Somehow he was too busy to do this, or so he believed. It wasn't until she tried to get out of the car while it was speeding down the freeway that he was shocked into taking a different look at his life and relationships. A painful divorce followed. Through the process of loss, he came to see his blind spots about connection, to accept that his need to be powerful in the world precluded the kind of vulnerability that could feed his own need for connection and bonding. Through his pain, he changed to become more aware of his own need for connection. As he became aware of this unanswered need in him, he was able to develop his capacity for connection and connected ways of knowing.

Not everyone needs to encounter this much pain to grow toward connected ways of knowing. Yet conflict often brings both pain and change in its wake. As we encounter conflict, struggling to understand and come to a new way or place, we may experience frustration and a sense of disintegration. These themes are present in a different kind of conflict—the conflict that accompanies quests to discover or invent something new. In this process, the would-be creator can expect blocks and puzzles that are not easy to solve. Unexpected, but also common in the process of invention is profound personal change.

This change sometimes takes the form of expanded awareness of the connectedness of humankind and the cosmos. The French astronomer Camille Flammarion reports being on a hillside at sunset, looking up at the dusk sky. Gradually, he was overwhelmed with a new realization that "there was an invisible bond which links all universes and souls in the unity of a single creation."[6] Whether we experience such profound moments of insight or incremental ah-ha's, conflict resolution invites us to change our perspectives and perceptions, even as we hold to that which is precious to us. We are called to pay attention in the moment to the many levels unfolding simultaneously.

Being Mindful

Connected ways of knowing are calls to mindfulness, bringing us exquisitely present with ourselves and each other. A sense of awe and wonder may be evoked as we are available in present tense to connected ways of knowing. There are many books about mindfulness, paying attention in the present, and self-observation. Mindfulness is about cultivating our inner observer so that we become more aware of all parts of ourselves: physical, emotional, intellectual, and spiritual.

Although spiritual traditions speak differently about the nature of the self and the role of self-observation, one thread that runs through many is the importance of recognizing that we are more than our emotions, ideas, and sensations. In Indian spiritual traditions, the analogy of the wheel is used. The hub of the wheel remains still while the wheel turns. So the inner self remains constant while the mind, intellect, emotions, and body swirl with experiences. From the still place at the center of the wheel, it is possible to observe and discern ways forward.

Mindfulness speaks to opening ourselves to life as it is, not as our habits would have it be. The German psychologist Max Wertheimer witnessed a conflict between two boys playing badminton.[7] The stronger, older player kept winning until the younger player threw down his racket and refused to continue. The older boy registered a variety of emotions—surprise, concern, reflection—and then suggested to the younger one that they change their goal. Instead of trying to win, why not see how long they could keep the shuttlecock in the air? Wertheimer later interviewed Einstein about how he had come to his theory of relativity. He discovered that Einstein's process was essentially the same as that of the boys: he pursued avenues until they no longer worked, then invented new ways of proceeding, of keeping the play going. In order to have new ideas, we have to open ourselves to life as it is. We surrender to reality—the reality we perceive from places of stillness in ongoing observation rather than relying on our perceptual and cognitive habits and assumptions.

We tend to be attached to our ways of seeing and our understandings of the world, and this keeps us in old patterns. Mindfulness means surrendering these attachments. The classic story of French physicist Henri Becquerel illustrates. Becquerel had the idea that uranium sulfate crystals could absorb radiation from the sun and then emit energy. He exposed the crystals to sunlight and then put them on photographic plates that recorded their emissions. One day it was cloudy and he was unable to repeat his experiment. Because he could not expose the crystals to sunlight, he put them away in a drawer. They happened to be placed next to some photographic plates. The next day, he was surprised to find that the photographic plates showed traces of energy.

He might have thrown these plates away in frustration; this was not what he was expecting to see. Instead he investigated further. He discovered that his theory was wrong, that uranium emits energy of its own that is radioactive. From this discovery came nuclear energy and nuclear weapons, arising from Becquerel's willingness to question his own settled ideas.[8] This willingness is a part of mindfulness, paying attention to ourselves and to the worlds around us for what they show us, moment-by-moment.

As we watch our processes of perception and decision making, we notice choice points. Connected ways of knowing call us to look for connections we might not have anticipated in places we might not have thought to look. They call on us to be particularly vigilant when we think we know the answer. Especially when others are involved, individual assumptions about the answer may be less helpful than a spirit of inquiry and joint dialogue. What other qualities of trainers and intervenors are inherent in connected ways of knowing? We explore this in the section to come.

Qualities of Connected Ways of Knowing

Connected ways of knowing are not unique to specific individuals or groups, though some of us have cultivated more of these capacities than others. Following are some of the ways that people who have made friends of connected ways of knowing tend to use. Not all apply in every instance, but together they are an impressionistic look at what connected ways of knowing look like embodied in real people and their experiences.

Gracefulness

Connected ways of knowing are marked by gracefulness. There is a fluid quality about people who employ them and often a sense of humility. One of my favorite stories is told by a woman who gives a great deal of time and energy to helping the homeless. She relates that she walked to work each day past a man who lived on the street. After some time, out of concern for his welfare she decided to prepare two thermoses of coffee each day, one to leave near him on the sidewalk and one for herself. Returning from work in the afternoon, she could pick up the empty thermos to fill again the following day. She did this for several weeks. Then it occurred to her that she could do the same with hot soup, providing better nutrition and making more of a contribution.

She always placed the soup on the sidewalk near the man, observing what she thought was a respectful distance. Each day the thermos was empty at the end of the afternoon, and she picked it up on her way past. One morning, after she had put the soup down on the sidewalk, the man picked up the thermos, opened it, and threw the hot soup back toward her. She was angry, indignant, and amazed. She picked up her thermos and left. Upon later reflection, she put herself in his place in a way she had not done before. What message did he receive from her actions? She had never acknowledged him, never asked his name. She was taking care of her own discomfort and guilt by leaving the soup for him, but until that day she had not considered how he felt. She had not pushed the limits of her comfort to meet and talk with him, human-to-human.

The next day, she took a thermos of soup as usual. But she stopped and talked with the man, introducing herself and asking his name. At the end of a short exchange, she left the soup in his hands. He had taught her something about humility, mutuality, and connection in a way that was painful but very valuable.

Connected ways of knowing are graceful, as they take others into account. They do not perpetuate inequity but are based on the ability of those who would help to step into the shoes of the others, understand their situation, and work with them toward self-belief and dignity.

Caesar Chavez, the pioneer of justice for Hispanic American farm workers, said it like this: "One of the most beautiful and satisfying results of our work in establishing a union in the fields is in witnessing the worker's bloom—the natural dignity coming out of a man when his dignity is recognized."[9]

Applying this to conflict resolution practice, we are reminded to personalize our approaches, acknowledging the legitimacy of meaning-making ways that are different from our own. The more divergent another's way of being, the more important it is for us as teacher or third party to try to understand it. Unpopular positions, minority views, or extreme ideas often have the effect of marginalizing the speaker. It is up to us as facilitator, mediator, or teacher to create a forum where diverse ideas are welcome. Doing this makes durable and satisfying resolutions more likely.

Gratitude

Connected ways of knowing are marked by gratitude for what is received. Maintaining a state of appreciation and a state of perturbed conflict at the same time is difficult. This is not to suggest putting a harmonic veil over real issues that need to be addressed. But it is to suggest that living from a place of gratitude is more generative, creative, and revealing of the possible than living from awareness of what is not. This principle accounts in part for the effectiveness of approaches like appreciative inquiry, where an emphasis on what works and what is valued forms the foundation for addressing issues in organizations and communities.

In mediation we see this choice illustrated again and again. Parties come with real grievances, traumas, and passionate views of how they have been wronged. The stories are reciprocal; each sees him- or herself as having been hurt by the other. Telling and retelling these stories amplifies them, possibly retraumatizing each party as the teller and the listener relive difficult times. With each new issue, the same story pattern may be retold, leaving parties acutely aware of the differences that divide them.

Conventional mediation practice tells us that it is important to uncover shared interests as well as reveal individual interests. These interests may be about the material things in conflict; they may also be social. What tends to be left out is the symbolic, meaning-making level. In encouraging expressions of appreciation in our processes, we invite participants to access this level. When appreciation is sincerely expressed, it is an indication that the thing mentioned has meaning for the speaker. What is appreciated and how appreciation is expressed is a window into how meaning is composed. Inviting appreciation also interrupts the cycle of naming and blaming that perpetuates the pain in conflict through generations.

Gratitude and appreciation can be modeled; opportunities to do so arise in the course of mindful engagement. Noticing that someone has remembered an issue important to another, we acknowledge it. Reinforcing even a small indication that one party recognizes something of meaning to the other can constructively shift the direction of a session. In a series of sessions, inviting appreciations and regrets at the end of each meeting gives an opportunity for parties to talk about what has worked well for them and where they struggled.

In my own life, I notice that expressions of gratitude are much more conducive to connected ways of knowing than their absence. When I begin the day aware of the many gifts I enjoy, I see more expansively, I express more creativity in my work and relationships, and I handle conflict more gracefully. This is harder to maintain if I feel threatened or afraid that I may lose something precious to me. Then my first tendency is to hold tightly onto what I believe I am entitled to, what I am sure I need. In short, I resist. Amidst the tightness of resistance, the field of the possible shrinks. Remembering gratitude expands the field again, bringing in other dimensions, even when loss is an inevitable part of conflict.

Gentleness

Gentleness is also invoked by connected ways of knowing. This gentleness is not soft or pliable; it is compassionate and caring, yet strong toward self and other in the context of conflict. Perhaps the greatest exemplar of the quality of gentleness was Mahatma Gandhi. He maintained courage, hope, and focus on injustice and righting conflict, even as he was gentle toward those around him. He did not separate people from the problem but recognized the dignity of people in the midst of their problems.

This quality of gentleness may be difficult for some of us to embrace. There is a receptivity about it—an acknowledgment of connection that individualist, action-oriented cultures may not habitually embrace. Our lifestyles tend to emphasize convenience, efficiency, and speed. Electronic communication, drive-through post offices and banks, even drive-in churches keep us isolated and task-focused in our dealings. This is not to deny that there are community connections and caring relationships among us. It is to suggest that our way of living further from each other in the privacy of our homes and further from family farms as agribusiness becomes our source of food may be contributing to less gentleness among us.

In Switzerland I was struck by an exchange between my Swiss friend and the proprietress in the village cheese store. She knew the alpage where the cheeses were made and the people who made them. She knew the kinds of cheese he preferred and inquired about our plans for the weekend. There was a gentleness to the exchange that set it apart from my visits to the suburban supermarket at home.

This is not to idealize an old way of being at the expense of modern life. It is to examine how our lifestyles do and do not encourage gentleness and civility with each other. Robert Putnam[10] speaks of this as social capital: how are we connected to each other, and what is the quality of our connections? Sadly, it is often through threat or shared victimization that we become aware of our connections and act as communities. We are sometimes galvanized into gentleness with each other through shared anger at a common enemy. Conflict resolution ultimately poses the question of how we can nurture and enact our connections as a global community.

How do we nurture this social capital—the acknowledgment of connections among us? There are many answers to these questions, most beyond the scope of this book. Here we treat just one suggestion: that we are most in control of *ourselves*—how we approach each other and which stance we take. How much do we allow inattention, habits, fear, or anger to stand in the way of our connected ways of knowing?

There is a wonderful series of photographs of Hudson, a husky dog in the Arctic, who was being approached by a polar bear just roused from hibernation. The polar bear was certainly hungry and weighed over a thousand pounds, but the chained Hudson did not howl in terror. He did not cower as the bear lumbered toward him. Instead, Hudson wagged his tail, grinned, and seemed to bow to the bear, as if in invitation to play. The bear responded with enthusiastic body language and nonaggressive facial signals. For several minutes, the pair tumbled around with each other. Then the bear walked away.[11]

As we cultivate gentleness within, refusing to conflate gentleness with cowardice, we tap connected ways of knowing as assets in conflict. We fail to meet the negative expectations of our adversaries that we will be combative or defensive, instead finding ways to invite divergent ways of seeing into our awareness. Even when it is not possible or desirable to sit down with the other, posing questions about the other's way of making meaning humanizes them in a way that gives us a broader set of choices for responding. In this way, we invite a generative quality into our processes.

Generativity

Generativity is about generating good things. It is about the fruits of creative efforts as they contribute to our lives and, in ripples, to the lives of others. Giving birth is the ultimate act of generativity; broadening this to include the birth of ideas, initiatives, projects, and processes includes a wide range of creators. Erik Erikson, the psychoanalyst, said that people move into concerns about generativity in their thirties, forties, and fifties. They come to realize, he observed, that "I am what survives me."[12] Generativity comes from meaningful engagement with others and the legacies that come of this engagement.

Noticing generativity as a product of connected ways of knowing is to take what is precious in the interpersonal realm and magnify it. As we center our processes on relationship and draw on connected ways of knowing, we create legacies of alternative ways forward. To go forward in these ways is to create positive processes and outcomes that generate hope.

Researchers have found that generative individuals are those for whom life is full of meaning. They are fulfilled in their work and relationships. They are altruistic, reaching out to others. One thing that distinguishes them is the way they tell stories about their lives. When people tell what are called redemptive stories about their lives, they are choosing generativity. As they identify turning points, they relate how these turning points led to positive, hopeful choices and eventual accomplishments. An African American retired police chief tells how he was discouraged and poised to leave the police force as a young member when he had a chance meeting with Martin Luther King Jr. King told him, "Don't give up. Don't let the dream die."

Connected ways of knowing lead us to generative outcomes. Just as King's admonition inspired the policeman to keep going, so we are challenged to develop the tenacity and creativity to keep dialogues going across difference. When a hurt has been registered, the conflict-avoidant among us want to walk away, to not speak of it lest more hurt be generated. The competitive among us want to exact revenge. Connected ways of knowing remind us to be mindful. We pay attention, seeking to expand the picture beyond our individual or cultural meanings, asking what learning is available from the conflict. Connected ways of knowing lead us into painful places, sitting with the hurt and the damage done by conflict. Neither reacting nor avoiding, we address conflict in practical ways.

Groundedness

There is a wonderful Sufi saying: "Trust in God, but tie up your camel." Connected ways of knowing are not about abandoning ourselves to some ethereal way of being that leaves the ways of the world behind in favor of a transcendent way of being. Connected ways of knowing are grounded.

A friend has lived this journey in a painful way. After high school, she went to a university and studied sciences. Two years later, she applied and was admitted to dental school. But during the summer before attending, she met some people on a bus who followed an Indian guru. She gave up her acceptance at dental school and went to live communally with them. A few years later, she was working at a natural foods store, struggling to get by, no longer following the guru. She realized that she had trusted in God but had forgotten to tie up her camel. Without the education she had once pursued, she did not have the resources to accomplish what was important to her in life.

The story does not end there. Her life has been generative; she has found her way to environmental advocacy and activism. She found her camel and secured it, as she composed her life in accordance with her deeply held values. The choice to give up some of the values her parents held led to a series of choices that were ultimately very satisfying to her; hers is a redemptive story. Perhaps much of our conflict practice is about helping parties compose redemptive stories they can live into.

How can we do this? How can we infuse connected ways of knowing in our practice while not metaphorically losing our camels? We do this by being sure that our intellect is not left out of the dialogue with our heart, our imagination, our intuition. Like a colleague who carries around a flip-open badge reading "Agent of Reality," we ask all the practical questions we can think of; we make sure that we have attended to everything we can do to set our processes up for success. As we do this, we remember that what is practical and sensible to us may be different to another. Inviting diverse ideas about how to tie up the camel does not mean neglecting to do it.

In some ways, this focus on practical action involves paradox. We act to take care of what can be taken care of; at the same time, we surrender, trusting each other and the wisdom that we each bring. We trust, and at the same time we pay attention. This way of being connected to the practical aspects of situations, as well as our choice to trust, informs our processes and our classes. We explore more of what connected ways of knowing look like in practice in the following section.

Connected Ways of Knowing in Practice

What does a practice valuing connected ways of knowing look like? Do we know one when we see it? We have said that connected ways of knowing are multifaceted and not prescriptive. This makes it challenging to identify any exhaustive way of weaving them into our practice. We can, however, find examples that inform us about concrete steps to take and show us ways *not to proceed* as we seek to infuse our work with connected ways of knowing. We begin by exploring how we exercise leadership in conflict, drawing on connected ways of knowing.

Process Leadership

As a third party in conflict, we are more powerful than we think. Just as students adopt a receptive mode toward a teacher at the front of the class, parties and their counsel generally accord a mediator respect and considerable latitude over the process. This power is ours to lose if we step outside the bounds of ethical guidelines or cultural expectations, but it is potent indeed. The cues we give about order of speaking, what is important, process expectations, and boundaries for interaction shape the climate of the process. The smallest decision to ignore an interruption or to amplify a suggestion can have profound consequences for the course of a session.

We exercise leadership in obvious and subtle ways, some within our own and the parties' awareness and some outside. As we intervene in conflict, we become part of the relational system that includes parties and their representatives. In this relational system, influence is dynamic and multidirectional. It is important not to let our professed neutrality or our techniques for building party ownership in the process blind us to the significant power we wield. Our nonverbal and verbal behaviors cue parties to what we believe, what we dismiss, and what we welcome. Thus we affect the substantive outcome of the conflict, whether or not we ever make explicit suggestions about solutions.

Given our influence as process leaders, cultivating connected ways of knowing becomes important. Parties in conflict have had their boundaries shaken; change is being asked of them where they most resist it. In resisting, their energy is tied up, and it is difficult to shift from cherished viewpoints to an attitude of inquiry, from personal agendas to a willingness to be surprised. When we model connected ways of knowing as third parties, we implicitly invite parties to access expansiveness and energy through connection and deep listening. As we operationalize connected ways of knowing in processes, stuck dynamics soften and boundaries are stretched in ways that interrupt limiting habits.

How we exercise process leadership depends on our reasons for engaging in the work of conflict resolution. Do we value participation, empowerment, connection, harmony, closure, interpersonal cooperation, or revolution? How do we order the things we value? Which of them are we willing to sacrifice? Which are so precious that we will protect them with all of our strength? What are the shadow sides of what we value? Do we value being in control, wielding power, being needed, being seen, being respected or revered, making money, making deals? How do these values inform what has meaning for us? How do we compose our lives, our work, and our processes to give effect to those values?

If we hold creativity and change as important values, we construct different processes than if we hold closure and clarity as central. If we hold social justice as primary, our processes look different than those driven by efficiency and cost-effectiveness. This is not to suggest that these values are opposites but that we internalize hierarchies of values that affect the way we design, convene, and unfold processes. Connected ways of knowing lead us to continuing explorations of the relationships between who we are, what we value, and how we work.

Another part of this exploration is to draw on connected ways of knowing in self-monitoring during processes. Using our bodies as instruments, we scan for tension or discomfort. We inquire whether we are screening off important sources of knowing within us in response to the limiting meaning-frames brought by others. When we are, we often experience tense muscles, constrained breath, or minor pain such as a headache. Then it is important to refocus and step into the expansiveness that comes from centering ourselves in relation to what we value, reaffirming relationships as the heart of our processes. In the midst of struggle, we are challenged to hold our center in a way that we remember what is important to us while being in genuine inquiry with others. As we exercise leadership in this way, we experience spaciousness that breathes fresh air into our processes.

Openness to Meaning Making

Our openness to engaging parties at the levels where they make meaning is another way to bring spaciousness to our processes. This does not mean inviting everyone to share their cosmology and deep beliefs when they have gathered to make a decision about the siting of an industrial facility. At the same time, imagining that the siting of the facility is unrelated to what matters to participants in a process is also an error. A conflict resolution process is likely to be more constructive and satisfying when the meaning of both process and outcome choices are considered by all involved.

To inquire about meaning is to go beyond our usual exploration of interests. It is to step away from a pretense of objectivity, inviting parties to explore and articulate their relationships to the subject of the conflict. In our example of the siting of an industrial facility, it is to welcome parties' histories, stories, and myths that connect them to the sites considered. It is to explore the sites relationally, surfacing associations and ties that link people to each other and to a sense of place and home. Doing this well nurtures relationship, emphasizing connections and shared anchors.

To engage conversations about meaning, the process must fit the parties involved. Recognizing this, the attuned third party remembers that ideas about order, turn taking, civility, and appropriate communication have assumptions about relationship and conflict built into them. Too often they include assumptions that screen out alternatives, whether those alternatives arise from different learning styles or different ways of composing meaning. If we guide our processes with connected ways of knowing rather than communication prescriptions, openness to examining our assumptions about communication and process structuring is ongoing.

For example, most everyone involved in conflict who is willing to engage with the other will agree that respect should be a part of the process. What does respect look like? For some people, respect means sequential but immediate turn taking. For others it may include talking over each other. Still other groups may, as a norm, leave minutes between speakers for reflection and consideration of what has been said. Taking another dimension of communication, active listening may be a functional sign of comprehension for some. For others it is offensive and patronizing. Third parties who draw on connected ways of knowing seek to operationalize respect in the process in ways both inclusive and comfortable for all concerned. They will do this in a range of direct and indirect ways, making adjustments as needed, inviting parties to monitor the ongoing fit of processes.

Meaning making relates not only to the procedural and material aspects of a conflict but to its deeper, symbolic genesis. Like the Americans who wore their shoes on the tatami mats sacred to their Japanese colleagues, parties to conflicts often have difficulty getting inside the meaning-frame of the other. It is easier to minimize or avoid conflicts than to address them. When we cannot ignore them, it is easier to externalize blame and demonize others than to inquire about what animates them. It is not easy to bring a spirit of inquiry when we feel aggrieved. Yet it is important to remember that we do not inquire to determine who was right; we inquire to understand. The meanings we each make are multitextured and reinforced by life experience and cultural norms. To the listener, they do not justify trespass nor violation, but they do expand awareness of the context from which actions were born. From this awareness, a wider repertoire of responses is seen.

As practitioners and teachers, how does dialogue help us invite meaning making to the table? Dialogue seeks to unfold multiple meanings rather than focus on a single meaning. It inquires to understand rather than to convince. It values communicating and mining levels of meaning over winning and imposing ideas. In this sense, it requires those in powerful positions or cultural frames to step outside their privilege.

Paulo Friere is eloquent on the subject. He writes, "Dialogue further requires an intense faith in man, faith in his power to make and remake, to create and recreate, faith in his vocation to be fully human (which is not the privilege of an elite, but the birthright of all men)."[13]

If those in power could get what they want without the support or participation of others, there would be no need for conflict resolution processes. They could simply impose their will on others, limited only by their own consciences or ethical understandings. Yet we live in a world where our interdependence is increasing rather than decreasing. Industry cannot proceed without the support of governments, community members, and workers. Governments cannot ultimately proceed without the support of constituents and other governments. Citizens are increasingly demanding a voice in decisions affecting them, moving in the words of Canadian author Peter Newman "from deference to defiance."[14] The defiance of the public may take a while to have an impact on policy (as it did in the case of the Vietnam War), but our Internet age has given us voice in ways never before possible in human history.

As more voices are heard, conflicts are surfaced and fractures made more visible. Conflict practitioners welcome this, recognizing that dialogue does not foreclose problem solving or inoculate against difficult trade-offs. It does deepen understandings, offering information for critical analysis and a foundation for empathy. As Friere observes, true dialogue cannot exist unless it involves critical thinking, that is, "thinking which perceives reality as process, as transformation, . . . thinking which does not separate itself from action, but constantly immerses itself in temporality without fear of the risks involved."[15]

As parties share what matters to them through processes that fit, they develop the capacity to build shared meanings in ways impossible if they had continued as parallel solitudes.

Building Shared Meanings

What would our processes would look like if we imagined them as opportunities for people to build shared meanings? They would involve not only dialogue but a wide variety of activities. Sharing silence is one powerful way to invoke a sense of connection initially or during a conflict resolution process. Introductions in which participants talk about the history and meaning of their names are another way of constructively emphasizing identity and relationship in processes. Generally, activities that invoke somatic, emotional, and imaginative ways of being prepare the ground for collaboration.

Experienced practitioners know the importance of framing interactions within connected ways of knowing. Good processes do not happen simply when participants are in each other's vicinities. Indeed, bringing adversaries together without awareness of relational dynamics and careful planning can worsen relationships and escalate conflict. At the Public Conversations Project in Watertown, Massachusetts, conveners direct careful attention to framing processes and formulating questions in the dialogue processes they convene. They prefer to bring parties together over a meal initially, understanding the powerful connecting effect of breaking bread. The ritual of eating together emphasizes common humanity and brings participants into a circle one with another. Following the meal, dialogue is structured around questions crafted by the intervention team after intensive conversation with parties. Often these questions invoke metaphors used by the parties explicitly or implicitly.

In one case, Public Conversations Project staff members facilitated a dialogue among members of a church concerning a set of divisive issues. Although many of our colloquial metaphors about conflict contain references to heat ("things got really hot in the meeting"; "the mediator suggested a cooling-off period"), it became clear to the staff that dynamics in this group were frozen by the conflict. As if in suspended animation, participants were reluctant to speak. Perhaps they feared that movement of any kind could cause more pain. Naming this frozen quality and inviting exploration of how a thaw could be accomplished was effective in engaging the parties in a more fluid exchange. It was important to name this frozen emotional tone before inviting any engagement on the substance of the issues among them.

The more scarred the history and the more divided the parties, the more essential it is to carefully design a process that situates stories in shared frames of respect and receptivity. Grounded in connected ways of knowing, we approach intervention with an awareness that timing is critical. We do not ask too great a leap from parties too soon, preferring instead to set them up for success by offering incremental steps toward engagement.

This reminds me of the first time I heard about using conflict resolution processes to address abortion. Frankly, I was skeptical. I worried about the volatility of bringing people together with incendiary histories. I envisioned protracted acrimony ending in feelings of confirmation about the evil nature of the other, reproducing the way that conflict has played out on the public stage. When Mary Jacksteit and Adrienne Kaufmann designed the Common Ground Dialogue on Life and Choice process in the early 1990s as a project of Search for Common Ground in Washington, D.C., they made process choices that shaped more constructive outcomes. They chose a forum and a process that interrupted the ways the abortion debate played out in public. The interruption their process represented made it possible for progress to spiral as participants used connected ways of knowing.

Adrienne and Mary centered their dialogue process in personal stories and girded it with strict ground rules. They reassured participants that they would leave with allegiance to the same position they came with. They carefully planned a series of small- and large-group activities, all facilitated, that provided safe and creative space for doing something different related to the abortion conflict.

In the end, they did not change people's positions, just as they had promised. But people did change, coming to care about each other and relax some of their negative "enemy" images. Coming together in a process that emphasizes common ground and mindful engagement rather than combative competition, they formed close relationships, even as they maintained their advocacy. We'll explore the dynamics and effects of the Network for Life and Choice process more in the chapters to come.

Another way that our processes can be designed to build shared meaning is when we think outside the box of what we mean by process. Search for Common Ground is a leader in this respect in our field. In Macedonia, they have worked since 1994 to defuse ethnic conflict. Rather than use a traditional approach of sequestering leaders in a room for a series of problem-solving activities, they leveraged their efforts. They built relationships with newspapers and television stations. They produced a children's television series titled Nashe Maalo (Our Neighborhood) and taped a public service announcement with interethnic casts, thus sending the message, "We want our neighborhood to be a peaceful neighborhood."

From an article in the *Wall Street Journal Europe,* we read the results:

> In most countries, children's television land is a soothing place inhabited by Big Bird, Barney, the purple dinosaur, and the Teletubbies, who love each other very much.
>
> But here in the Balkan nation of Macedonia, television's hottest show for kids, "Our Neighborhood," takes place in a graffiti-spattered jungle of concrete. . . . The music is rap and today's lesson is ethnic tolerance, not arithmetic. . . . Three quarters of Macedonian kids watch the show every week.[16]

How often we deplore the effects of the media, with their inflated and inflammatory images. Here is a case of a group working with the media, recognizing its power, and using it to send a potent message about interethnic cooperation.

Search for Common Ground has done the same in a number of other instances, publishing articles on mutual understanding and dialogue through the Middle East Common Ground news service. They have organized a music festival in Burundi, sponsored live drama in Liberia, and helped produce a peace song in Angola. They have organized an exhibit of Iranian art in Washington, D.C., and a film festival of films depicting common ground that is making the rounds in the United States and around the world. Evoking emotional and aesthetic engagement, these projects challenge us to think outside the box in the interventions we design, whether within divided societies or stressed families. They also expand our traditional thinking about processes and parties. In these ways, their work broadens the base from which shared meanings are built.

Legitimizing Connected Ways of Knowing

To create more possibilities for using connected ways of knowing, we are challenged to examine our language. How possible is it in our conflict resolution processes to talk about intuition, gut knowing, inspiration, or perception outside usual channels? Do we welcome ways of knowing that are the wind on the water—hard to measure or describe precisely but meaningful to the speaker? Do we celebrate relationship, not simply think of it as a problem? How much curiosity and patience do we bring to the process of stretching our comfort with language?

Perhaps I am more concerned with this than most because I have spent more than a decade in a university. There language marks territory, and intellect is the legitimate mode for traversing it. This is intensified in the field of law, where many conflict practitioners find a disciplinary home. We can follow the lead of the plain language movement within legal circles—a movement that has as its objective making laws and legal language accessible to ordinary people.

Some of the principles of plain language drafting include

- Avoid unnecessary formality.
- Consider your reader and write with that viewpoint in mind.
- Use simple, everyday words.
- Use words consistently.

Applying these to conflict resolution, we are challenged to consider the jargon and technical terms we have developed. Can we describe our processes in everyday language? Do we remember that our processes are primarily about relationship and use language that builds relationship, acknowledging a wide range of experiences and ways of making meaning? Do we invite the "whole person" into our processes by our modeling, our language, and the ways we shape communication among parties? As we do so, our processes will serve the grassroots from which they sprang. If we do not, we may find that conflict resolution processes are most comfortable for only a narrow range of participants but do not create safe space for a diverse range of people.

I remember the first conflict resolution training I attended back in the early 1980s. The presenter was speaking about "interest-based bargaining." I heard it as "interspaced bargaining," and I puzzled at its intergalactic implications. Although I since learned the meaning of "interest-based," I continue to struggle with finding words to describe what we do as conflict resolution practitioners in ways that are elegantly descriptive, easily understandable, and cognizant of multiple ways of knowing and being. I reflect on processes I convene and classes I teach, assessing the degree to which my language acknowledges connection, relationship, and interdependence. Writing this book is one of my contributions to legitimizing connected ways of knowing in our language and in our processes.

Exploring Our Connections

Employing connected ways of knowing in our practice, we are moved to ask how our work connects to the bigger picture. How does it connect to those who will inherit our legacy? Some First Nations people have a clear way of describing this dimension. As they make decisions, they consider the effects on their descendents seven generations in the future. As we stretch the timeframe across which we measure the impact of our conflict resolution processes, we may see different values or priorities than if we are only present-focused. As practitioners, we ask ourselves who our processes serve and who they exclude in the present. We also ask what impact our processes may have on others not identified or people who might be affected in the future. From the perspective of connected ways of knowing, these questions are as important as any.

I have heard First Nations people speak about their concern for seven generations in the future. I have seen government representatives at the same table roll their eyes at the prospect of having to consider such a long and speculative question. As a third party in such a setting, I remember that relationship is at the center of process. How can relationship be built among these participants?

I plan activities where they come to know and trust each other, person-to-person. From this base, they can speak together about what relationship means, how it is understood, and what responsibilities it carries in each of their frames of meaning. Informed by these exchanges, progress on substantive issues shows itself on the horizon of possibilities.

Synthesis

With awareness of the importance of connected ways of knowing, we come full circle to a final look at our processes. These processes have silence as a part of them. There is attention paid to the needs of participants for self-observation and inquiry into perceptual habits and blocks to curiosity. Participants in processes that celebrate connected ways of knowing are acknowledged as leaders, exercising leadership in the way they direct their own lives and participate in resolving conflict. They are encouraged to unfold and articulate their own purposes and what they hold meaningful, using these as a touchstone to energize their engagement and to measure progress and outcomes.

When connected ways of knowing inform processes, attention is paid to metaphors as windows into meaning making. Processes are unique, arising from the meanings that matter for group members rather than formulas or prescriptions. They employ rituals that may seem strange or incomprehensible to outsiders—rituals that bring them together and keep them connected. They are present-focused, with an emphasis on paying attention to interpersonal and intrapersonal messages whether intellectual, emotional, or physical. At the same time, there is a sense of connection to those not at the table and to future generations, as the legacy of the process is considered. Connected ways of knowing bring the gifts of energy and inspiration to animate processes. This energy arises from stories, metaphors, and rituals. All of these are explored in the chapters to come.

~~~⟨⟩~~~

PART THREE

Tools for Bridging Meanings and Identities

In Part Two—Creative Ways of Knowing as Resources for Bridging Conflict—we explored four ways of knowing that complement existing conflict resolution theory and practice. Together, somatic, emotional, imaginative-intuitive, and connected ways of knowing contribute to the deepening of relationship. As they invite us to move outside our accustomed ways of relating to each other in conflict processes and classrooms, they stimulate creativity. The creative process of bringing something new into being, whether an idea or a product, draws on all these ways of knowing. We use our imagining selves to picture it, our sensing selves to experience it, our emotional selves to feel it, and connected ways of knowing to integrate our learning.

Conflict asks us to find ways to bridge differences that uncover and respect diverse ways of knowing. It asks us to notice not only issues and relationships that befall each other but the deeper levels of symbol and meaning that fuel the collisions. Recognizing the need for tools that draw on these four ways of being, we search in the realm of the creative. We need creative tools because they have currency in the places where meaning is made and where expression is symbolic—levels not easily accessible through analysis.

Metaphor, ritual, and story are tools to access this level. They give us a window into each other because they convey not only thoughts but feelings, not only facts but perspectives about facts, not only ideas but values. Grounding what we learn in sensory experience, metaphors, rituals, and stories gather listeners and tellers into the same circle of human connection.

Metaphors are rich with images and information about who we conceive ourselves to be in relation to the images. They are a passage into what matters; third parties who listen for and invite metaphors are more likely to convene and facilitate processes that speak personally to those involved. Teachers who invoke metaphors will find their classrooms livelier places, where a range of expression is invited and welcomed. Metaphors are explored in Chapter Six.

Bridging conflict always involves stories. We keep our past alive through stories; we story our lives as we live into who we are. Transforming conflict involves co-creating new stories, or parts of stories, from which we can live into change. Chapter Seven examines how stories can confine or free us and how we can draw on the power of narrative in our processes.

All successful conflict resolution processes involve change. Rituals help parties transition, heightening awareness of sensing and feelings as anchors when new roles are enacted or achievements are marked. They both facilitate and celebrate change, communicating shared meaning on levels beyond words. They are dynamic and adaptable, flexible and comforting. Chapter Eight examines how rituals help bridge conflict.

With the tools of metaphor, story, and ritual, we have concrete ways to tap multiple ways of knowing in our processes. We begin with an exploration of metaphor—a tool both rich and versatile for conflict practitioners and teachers.

CHAPTER SIX

Symbolic Tools
Metaphors as Windows into Other Worlds

A Russian friend recently told me the story of the demise of her marriage. The relationship had become strained, stressed by unemployment, imbalance of responsibilities, the arrival of a child. Her husband got closer and closer to a female coworker. When my friend confronted his infidelity, he admitted it. She asked him why, struggling to understand his choice to risk family and home for someone who offered less. "Sometimes after you have had chocolate," he told her, "you want to have a pickle."

Metaphors are vivid windows into our worlds. They convey flavor, texture, sensation, and perspective. They reveal ways we make sense of our lives, sometimes heightening our differences, sometimes emphasizing our commonalities. The metaphor used by my friend's husband had a powerful, clarifying, if divisive, effect. It catalyzed her resolve to obtain a divorce.

Many metaphors are neither this stark nor surprising. We use them every day, every time we speak, even in our thoughts. We engage metaphors to make sense of the unfamiliar, to express feelings and viewpoints, to convey emphasis, to explore meaning. They communicate directionality ("It's an uphill battle"), ranking ("I'm on top of it"), or desirability ("That's scraping the bottom of the barrel"). They reference physical, sensory experiences, matching them to feelings and ideas. They communicate whole systems of meaning.

Our metaphors for health, the future, and rationality tend to be upward and positive, as when we say, "I'm feeling up today" or "I got the discussion back up to a rational level." Metaphors for illness, the past, and emotionality tend to focus downward and have a negative tint. So we say, "Is she still feeling down?" and "The session sank into emotionality." Arising from our physical experience of walking upright in the world, metaphors not only reflect our understanding but pervasively structure our thinking and shape our expectations.

Many metaphors are unmarked, meaning that we are not conscious of their presence. Metaphors associate two things without making the comparison obvious. A common example is the phrase, "Time is money." We know it is not literally true, yet it is so often used and embedded in our language that no attention is drawn to the comparison or the values it communicates. In this way, metaphor asserts a relationship or an analogy assumptively, without inviting a different perspective or even acknowledging the possibility that a different perspective exists. Conflict arises when parties see issues, roles, and processes through different metaphoric lenses. Because these metaphors are unmarked, they are not explicitly addressed or negotiated, and conflict escalates.

Metaphors are more than poetic ways of looking at what we do. They are windows into who we think we are, our purpose, and our approach. They show us what our blind spots are, where our attention is likely to go, and how we situate ourselves relative to others. Conflict intervention means paying attention to many levels simultaneously. But we cannot pay attention to everything. Metaphors give us clues about what we feature on our radar screens and what may be missed.

Metaphors are powerful tools for third parties who understand and use them artfully. They help make explicit what are otherwise hidden: assumptions, perceptions, judgments, and worldviews. They offer enormous potential for clarifying and enhancing roles and relationships, not only among parties but among practitioners and educators. In this chapter, we explore the multifaceted gifts that metaphors offer, including ambiguity, economy, and invention. We examine how metaphors reflect our roles as third parties and how they help bridge differences, especially across worldview or cultural divides. Finally, we consider the versatility of metaphor as a tool for process design.

Conflict Metaphors

Our understanding of metaphors has moved a long way past grade school searches through dusty books of poetry. No longer do we see metaphors as remote, arcane, and literary. Lakoff and Johnson[1] showed us the pervasiveness of metaphors in their book *Metaphors We Live By*. The book is perfect for conflict resolvers; it begins with an exploration of war as a metaphor for conflict or argument. Words like *battle, attack, target, shoot, strategy, shot down* are ubiquitous in our culture when we talk about conflict. What effect does this have on our attitudes and behavior? It has shaped negative associations, expectations, and approaches. It is not accidental that groups of people who have not had conflict resolution training (and some who have) volunteer mostly negative words when asked to brainstorm associations with conflict. The war metaphor forecloses other understandings and ways of being in conflict. It literally structures what we do when conflict arises and how we understand what we are doing.

If we call conflict a war, two possibilities suggest themselves: winning or losing. It makes sense that we would want to do our best to achieve a win. If we can't win, then we may try to paper over the difference with compromise to avoid damage or save face. Collaboration and creative interaction in the service of conflict resolution do not suggest themselves. Neither are third parties valued who want to do something other than support one side to win against the other. Fortunately, new metaphors associated with conflict have arisen in the past two decades. Along with new metaphors for conflict have come new ways of looking at ourselves as intervenors.

Consider these questions:

- Who are you?
- What are you trying to do in your work?
- When you intervene in conflict, what is your purpose?

Chances are, as you answer these questions you draw on metaphors. You might call yourself a peacemaker, a peacebuilder, or a listening ear. Stepping further into the realm of imagination, images of a gardener, a trickster, a trail clearer may come to mind. Each of these has different purposes, roles, and modes of operation. Trail clearers pay attention to getting trees and brush out of the way after the winter freeze; they are less likely than gardeners to concern themselves with nurturing seeds in the form of relationships. Neither role is wrong for conflict intervention, but they serve differently. Because energy follows attention, becoming aware of metaphors that direct our attention is important.

Over the past several years, I have asked hundreds of mediators, facilitators, and conflict resolution trainers to identify metaphors for themselves in practice. I have heard a wide range of images, from firefighter to amoebae, from clown to electric current. This wide array of metaphors belies diversity in the field. People involved in conflict resolution do different things in different ways to achieve different results. The patience of the gardener and her focus on sowing seeds has a very different tone and character than the power and urgency of the firefighter. The willingness of the clown to push boundaries and act against expectations contrasts with the physical principles by which an electric current predictably energizes a system. Metaphors open conversations, internal and shared, about our roles and approaches.

In a relational approach to conflict, these explorations are vital. They help us discern where our common sense of practice is rooted and where our paths diverge. They invite us to examine our assumptions against our values centered in relationship, connection, and possibility. They help us assess our standpoints, our flexibility, and our openness. They can also help us assess third parties and trainers. If you were involved in a workplace conflict, would you rather have the services of a third party who saw himself as an orchestra conductor or a magician? Would you prefer the listening ear of someone whose image for herself was a plumber or someone who saw her role as leader of an improvised dance?

The answers to these questions may not be as simple as they seem at first glance. A plumber may bring insight into the system and tools to bring it to a level of functioning; a dance leader may bring an attitude of flexibility and creativity. Both capacities may be useful in addressing the conflict. The question of fit depends on the culture and lifecycle of the workplace, the needs and learning styles of participants, and the ways metaphors for practice inform the third party's approach.

Some metaphors for practice may fit better in particular venues than others; the mediator who sees himself as a plumber may find it difficult to work with faculty in an art school. The improvisational dancer may find it challenging to relate to a highly technical dispute. But not necessarily. The beauty of metaphor is that it is spacious. It invites us into the possibility of connection. What might a dancer have to offer a group of engineers? What could a plumber bring to an art school? Dialogue in a spirit of inquiry may help everyone clarify appropriate choices.

Metaphors are useful, not because they provide prescriptions about third parties but because they invite us into imaginative conversation. They pose the possibility that roles shift and change over time as we grow, develop, and encounter new situations and that it is possible to bring a variety of approaches to the table at different points in a conflict lifecycle. In addition to their use as a medium for conversation, they are essential tools for third parties in conflict. Metaphors offer shorthand ways to enter other worlds of meaning, bridging difficult conflicts and deeply divided communities.

Limitations of Metaphors

As useful as metaphors are in conflict intervention, they also carry limitations. I recently took a class to a modern art museum. We saw beeswax structures, pigmented polystyrene eggs, and paintings with objects protruding from them. We saw colors and textures and forms that mystified, repelled, and intrigued us. If you are like me, you may not have a close relationship with modern art. I found it difficult to fathom and so preferred the literal comfort of impressionist paintings that invited me into gracious gardens and early morning views of misty cathedrals.

We came to a painting by Mark Rothko titled "Blue, Orange, Red." It was just that: blue, orange, and red—rectangles of color juxtaposed with each other in a piece that stood twice our height on a stark white wall. I was confronted by my complete uncertainty about what it represented, what it meant. I was not alone. As we spoke of our experiences of the piece, we quickly moved from literal descriptions like, "The blue is intense and feathered at the edges" to metaphoric responses such as, "I see an invitation to eternity." The experience reminded me how difficult it is for us not to use metaphors, not to make stories. As soon as we name the blue "eternity," we foreclose a whole universe of other experiences the blue might have evoked.

When we encounter mystery (and conflict is often mysterious, tangled as it is in relational, personal, and cultural dynamics), we seek to understand it. Often we do this by finding a metaphor. We call the painting harsh, uplifting, forceful, shallow. We use words that connote space, direction, depth, and intensity. Labeling the painting with one of these metaphors, we feel better, a little less uncomfortable. But the metaphors do more than foreclose other understandings. They also contain judgments. They may dismiss, minimize, categorize. The effect of this is that we are less able to do what Rothko intended, to use his painting as an invitation to move through a range of experiences, exploring what is beyond the medium and the contents of the frame. Metaphors can limit our understandings as well as expand them.

Our metaphors for conflict also contain limiting assumptions, inhibitions, and emotional judgments. Think of a serious conflict you have faced. What metaphors suggested themselves to you as it happened? How do these metaphors reveal the choices you perceived, the way you characterized yourself and others, your experience of power dynamics, and your expectations of outcome? Notice whether your metaphors for that conflict have changed over time. Have they become more expansive, less limiting, less judgmental? If you feel some resistance to changing old metaphors, you will have increased empathy for those who trust you to work with their conflicts. To draw effectively on metaphors in our teaching and intervention, we need to explore more about how they work.

Dynamics of Metaphors

We have seen that metaphors are most often used unconsciously as essential parts of our everyday language. They help us explain and understand things that our logic cannot comprehensively address. Metaphors connect the realms of emotion, sensation, imagination, and creativity to logic and rationality. They contain stories in succinct form—stories that link not only phenomena but ourselves, our values, and our deep convictions. Metaphors are associative, bridging different systems of logic and ways of making meaning. Because I cannot understand your world in context through applying the logic that reflects my way of making meaning, I have to rely on another resource. That resource is metaphor. The great thinker Gregory Bateson explains that logic does not work well to help us understand complex natural phenomena or relationships. Metaphor, he says, is "right at the bottom of being alive. . . . [It is] how this whole fabric of mental interconnections holds together."[2]

Richness of Metaphors

Try to speak without using metaphors, and you will find it difficult indeed. Their value arises from their sensory nature coupled with ambiguity. They give us known referents that help us connect more directly to ideas, while at the same time leaving room for interpretation. This poses special challenges across cultures and even personalities; my interpretation may be different from yours. If we do not surface these differences, we may believe there is accord when there is not, leading later to manifest conflict. Suppose I call our friendship a cocoon. I believe I am communicating warmth, safety, comfort. My friend is hurt. He associates cocoons with limited light and space, with feeling trapped, with waiting to become something better and freer. Most of us have had the experience of miscommunicating through metaphor, leading to sometimes uncomfortable results.

This very ambiguity can also help save face, however. In a workgroup meeting, a new member of the staff suggests changes to the office layout, ignorant of a recently resolved contentious conflict about that issue. The room is silent. Rather than confront or dismiss the suggestion, a manager observes, "That ground has been well-tilled in past weeks. Jerome will fill you in later and let you know the process we adopted for space suggestions." No comment is made about the suggestion or its propriety, yet the employee's contribution is acknowledged and a way forward suggested. The metaphor of well-tilled ground represents the energy and depth of the conflict without blame or evaluation.

Metaphors are remarkably economical. Earlier, we referred to them as shorthand for their concise way of conveying information. Like the grain of sand that holds the world, they communicate more than facts or information; they communicate feelings, beliefs, meanings, and structures through physical and sensory imagery. If I say to my friend, "I had a hard day," much less is communicated than when I say, "Today, I was swept up in a whirlwind." The second statement communicates feelings (tiredness), position (in the center of activity), meaning (lack of volition), and magnitude (something bigger than me was at work). When we ask parties to talk about what an issue means to them, we invite metaphors. Listening closely, we learn a great deal from few words.

Metaphors also make it possible to invent new ideas and applications. The metaphor of the pump, when applied to the human heart, revolutionized the way we think about the circulatory system. The pump metaphor also inspired ways to apply paint more efficiently than using an object with bristles to smear color across a surface.[3] Similarly, the metaphor of the forest as a farm gave rise to contemporary practices in forestry, with concepts of "harvesting" (what foresters do to trees), "weed trees" (economically undesirable species), and the goal of maximizing "yields." As this farming metaphor became embedded within the field of forestry, it went largely unquestioned.[4] Only when we hear alternative or competing metaphors such as "the forest is the hair of Mother Earth" do we mark or notice them. It is tempting to devalue metaphors when they challenge conventional or accepted views. We will see how this phenomenon plays out later in the chapter.

Metaphorical Shifts: The Abortion Issue

Metaphors lend a pervasive valence to things and ideas. Think again of the example Lakoff and Johnson[5] gave of conflict as a war. If we metaphorically construct argument as war, then we see the person we are arguing with as an opponent. We attack our opponent's positions; we defend our own. We gain and lose ground. We plan and use strategies. If we find a position indefensible, we abandon it and take a new line of attack. We wage divorce battles and partisan contests in Congress. And all of it seems natural. Given our choice of metaphor, it is.

When Fisher and Ury wrote their hugely popular *Getting to Yes* in 1983,[6] they proposed a new approach to conflict. Readers were invited to rely on four simple principles and an ordered, rational process. Fisher and Ury suggested that parties in conflict should be objective and empathic, putting themselves into each other's shoes. Even as they suggested a fundamental shift in the way conflict is seen, Fisher and Ury continued drawing on the pervasive metaphor of war. "Attack the problem without blaming the people,"[7] they suggest. Arguably, their book would have been even more powerful if it had been grounded in a coherent alternative metaphor, as their later work has shown.

What happens to our attitudes and behaviors when we change metaphors? Lakoff and Johnson[8] propose seeing conflict as a dance. If conflict is a dance, then participants are performers, and the goal is to perform in a balanced and aesthetically pleasing way. In such a frame, people view arguments differently, avoid less, are less judgmental of themselves and others, and demonstrate more awareness of the flow or the shape of conflict, increasing the possibility of a harmonious conclusion. The focus changes from winning to connecting with the music, each other, and the audience. In short, conflict a dance is a metaphor that draws our attention to connection and relationship rather than disconnection and destruction. From this place, we have more room to move.

Part of our work as conflict resolvers is to invite participants to adopt generative metaphors that encourage and reveal possibilities. Metaphors help us map familiar worlds onto our experiences. Yet it is important to ask, Which worlds? Conflict-as-war limits us, as does calling life a battle, age a curse, or love an illusion. Mediators can draw on the power of metaphor to make our role in constructing our "reality" evident.

Metaphors are also useful in addressing conflicts because they provide the opportunity to shift perspectives. Our mind works largely through metaphor (relating to images and felt experiences) and comparison, not by logic or pure invention. When we are caught in a perceptual or conceptual trap, the best exit may be a change in metaphor. This is not because another metaphor is necessarily superior but because we need a shift to another perspective and the possibilities that it may reveal. Let's look at the issue of abortion in Canada and the United States as a way of exploring the effect of shifting metaphors in conflict.

Listen to the ubiquitous news reporting on the issue of abortion and ask which metaphors predominate. References to war, battle, wins, and losses abound. After a successful judicial or legislative "victory," representatives from either side are likely to caution, "We've won the battle but not the war." These word choices are not coincidental, nor are they insignificant. It is difficult when in the heat of battle to even imagine peaceful coexistence. In war there are enemies. Getting to know "them" or working with "them" is undesirable and dangerous.

Now come with me to a Saturday morning meeting of a group of people gathered for a dialogue about abortion. They begin in a circle, having agreed in advance to ground rules that promise speaking from personal experience, bringing genuine curiosity, and making no attempts at conversion or persuasion. There are ten pro-life and ten pro-choice activists, men and women, young and old. There is an air of nervousness and sparse social chatter as they get coffee and find seats. Here are veterans of the "war" over abortion, riders on a train that some have said is carrying a load of freight related to all kinds of social conflicts in the United States and Canada that are harder to identify and quantify than abortion itself. And they are sitting in the room with others who are averse to violence, tired of the boxes built by debates, or simply curious. They have come because they want to find a better way than violence, escalation, and destruction.

Taking first steps is difficult. There is a freeze in the air, born of choosing a new, untried way. Introductions proceed, and participants fill out a questionnaire about their views on abortion, premarital sex, and unwanted pregnancies. There is some comfort in this; filling out a questionnaire is an unthreatening, individual activity. Once they are finished, the facilitators ask them to fill out the questionnaire again—this time as they believe someone from "the other side" would fill it out. Later the results of these questionnaires will be tabulated and reported back, invariably showing that the respondents are closer to each other in their views than they anticipate. Each tends to rate the other as more extreme than they rate themselves. This use of quantitative data is a powerful way to interrupt metaphors of war and distance, inviting a closer look.

Moving into small groups, participants share stories about how they came to their views. Listening in, we hear accounts of struggles, confusion, frustration, and conviction that turn flat stereotypes into multidimensional beings. As stories are shared, war metaphors give way to images of discovery and illumination arising out of difficult transitions. There are surprises along the way. One woman in her forties tells a story of how she was touched by her sister's unplanned pregnancy. A while later, a man in his fifties shares events from his life that are strikingly similar. The main difference that marks them is the conclusion. One finishes by saying, "And in that moment, it was clear to me that every child should be a wanted child. I felt a burning need to work for abortion rights." The other concludes, "And so I promised myself and my sister that we would hold the torch to make sure that no more unborn children are lost."

Two stories have been heard—stories with similar themes leading to two different conclusions. The effect in the small group is palpable. Empathy is present; everyone can feel with the storytellers. Although the conclusions are different, many things are shared: the need to make sense of difficult times, to take a stand, to work on an issue that has touched your life. The storytellers have become more than a label. They are parents, neighbors, siblings, business people, citizens who care, people who could not prevent pain in their families though they deeply wished to. In the dialogue that follows, new metaphors emerge. No longer is the ground frozen or the group embattled. Participants speak of linkages, thawing ground, and tender shoots of spring flowers as they move to plan joint research into adoption and negotiate limits and acceptable behaviors outside clinics.

As powerful as the metaphor of war associated with abortion has been, the journey metaphor comes to fit better for these activists who have begun to develop relationships with each other. To test the power of metaphor, we can use ourselves. Consider the metaphors of war and journey. Words and images associated with each term register in the body, producing different sensations and responses. Battles arouse tension, concern for security, guardedness, and defensiveness. And journeys? They may evoke curiosity, excitement, anticipation, and openness. When we envision journeying together in spite of fundamental disagreements about an issue, we sow the seeds of new relationships. Understanding grows

through shared experiences and stories; blaming and personaliz-
ing issues decreases. Respect and safety become paramount as the
boundaries between "them" and "us" are broken down, and everyone has less tolerance for violence, polemic language, and demo-
nization.

I will never forget visiting in a Western city with a group of
clergy from several denominations active on both sides of the abortion issue who had been meeting regularly for nearly two years. All
of them were busy, yet some traveled for over two hours to attend
meetings and return home. They were passionate about their
views, well known in their communities as leaders of pro-choice
and pro-life initiatives.

The question that came to me as I sat with them was, Why?
Why were they making this effort, when it was so much more difficult than continuing their advocacy? Why did they spend hours
each month sitting together and talking with those they had previously avoided or encountered only in debates and court contests?
When I asked this question, there was silence. Then, with tears in
his eyes, one of the participants softly answered, "As we walk
together, I see God in these others." The others nodded their
agreement, some reaching out to touch the hands of those seated
next to them.

I kept this experience inside, feeling privileged to have met
these men and women. Here was a group of people who had
found a way to be in relationship with each other, even in the midst
of deep disagreement about an emotional and difficult issue. Here
was a group who were enacting their values of respect for difference and love. They were doing something unpopular with those
they served, many of whom were suspicious and concerned that
their leaders were selling out or losing their resolve. Yet their advocacy was strong, their beliefs undiluted. They were finding new
metaphors for conflict, drawing strength from each other to reject
"war" and explore more generative ways of moving forward as leaders, community members, and advocates with a broader understanding of issues and strong relationships with those on all sides.

Common Ground groups learn firsthand about how
metaphors set the tone of conflict, influencing behavior and attitudes. Metaphors both help them change the tone of interaction
and show them their progress. Metaphors also mark or ritualize

their steps onto common ground. By sharing metaphors in a word collage at the end of their first annual conference, participants from dialogue groups around the country acknowledged their progress, celebrated their discoveries, and confirmed their connections. Common to these metaphors were light, energy, and relationship in the forms of rainbows, big skies, hands held across canyons, and caterpillars emerging as butterflies.

How does this metaphoric change occur? Do the facilitators of Common Ground dialogues on abortion suggest new metaphors, or do the old ones fail to fit and the new ones arise organically? As with so many aspects of process, there is no one answer. Different dialogue groups adopt different metaphors for their relationships and their work. Sometimes facilitators observe and reflect metaphors implicit in dialogue; sometimes participants name them. Transformation marked by the adoption of a new metaphor only occurs as it reflects what is genuinely felt in the room.

Third parties or trainers who try imposing metaphors early will encounter resistance. Absent shared experience, suggestions to substitute journeys for wars will not be supported by the attitudinal and relational change necessary. As participants in dialogue are assured that they will not be pressured to change their views on issues, metaphors may arise that simulate change, indicate movement, and anchor progress. Third parties may suggest metaphors implicitly or explicitly with sensitivity to timing, fit, and culture. The next section discusses this and other uses of metaphors.

Uses of Metaphor in Training and Intervention

Because metaphor is so powerful and versatile, there are many constructive ways it can be used, as well as ways it can cause or perpetuate damage. The longstanding Arab-Israeli conflict is a powerful illustration. Each side uses metaphors and images that divide, demonize, and diminish, perpetuating a siege mentality. An Egyptian colleague reports his experience of growing up in Egypt in the 1960s, watching a German anti-Semite movie titled *The Smile of the Serpent* on Egyptian television. Jews were portrayed as money-hungry and manipulative, invoking the image of the serpent and its associations with stealth and evil. In turn, some Jews have dismissed Arabs as an accidental creation, rejected by God as a mistake. Both sides see the other as misguided appropriators of land. Given these metaphors, a relationship of fighting is not only heroic; it is natural.

Metaphors, like the language in which they are embedded, are relational tools. They promote or weaken relationships, depending on how they are used. Whether rough, crude, expressive, or lovely, we draw on metaphors when we have a problem to solve together or a plan to formulate. Using metaphors can help by

- Promoting constructive communication
- Informing cultural or worldview dialogues
- Building safe spaces
- Acknowledging creativity
- Enhancing process mutuality

Next I explore each of these themes in turn, with examples of how they have been used in interventions or trainings. These categories are not distinct; they are overlapping. They are representative of ways that metaphors are helpful. As you read, you may think of other ways you have encountered metaphor. Our understanding continues to unfold and develop as we reflect on our experience and try new approaches.

Promoting Constructive Communication

Some ways metaphor promotes constructive communication are to

- Set or invite a positive climate or tone
- Communicate meaning and shades of meaning or emphasis
- Reveal symbolic issues
- Clarify communication

Set a Tone. Metaphors are useful in convening and setting the tone for processes. They may suggest positive momentum, shared goals, and a reliable route. They may communicate positive expectations, strong leadership, and collaborative values. As we have seen, metaphors in dialogue or mediation processes may become touchstones. Sometimes metaphors are general, like a journey; sometimes they are more specific, such as a reference to a train trip.

Specificity may be helpful, giving participants language to call for focus by observing that the process is "off the track" or to reassure each other that "the station is in sight." Kinesthetic experiences evoked by metaphors remind us to bring all of ourselves to the process.

One class developed the metaphor of dancing as a way of framing their interactions, shared responsibility, and creative approaches to learning. This particular group of participants did not go through the stages once thought "normal" for groups: forming, storming, norming, and performing. They got along remarkably well during the year-long training in community counseling and conflict resolution. Here is how instructor Jo-Anne Stoltz[9] describes what happened:

> Early in the year, I had brought a tape deck and music for a specific training exercise, and we had enjoyed some freeform dancing at the break. Before long, we were beginning each session with music and dancing, each person engaging in whatever form of movement felt right before settling in for the long evening of sitting and learning. We felt connected with each other through movement and music on kinesthetic, intuitive, and irrational (i.e. goofy and fun) levels, and not in pairs but as a group.

As a result, Stoltz observes, the group worked together with more respect, care, and mutual support than other groups. They were able to draw on dancing as a metaphor for learning together. When they needed to shift negative energy, they referred back to dance as a way of coming together, moving through difficulty, and reaffirming their shared values of connection, play, and imagination.

Communicate Meaning and Reveal Symbolic Issues. Metaphors may also be useful in revealing the symbolic nature of issues and uncovering shades of meaning. In the Northern Forests Lands process I refer to later, one participant described the conflict over forestry, saying, "If we keep going the way we're going, we're going to hit the wall." This choice of metaphor communicated strong feelings but also raised questions:

- What form would the wall take?
- When might we hit it?

- How would hitting it look?
- Could we avoid hitting it, and if so, how?

Questioned about the meaning of his metaphor, the participant explained his worries about development, road building, and human impact in wilderness areas. These worries related to concerns about the symbolic importance of forests as legacies for future generations. Asking him about his metaphor revealed much more nuanced information and surfaced symbolic dimensions that may otherwise have remained hidden.

Clarify Communication. At the same time, we must remember that metaphors evolve through cultures over time and are not necessarily accurate vehicles for communication across cultures. Allusions like "the straw that broke the camel's back" may be as mysterious to new speakers of English as an unknown language would be, if they try to understand them literally. Other expressions may be not only mysterious to those from outside the linguistic culture but offensive to those within it. The frequently used expression "rule of thumb" actually refers to the old rule that a man could not beat his wife with a switch wider than the circumference of his thumb. So caution is in order when using metaphorical expressions, and good facilitators watch for times when translation or explanation may be needed to turn a confusing metaphor into an opportunity for learning and clarification.

Experienced facilitators and teachers have stories about how they learned this the hard way. Here is mine. At the end of the day during an intensive class, a participant described his experience of trying to process the large quantity of information as "trying to sip from a fire hydrant." A fellow participant whose first language was not English understood him to say that he had been "trying to sniff a fire hydrant." When the mistaken interpretation came out in a later discussion, the listener revealed that she had given him "a lot of space" ever since his statement, as she took it to be a crude reference. I made a note to be sure that metaphoric expressions are clear to everyone present. Only when we are attuned to metaphors that may not be understood by everyone can we be sure that they truly clarify communication.

Informing Cultural or Worldview Dialogues

Conflicts often involve cultural or worldview differences. In these cases, metaphor helps to

- Make the meta-level visible in framing or implementing a process
- Connect with diverse parties through communicating understandings of ways people see themselves relative to an issue, relationship, or situation
- Empower parties

Exploring these applications requires some attention to the nature of cultural and worldview conflicts.

Many conflicts involve cultural or worldview differences. Cultural differences, broadly defined, refer to the way members of any given group behave, relate, and perceive self and others. Cultural groups may be organized around an activity, a set of beliefs, geographic origin, ability or disability, age or generation, or identity. Viewed this way, all of us are members of many cultures. Which set of values, beliefs, and prescribed behaviors we act from depends on context, relationship, and many other factors. For example, I may respond from the culture of my legal training and identity as a lawyer when faced with an apparent injustice to me or a family member by a public official. This set of cultural messages did nothing to prepare me for how to behave in the Indian orphanage where I found myself one hot morning in Chennai. There my cultural training as a woman and a mother was a resource, as I helped a group of undergraduate students relate to dozens of clinging children crying for touch and attention.

Worldview differences are even more complex because they include cultural identities yet are less explicit. Consider the famous metaphor of culture as an iceberg where only the tip is visible above the water. Worldviews are the ocean in which the iceberg floats. Oscar Nudler reminds us that "most of the time world views are just part of the assumptions or pre-understandings on which theories [and behavior] rest, and so they are excluded from awareness or focus"[10] and, therefore, from our processes. The result, he cautions, are theories and practices unconsciously permeated by the particular worldview of the people who developed or adopted them.

This is particularly problematic in conflicts involving ethnic, religious, environmental, generational, or other kinds of deep differences. In these cases, engaging in dialogue about metaphors brings the meta-level into awareness, opening the possibility of designing processes responsive to worldview differences. As this is done, metaphor becomes useful in facilitating communication and empowerment. We begin with the opportunity metaphor presents to make the unseen visible to everyone involved.

Make the Meta-Level Visible. Worldviews reflect how we make sense of the world and our place in it. They include ways we learn, how we order what we know, what we value, and ideas about the nature of the universe. These are not things we name or negotiate; they define what we consider "normal," "right," and "usual." Consider two worldviews about the natural environment and humans' place in it.

Traditional aboriginal and pagan cultures see spirit everywhere—in rocks, trees, and animals. No entity is greater than any other; each has its own wisdom. Humans are a part of the system. Their role is not dominance but harmonic coexistence. Knowledge among aboriginal and pagan cultures is passed orally through traditional rituals, gleaned from experience in the natural world.

Dominant culture views of science and discovery involve manipulation of elements in controlled environments. Humans are seen as uniquely gifted with reason, emotion, and the ability to document through writing and information processing. Knowledge is developed through scientific inquiry and passed on using written conventions and symbols.

When a conflict resolution process seeks to bring together members from each of these groups, they will be frustrated and confused rather than engaged in meaningful dialogue unless ways are found to address worldview differences. Metaphors offer the opportunity to have these conversations. Later in the chapter, we will explore ways this might be done.

Connect with Diverse Parties. As we have seen, metaphors are a potent way into worldview dialogues. The skilled mediator listens for the metaphors used by each party in early conversation. Suppose one party shows a strong preference for "levels talk" (ranking metaphors), another party prefers "circles talk" (systemic, connecting metaphors), and still another uses "sides talk" (relationship metaphors). The mediator can be sure to include a variety of directional or spatial references in her or his description of process. This will let parties know that their perspective is being understood and reflected. It is also possible to make explicit use of these metaphors, engaging parties in a discussion of how they will evaluate issues, criteria, and eventual solutions to their conflict, given diverse ways of seeing the world. In this way, parties are invited to acknowledge differences and treat the process as mutually educational.

Empower Parties. Through a discussion of metaphors, parties are empowered. They become aware of their own and others' metaphors and thus have the language to question subsequent situations in which one party may seek to impose a process or an idea grounded in one worldview that excludes others.

I remember well a situation in which metaphor awareness fostered empowerment. I was facilitating a three-day meeting of a group of diversity consultants who had come together to share practice ideas and experiences in a large city in the eastern United States. Gathered were about twenty men and women from various ethnocultural backgrounds with a wealth of experience in intercultural conflict and diversity work. As part of convening the group, I proposed a set of guidelines for communication and invited feedback or suggestions. These guidelines referred to taking turns when speaking, speaking in the first person, demonstrating respect for others, and balancing participation in ways that allowed everyone's ideas to be heard. In my experience, introducing guidelines may lead to discussions of confidentiality or ways of ensuring equity in participation. Other times, groups simply accept the proposed guidelines, anxious to get into the substance of the meeting. In this case, an African American participant rose and challenged me.

He characterized the proposed guidelines as a muzzle—a political act by those who might want to constrain the discussion to calmness, docility, and harmony, even in the presence of real disagreement and conflict. He proposed that we govern ourselves by the principle of authenticity alone, trusting that issues that needed to come up would come up and that we would find ways to address them by staying engaged in the process. He pointed out that we would not be able to foresee or prescribe these in advance.

There followed the most spirited discussion of communication guidelines I have ever witnessed, galvanized by the powerful imagery of the muzzle and counterimages proposed by others. Some suggested that we see ourselves on expandable leads or constrained by a fence at the periphery of our discussions. We struggled with balancing concern about respect and boundaries with our desires for openness and free exchange of ideas. Amidst the suggestions, consensus emerged about a way forward. We adopted an open space approach; participants self-organized in thematic groups, sharing what they had learned and their action plans during plenary sessions. This provided latitude and some structure without imposing ways of knowing or doing on those who wanted to pursue areas of shared interest and passion.

This experience made the rules of the process negotiable in a meaningful way, engaging everyone in inquiry about which worldviews and cultural assumptions would frame our participation. Not everyone would feel so empowered or so motivated to challenge a proposed frame. Engaging in some discussion of whose ideas of process and order are informing a process is useful whenever cultural or worldview differences exist. If not done, the unspoken assumption that the rules of the dominant culture prevail may foreclose meaningful participation for others. We will see a poignant example of this later in the chapter in the context of a public policy negotiation process.

Building Safe Spaces

Some measure of safety and security is a precondition for effective dialogue and conflict resolution. These issues clearly overlap with sensitivity to cultural and worldview differences. When cultural and worldview differences are acknowledged and reflected in practice, safety is enhanced, promoting participation. Metaphors can help

- Surface existing levels of conflict
- Suggest alternative perspectives

- Enhance relationship through acceptance and empathy for others' experiences
- Convey questions, objections, or inconsistencies about others' views without loss of face

Surface Existing Levels of Conflict. Imagine a training session that is being held jointly for loggers, conservationists, and forest industry representatives. A negotiation process is to take place, and training is being offered as a way of developing skills and coming to know each other. During the initial round of introductions, a logger gets up, holding a long metal tree spike that had been placed in the forest by an opponent of logging. When loggers hit a spike with their chainsaw, they can damage their equipment and be seriously injured. "This is a lost limb," he says in a gravelly voice, shaking the spike at the group. "I'm here to stop it."

Silence reigns. The impact is felt. Confrontation confirms early feelings of discomfort. It is not a safe space. Not yet. Conflict generally exists in an atmosphere of distrust, suspicion, and relational strain. It metaphorically backs parties into corners. If they could have found a way out by themselves, they would have done so. Although the route may seem direct and clear to me or to their counterparts on the other side, a person will not venture out of the corner until she or he has experienced some measure of safety. Naming the extent of the conflict diffuses the potency that could build if it were held under the water like a rubber ball and suddenly released during the process. The tree spike brought "the war in the woods" into the room and focused participants on working hard to build another way. Choosing another way is often more threatening and difficult than we anticipate.

Suggest Alternative Perspectives. I had a dream one night that I was in a large, grand house. One of the rooms was flooded with light from huge transom windows trimmed with beautiful yellow silk curtains rippling in the breeze. The high ceiling was adorned with exquisite chandeliers; the rich oak floors were the color of honey. It was the kind of room that invited dancing or quiet enjoyment on the warm summer afternoon of my dream. But I was not in the room. I was next door in a tiny closet, dark, close, and cluttered with dust balls and straw from discarded brooms. I stood facing into the shadowed corner, vaguely aware that there were other parts of the house to enjoy. I stood there for a long time, feeling despair and sadness. I wanted to leave, but I was also afraid and somehow strangely comforted by the small space and the darkness. At last, I realized I could simply turn around and leave the closet, stepping into the beautiful room.

People in conflict are often like this. They know there is a more beautiful, restful place. But they are invested and stuck, imprisoned by their intentions, perceptions, understandings, and pain. Third parties can help them know the bright room is still there when the closet walls sccm to close in and have the courage to turn around and walk out of the familiar, close space.

Enhance Relationship Through Acceptance and Empathy. Metaphors may help, just as my dream posed the question for me of how I was standing in my own way. Listen to the parties. If they say they feel as though they are walking a tightrope, explore with them whether there is a safety net, what supports they could use to help them maintain balance, and what they need from the process to help them across. If they say they are holding up the sky, see what kind of help they would accept from the other party or what other resources they can summon. Metaphors are shorthand for whole stories; help parties discover what they are, how they limit, and how they hold the keys to untangling conflict.

Another way metaphors enhance empathy is through deper-sonalizing or deflecting blame. In a conflict in a church commu-nity, the facilitator helped normalize discomfort with a high level of disagreement. She invited everyone into a spirit of inquiry by suggesting that they find ways to metaphorically open the windows and let out the smoke. Only then could they see where the fire was, its size, nature, and threat. As they "opened the windows" by sur-facing some of their fears and their genesis in the history of the congregation, space emerged for deeper dialogue. Participants spoke about how the fire started, what the fire had illuminated, and how to put it out rather than blame or accuse fellow members of the congregation. Empathy developed as they shared their feel-ings about the fire in a way they may not have done without the space provided by the metaphor.

Convey Questions Without Others' Loss of Face. Metaphors can also help by virtue of their ambiguity. They allow speakers to send messages containing principles without imposing an entire structure or outcome. This process invites the listener to use imagination and save face without directly challenging their point of view. For example, if a party responds, "It takes two to tango," to an accusation from their counterpart, a different perspective has been suggested. At the same time, no degree of accountability is specified, nor is the challenge as direct as simple denial or contradiction. The speaker appeals to the listener's understanding of dance and its impossibility when one of the partners is passive or unengaged, while implicitly recognizing some responsibility themselves. As John Haynes, a family mediator who contributed richly to our understanding of metaphor, points out, even if the speaker believes they have just 1 percent of the responsibility, the statement represents a shift from outright denial, and forward momentum is achieved.

Acknowledging Creativity

As we saw in Chapter One, creativity is a core competency for third parties, trainers, and parties in conflict. There are many definitions of *creativity*. Simply stated, creating is making something new. The new thing may be an idea, an invention, or a way forward in conflict. As Betty Reardon observes, "The failure to achieve peace is in essence a failure of imagination."[11] When creativity is acknowledged as relational and available to everyone, it becomes a pivotal resource in conflict. Metaphors help access and enact creativity. They can be used to

- Invite imagination into a process
- Guide assessment or exploration
- Unlock impasse and energize inquiry
- Help enact group dynamics and effect change

Contrary to popular misconception, creativity does not demand great skill, nor is it an attribute of the very intelligent. Being creative does not mean having extraordinary artistic ability; it does not mean madness. Creativity is essential to effective conflict resolution because it means doing something differently from the way we have done it in the past, sometimes with the same resources. Of course, if we do what we've always done, we'll get what we've always gotten. If conflict is the result of our ways of relating, then creativity helps us explore new, more generative ways.

Invite Imagination. By their conscious use, metaphors invite us to be imaginative. When we ask parties for a metaphor for their experience, we ask them to delve into that place where they dream, where physical sensations inform and mirror thought, to reflect beyond logic or analysis. Think of a process you have convened, and let a metaphor or an image arise in connection with it. What does the metaphor show you about that process, your place in it, your sense of closure about it, your perception of others in it? Don't try to invent the most clever or most literal metaphor, and don't worry if one does not come to mind immediately. Take a quiet moment and let your breath clear your mind of thoughts. See what comes. Absurd or mysterious as the image may be, ask what it shows you. You may be surprised at the richness and the wisdom efficiently contained in one image.

Guide Assessment and Exploration. I once intervened in a county agency with serious problems related to race and gender. The problems had ballooned into court cases and letters to public officials, leaving the workplace fraught with tension and low productivity. After I had met with the staff a couple of times, I saw a clear image of myself in crossfire. Whenever I made a procedural suggestion or even asked a question about the past, objections came quickly and sharply from one side, then another. I began to understand why the workplace was uncomfortable for so many employees. The image of crossfire showed me that I had to think about issues of security and protection as they related to intervention and to how employees related to each other on a day-to-day basis. It also helped me think about how I could avoid being in the crossfire myself.

As our work proceeded, the group worked with metaphors of their workplace in the present and in the future, functioning optimally. The metaphors were graphic and telling. For the present, there were eggshells, walking a tightrope without a net and thin ice. All of them spoke to tension and a sense of precariousness. Future images included a space station where communication is open and clear, an ecosystem where there is balance and functional diversity, and a clock where every part contributes to the whole.

Together we worked through ways of moving from embattled images full of fear and anxiety to hopeful, generative images of synergy and participation. Metaphors helped us think outside the box, deriving solutions other than firing problem employees. With so-called problem employees gone, the systemic issues would have gone unaddressed, and the conflict would have continued. Metaphors helped build ownership in a creative process that moved beyond myopic solutions. Other examples using metaphor in organizational conflict can be found in the work of Barrett and Cooperrider.[12]

Unlock Impasse and Energize Inquiry. Other ways that metaphor can stimulate creativity include asking people to draw their conflicts or issues. Temporarily prohibiting words turns the mind to visual, auditory, and kinesthetic images without the constraints words impose. Edward de Bono[13] reminds us that new ideas tend to occur more often to those who are able to escape the rigidity of words and classifications.

Another important aspect of creativity related to metaphors is knowing when to stop trying. There are countless stories of inventors who worked diligently on problems and finally took a break, only to discover "the answer" in an image in nature or a metaphor that came, unbidden, to mind. I recently read a quote: "Ask a difficult question, and the marvelous answer appears." I would reframe it to say, "Ask a difficult question, wait, and the marvelous answer appears."

Metaphors are also useful and important for creative problem solving. Techniques include free association with a chosen metaphor connected to possible outcomes or brainstorming images of solutions. If stuck, try doing something unrelated for a short time, like making connections between two seemingly unrelated metaphors as a way of loosening the mind. Ask yourself to identify connections between a bridge and a moth, between a waterfall and a piece of paper, between a badger and a brief case.

Then go back to the problem. If nothing else, you may bring a more playful spirit to the exercise.

Enact Group Dynamics and Effect Change. Finally, metaphors are very useful when we enact them, bringing reality testing and life to our ideas. We call these kinesthetic metaphors. Kinesthetic metaphors can help a group discern where it is in a process and the dynamics of power, leadership, and creativity needed to move forward. An example is the knot. Participants are asked to form a circle. Each crosses her or his arms and joins hands with two people on the other side of the circle. The group is then given the task of untangling the knot without releasing hands. Debriefing can focus on leadership and communication, on team building and problem solving.

Another kinesthetic metaphor relevant to conflict is "the edge." Participants are asked to pair up and actively explore a variety of edges: the edge of a sidewalk, of a carpeted area, of a counter, of a stair. As they explore, they are asked to pay attention to their experiences. What is it like to approach an edge, to look over an edge? What does retreating from the edge feel like? What is it like to walk the edge? How does it change if your eyes are closed and you are relying on your partner to guide you? Experiences of edges can give participants insight into their responses to disequilibrium or dissonance. They are also valuable in exploring interactions that cross culture or worldview divides; often these involve feeling "on the edge" between the familiar and the unknown.

When metaphors like this are used in training or intervention, creativity enlivens participants. Analysis and mental processing are complimented by experience. I might know that I find transitions difficult, that I dislike standing on the edge of a cliff and looking down. Actually putting myself into the situation gives me insight into what happens when I am there. Am I likely to freeze, go toward the experience that scares me, or run the other way? Given my tendency, what could I do next time I feel myself in a transition or on the edge to make a choice that supports me and those around me? My answers to these questions will be more informed after I have had the sensory experience of edges than if I try to answer from my mental understanding alone.

Enhancing Process Mutuality

A relational approach to conflict emphasizes relationships among parties, between parties and intervenors, and within all participants. Our internal state has a huge impact on intervention and teaching. A relational approach offers parties ongoing input into process framing and design. Metaphors are useful in posing questions, marking progress, or naming choices in a way that invites everyone to participate in moving forward. Metaphors help parties

- Share ongoing analysis
- Build rapport and shared ownership in processes
- Understand worldview differences and assess processes
- Enhance team effectiveness

Share Ongoing Analysis. An example of using metaphor in assessment is the invitation to members of a process to share their metaphors for conflict, which are then listed on a flipchart at the front of the room. By making the invitation to the group, everyone becomes more aware of their image and how the group images cluster or vary. Metaphors remind us of something we frequently forget: that problems are not given but constructed by humans in their attempts to make sense of complex and troubling situations.[14] Many people volunteer metaphors that are heavy, negative, and tension-filled when asked to do this exercise.

The facilitator may ask people to work in small groups with their images. If there are words that are not metaphorical (for example, *terrible, frustrating*), ask, "What does terrible look like? What does frustrating feel like?" to get to a metaphor. Encourage participants to make the words concrete. Then groups can consider three questions about each conflict metaphor:

- What does the world look like from inside this image?
- What kinds of actions can you perform that fit with this metaphor?
- What kinds of actions would not fit with this image?

Through this experience, participants deepen their understanding of their common sense of conflict and ways it may constrain, inform, and free them. Thus they participate in self-assessment and build rapport with each other.

Build Rapport and Shared Ownership. Another way to use metaphors in practice is to observe their physical qualities. As we've seen, metaphors may be directional, spatial, or system-oriented. Spatial or directional metaphors are useful in monitoring and communicating progress. Often these metaphors are so embedded in our speech that we don't recognize them. Examples of directional and spatial metaphors include "We're back on track," "I've got it in hand," "I see the light at the end of the tunnel," and "We're getting there." System-oriented metaphors include describing a forest as interlocking parts and pieces, change as a force, and linking healthy forests with healthy economies.

Metaphors may come from a group, as when a third party notices that several group members refer to the same image repeatedly. "We have to step toward change," they may say, and later, "Let's sidestep that question." The third party wisely embeds the metaphor of steps in communicating, observing things like, "We've taken some big steps today toward addressing the issues." Parties will feel listened to and more comfortable with a third party who respectfully and appropriately adopts their metaphors. Neurolinguistic programming practitioners have studied this extensively.[15]

Sometimes no metaphor suggests itself. It may then work to suggest one, either explicitly or implicitly, and watch to see if the parties adopt it. If it is not adopted, try another. The more comfortable the fit for parties, the more effective the metaphor is likely to be. One way of unfolding a metaphor is to consider the parties' frames of reference, their professional contexts, their shared cultures. A group of chefs might respond well to a metaphor about taste and composition; a group of history professors are more likely to adopt an image related to legacy or artifacts.

Understand Worldview Differences and Assess Processes. As we have seen, there are several process-related uses for metaphors. Facilitators may check for false consensus by making sure that parties have the same general association with metaphors being used. They can ask parties to talk more about their chosen metaphors as a way of expanding understanding and inviting joint discussion of symbolic issues and their importance. In the Northern Forest Lands Council process I mentioned earlier, a group of scholars from George Mason University studied metaphors as a resource for understanding worldview differences and assessing process mutuality.[16]

The Northern Forest Lands Council process was intended to make consensus-based recommendations for forestry policy in four northeastern states. It involved a series of public listening sessions in each of the jurisdictions. Transcripts of these sessions were analyzed, and participants were asked about metaphors they had used. Researchers uncovered information about levels of consensus and understanding, as well as about the effectiveness of the process. One conclusion researchers drew was that there was very little consensus on what constitutes a "forest," leading to difficulties in using the information gathered to design forest policy. Another observation was that metaphors were shorthand for a wealth of information that remained untapped when not pursued.

One person said, "The greatest gift we can leave our kids and grandkids is the gift of undomesticated wilderness areas." What had he meant by "wilderness area"? In his view, would some forestry or recreational activity be appropriate? What did he mean by "undomesticated"? The researchers sought him out to ask. He answered that wilderness "really means roadless, no extraction; uses are all minimal uses that are designed to create a sense of untouchedness, as opposed to what many people think is wilderness." Policymakers did not have the benefit of this expanded answer. It is difficult to know how his comments were categorized and used. If inquiry into his metaphors had happened, process mutuality would have been enhanced.

Enhance Team Effectiveness. Participation and process mutuality are particularly critical when we work in intervention or teaching teams. In this situation, too, metaphors are useful. A key metaphor in this instance is "the lens." The lens metaphor is useful because it draws attention to the omnipresence of something we look through. No one is able to see things "just as they are" without interpretation and inference related to their cultural experiences, personal histories, and individual cognitive and emotional functioning. As we are aware of the constant existence of our lens, we can begin the exploration of how these factors color it, shape it, and determine both what we see and what we do not.

From this place, it is possible to move to an exploration of working relationships. Do our blind spots coincide? If they do, what are we likely to miss when we intervene in conflict? Do recurrent conflict patterns distort our lenses? Which kinds of issues are we most likely to miss, based on past traumas, deep experiences, or closely held assumptions? How do our styles complement, unsettle, or challenge us when we work together?

This exploration can be taken deeply or more simply. The conversation sets us up for shortcuts later as we check in after cofacilitated sessions. "Aren't you looking at this through rose-colored glasses?" or "How has your experience of being injured in an automobile accident affected the way you are seeing this claim?" are both questions that refer to lenses. Once imported as a reference, the metaphor allows us to answer without admitting weakness; our lenses are not good or bad; they simply exist. We can entertain the idea that we may need to check our prescription or that there is something clouding our lens without acknowledging pervasive fallibility. As we engage in productive dialogue with colleagues, we enhance process mutuality for everyone involved.

Using Metaphors to Bridge Worldviews

We have seen many ways that metaphors are powerful and useful in resolving conflicts. They enhance communication, relationship, and participation. They communicate emphasis and link the unfamiliar to the familiar to enhance understanding. Metaphors may even be useful in bridging worldviews by drawing explicit attention to the presence of fundamental meaning-making differences among parties. This use is the most subtle and demanding of all.

Metaphors for a Mountain Valley

Metaphors are laced through language so that identifying them is not just a matter of listening for particular images but asking about the gestalt or the whole image. This was the case in the facilitation of a multiparty process concerning the future of a magnificent mountain valley that was threatened by competing activities and development. Participants included representatives of local business, governments, scientists, recreation outfitters, guides, and conservation groups. A talented facilitator and good administrative support assisted them. Here was a well-designed opportunity for comprehensive planning rather than reactivity to disputes that had played out for many years over limits on development, permitted recreational activities, and wildlife management. Recreation outfitters talked directly with wildlife biologists about how humans affect wilderness; both communicated with government representatives responsible to write and enforce regulations. Everyone worked together to come up with agreements on issues of interest to the whole community and to those who came from around the world to visit the valley.

After eighteen months of regular meetings, the group reached consensus on several points. They announced their achievement with considerable pride at a press conference attended by the community. But a few months later, the participant who had represented conservation groups at the table felt unsettled. By all reports, he had participated effectively. He was articulate, respected, and passionate. He acknowledged that the process had indeed provided an important forum for surfacing and exploring issues and coming to common ground. At the same time, the metaphors that were at the heart of the conversation did not make his values or concerns seem welcome or legitimate in the ways that he would have liked.

What were these metaphors? The valley was talked about as a precious resource to be shared, preserved, and used. Sometimes the metaphors of farming or ranching were implied, as representatives spoke of managing, returning areas to wilderness, and protecting wildlife corridors. At other times, the metaphor of banking and trusts was invoked, as participants spoke of investing in the future of the valley, discharging a trust as stewards of capital that should not be spent but grown and protected. Some spoke about balancing the fulcrum, with preservation on one end and public use on the other.

As diverse as these metaphors are, they have some things in common. To some extent, they contemplate use and active management. Resources are to be exploited and preserved for future profit. Implicit in those metaphors is the assumption of human status, wisdom, and entitlement to regulate the natural ecosystem. Farms or ranches exist to produce products to market; they require careful attention and cultivation. If the product in this case is tourism, it has to be marketed just as soybeans or rice are sold on world markets. Banks and trusts manage investments, seek high yields, and divide balance sheets into various accounts and commodities. So the economic effects of decisions on local business and residents were important considerations at the table. Balancing the fulcrum conjures the image of attending to both communities of interest: preservation and public use, and finding an appropriate proportion of each.

The Values Implicit in Metaphor

The conservation representative did not see his values represented fully in any of these metaphors. He did not agree that use and management were the central concerns for the valley. Rather, he questioned the metaphors at the root of these ideas and the assumptions that flowed from them. If he had articulated this concern during the process, it would have been difficult to know how to address it. Addressing it would have meant a renegotiation of the process, of what was considered relevant, of how issues were discussed.

Picture this: It is the middle of a busy and pressured two-day meeting, and people at the table have their sleeves rolled up. They have flown in from many places with reams of documents and compilations of studies. They are wading through mountains of scientific data with the assistance of wildlife biologists, hydrologists, geologists, and engineers, trying to keep all of the various interests in mind as they grapple with questions of whether the local airstrip should remain open and how wildlife corridors should be maintained in the face of rapid development.

Where is space for the perspective of someone who sees the valley, not a resource or even a trust but as a sanctuary, a paradise, a sacred part of the body of Mother Earth? For him, how to use the valley appropriately is not the question; restoration, harmony, and nonintervention are the objectives. His questions relate to how these can be accomplished in ways that respect ecosystem integrity and the inherent wisdom of Mother Nature. There is no top-down or paternalistic relationship of the kind implied in farming or managing a trust; there is reparation, humility, and a spirit of inquiry about what Nature has to teach us about regeneration.

Certain conversations were legitimate at the table. These conversations could be identified by the metaphors that were laced through them. Others were not; they were either unheard or dismissed as not serious, not viable, too extreme. The conservationist experienced this firsthand but could not address it. His needs fell prey to the momentum toward consensus and results ("Better that we come to consensus recommendations than leave it to government to impose solutions") and to the generally accepted metaphors that set the climate and framed the discussions. From these metaphors came values of efficiency, economic viability, and closure. Because most people at the table accepted use and management as givens, solutions arose from these frames. His views were marginalized, often unspoken, and diluted.

Not many public policy processes take metaphors into account to guide process design. It is also true that some public policy processes eventually proceed without the input of a range of conservationists. Disillusioned, they may leave the process before it is over. Worse, representatives of other sectors maintain that they "are conservationists, too, just not extremists." Everyone claims to care about the environment. But not all views about the environment are equally welcome. It is difficult to find ways to incorporate and legitimate views coming from different ways of ordering and thinking about the world. It is uncomfortable, hence the pejorative adjectives often associated with environmental representatives—words like radical, unrealistic, idealistic.

Process Design Using Metaphor

How could the experience of this conservationist have been different? His problem could not be addressed by talking about the issues as they had been defined. It could not be addressed just by adding particular concerns he brought to the list of issues on the table. The problem did not occur at this level but rather at the level of process design. Because there was substantial agreement among people at the table about management and use flowing from metaphors of trusts, fulcrums, and agriculture, the worldview giving rise to different metaphors and therefore different issues and solutions did not emerge. If Mother Earth is to be cherished, not managed; if She is a teacher from whom we learn, not someone whose body we use, what are the implications for our relationship with the natural world? Are we willing to engage the questions of how unmarked metaphors, like agriculture and trusts in this example, are given power, while others are marginalized to the point of being unspoken?

What if the participants in this process had been engaged in a metaconversation? The facilitator could address not only the question of what we would talk about (issues) and how we would talk about them (process) but which values inform our process and how we could invite a divergence of views. Through paying attention to metaphors used in convening stages of processes, facilitators may be able to identify divergent metaphors as signposts indicating the presence of different worldviews. When there are different worldviews, those of the most powerful or dominant parties will shape the discussion unless the facilitator does something to change this predictable course. Like water, conversations flow into already established channels unless there is a shared intention to do something differently.

Several groups have explored using metaphors in conflict dialogue. Among them are Search for Common Ground, the Institute for Multitrack Diplomacy, and the Public Conversations Project.

Generally, metaphor dialogue includes

- Noticing, naming, and sharing metaphors
- Unpacking and exploring the implications and dimensions of the metaphors
- Comparing metaphors
- Generating inclusive metaphors

And based on this, metaphor further includes

- Designing a process that respects and invites participation from multiple frames of meaning

Such a process may yield wiser and more complete solutions to complex issues faced by communities of people. Acceptance of the approach requires more research and testing. But most important, the approach requires a willingness by those holding dominant views to share power. Power is shared when the powerful see that they can get more from working together in diverse groups through meaningful processes than they can by proceeding alone or in homogeneous groups. Parties with alternative metaphors enhance their power when they articulately address the needs and benefits of surfacing meanings and worldviews.

Whether dealing with complex multiparty conflicts or simple, repetitive disputes, third parties who make friends with metaphor offer more to their clients. By simply cultivating an awareness of metaphors used in their daily lives, they find themselves noticing and using that awareness in their training and their interventions. Aware of its possibilities and limitations, they are on the forefront of resourceful and responsive process design and imaginative, creative training.

CHAPTER SEVEN

Narrative Tools

Stories as Paths to Transformation

I'll tell you a story. Come close to the fireplace and listen. I'll tell you a story. As the cold night gathers outside, the story will cozy and change us at once.

What follows this opening? A universal act—an instinctive choice to weave words together, inviting listeners into a circle. It is an act both ordinary and powerful. The telling reveals meaning and makes meaning at once. It is an invitation to connection, mystery, and learning.

One of the most powerful stories I know is about a man whose love had disappointed him, leaving him despondent and alone. Not wanting to trouble his family, he determined that he would commit suicide in a distant city during a conference in a hotel. He just happened to choose the conference where I was presenting on intercultural conflict and signed up for my session. On the third and final day, I asked participants to choose someone with whom to share stories about conflicts in their lives. We had worked hard on developing skills of deep listening and empathy; here was an opportunity to apply them.

He looked around the room and his eyes met Kate's, not knowing that she too had experienced abandonment and despair after years of relationship. As he related his story, she listened to him in concentrated silence, not telling him of her experience until he was finished. He had made a decision to disconnect from the world and then experienced connection through telling his story. In the process of relating it, he came to see with new eyes—eyes that could see beyond the story as well as into it. Telling it to someone who resonated deeply with his words was so powerful that he reconsidered his decision, coming with tears in his eyes to tell me about it.

"Tell this to anyone you want to," he volunteered. "Perhaps this will help others realize how important it is to tell their stories before making irrevocable choices."

Some stories stop us in our tracks. Some intrigue us and yield new questions we had not thought to ask. Stories may comfort, coax, or kindle; they may incite, disturb, or rearrange. How we listen, hearing one another into speech, is at the center of a relational approach to conflict. The process of telling and receiving continues seamlessly until a circle is made, and circles within circles. Where and how our stories are told has a lot to do with how they are received.

In the far north, stories are told on long winter nights, passed from elder to daughter, from old ones to young ones through the telling. They are whispered above the raw Arctic wind, seeding themselves deep into children's hearts, passing on the legacies of wisdom, strength, and relationship that have long sustained life in one of the most remote regions of our planet.

I once read an account of an anthropologist who visited some Inuit, smuggling in a flashlight and a notepad so that she could write the stories down as they were told. Every time she switched the light on, the stories stopped. They were to be told only in the hush of darkness. They were stories for the heart, sacred in their telling, alive in the living words that conveyed them. They were to be received in the timeless moment, not captured for others or extracted onto a page. This reverence for stories informs our exploration of stories at the center of a relational approach to conflict.

Seed Stories

Many of us are fortunate to remember what I call seed stories. These are stories that contain the germs of our beginnings, told to us or overheard when we were small. As a child, I slept under quilts sewn by hand by my grandmother and her women friends. These gentle, gray-haired women with weathered faces created quilts in a day or two, crowded around quilt frames that filled their living rooms. As they worked, they told stories, sewing memories into the quilts in the form of fabric fragments from outgrown dresses, blouses, and discarded ties. Now, long after my grandmother's death, the quilts evoke childhood summer days and the texture of the reedy leaves in which we captured ants and beetles many years ago.

I played under those quilt frames and listened to the stories, never dreaming that I was hearing myself into being—that through these stories I was being taught who I was, where I came from, and what mattered. I wonder now whether the women were aware of me under there, building tottering castles out of wooden spools. Did they choose their stories to teach me, or were they simply using them to come closer to each other, to smooth out edges among them, to secure loose ends and communicate understanding in ways both lyrical and ordinary? Much of what they said has left my memory; instead, I remember their warmth, their humor, and their determination. These were homesteading women, veterans of hard lives, doing what women and men close to the land have always done, working well and sharing stories.

Stories connect us to other times, helping us to make sense and meaning of our lives. They carry hope, values, choices, and reasons. Stories give our lives place, identity, and context; they communicate this to others. They connect us in relationship through content, feeling, and meaning. Often the feeling and meaning linger long after the content has faded from our memories. They help us build relationship, and they also trace the contours of the ruptures and crevices that divide us from others. Stories are always present, both in conflict and in harmony. They can be barriers to resolution. They can be resources for change. It all depends on how we construct, tell, and receive them.

This chapter is about the importance of stories, about ways they can be woven and rewoven to enhance relationship, giving us space to reinvent ourselves, poking new openings in the fabric of our lives. Though we may resist these openings, stories are the way that light gets in, especially in conflict. Stories remind us that addressing conflict is at heart an art, drawing on our capacities to create, shape, interpret, and reinterpret our experiences. As we develop our artistry, we find that we are engaged, like the quilters, in working well and sharing stories.

Patterns in Stories

When a quilt is made, it is first blocked. Blocking is the process of assembling fabric scraps into a pattern and attaching them before sewing them to the filling and the backing. This gives order and coherence to the otherwise disparate colors, shapes, and textures of the fabric remnants. In this chapter, diverse stories act as the blocking for our explorations. With these stories in our midst, we uncover collected wisdom, surprising perspectives, and novel juxtapositions. We create a quilt that contributes to our processes like eiderdown, both light and substantial.

You may be reading this chapter in hopes of finding ways that stories can enhance your practice. Your questions may center around what you need to know about stories, when to use them, and how. We will unfold answers, but I ask for your patience. For conflict was not just invented. It has been with us always. Though we are not historians, we seek what can be learned from the past. Though we are not mythologists, we seek to invite old stories into this mix to see what might be added to all that we assemble. These stories show us aspects of ourselves in conflict and ourselves as leaders that will inform our practice. They remind us that there is both simplicity and complexity in any subject worth examining. And stories are the vessels for our most precious subjects.

The Power of Stories

We begin with a story of lethal conflict—the story of Scheherazade. Scheherazade is a young woman living in a kingdom ruled by King Shahrayar. Both he and his brother are deeply upset by the infidelity of their wives. So outraged is the king that he wants revenge beyond killing his wife and her lover. King Shahrayar decides to take a new young bride each night into his bed and have her killed the following morning. In this way, he plans to rid his kingdom of the "menace" of potentially unfaithful wives.

After a few nights and lost lives, the daughter of the man commissioned to escort these women and later kill them requests to be the next wife. Her name is Scheherazade. With the aid of her sister, Scheherazade tells an endless stream of stories. She becomes a master of control, breath, gesture, facial expression, hand and body movements, telling stories each night up to a certain point, then stopping. The king does not kill her because he wants to hear the end of her stories.

This is a potent illustration of the power of stories. They are an opening into whole worlds. They are keys to a locked garden—one we do not want to leave until we have explored its corners, its surprises. The characters call us into their realities; the narratives keep us moving in time, shifting us in unforeseen directions. The mood and tone play on our sensibilities, and details snare us further from who and where we are. Stories attract us through and away from our own reality, if only to give the reality back to us with new perspectives.

Generally, we tell stories that are cohesive, providing description and explanation as a way to make meaning of events. When the stories we tell involve ourselves, we tell them in a way that justifies, explains, and presents our behavior in a positive light. In conflict, parties are even more likely to do this as a defense to anticipated opposition. Because individuals perceive and process information and experiences differently, it is possible to hear two completely different stories about the same events. And because each story is threatening to the other, there is little openness to receive the other's story.

As third parties, one of our jobs is to help create openness to alternative stories, both those related by individual parties and those re-created by the parties together. In their book *Narrative Mediation*, John Winslade and Gerald Monk[1] suggest that openness is encouraged when we see stories as dynamic, cultural products rather than representations of reality. This perspective reminds us that we are all engaged in actively constructing our realities minute-to-minute, immersed always in the medium of culture. These realities reflect different ways of knowing and being, different habits of attention, different core concerns and values.

Seen this way, stories become windows into our ways of situating ourselves in our worlds rather than vehicles for triumph in a contest over competing realities. Our attention is drawn away from constructing logical, tight, right explanations and into the choice-points along the way. Third parties function as guides for this journey, noticing where we are fused with our stories—where we have become so attached that we have assigned "reality" to them in such a way that we cannot see another way. They help us find the spaciousness and the gracefulness available when we step away from seeing our stories as the only truth to seeing our stories as containers for meaning that may have to be adjusted as multiple meanings come together.

From this perspective, the third-party role is challenging. We need only remember Scheherazade to know that putting ourselves in the midst of parties' stories has its hazards. The role of the third party in conflict is not for the faint of heart. It is for those who bring courage, an awareness of the power of stories, and a facility for working with and through them.

Scheherazade also illustrates that stories are more than entertainment and more than truth. Graceful, they intercede where direct pleas would fail. Powerful, they intervene to prevent loss, destruction, and violence at the same time that they restore faith and transform values. After all, when the thousand and one nights of storytelling have passed, King Shahrayar does not slay Scheherazade. Nor will he put her or any other concubine or wife to death in the future. Shahrayar comes to realize through the stories that the female gender is not genetically tainted, as he had believed, but that women, like men, are individuals and can be admirable. The king comes to see women as other than sexual objects and appreciates the subtle intellect of women, their artistry, their capacity to love and be loving.

Scheherazade used stories to build relationship, which is our central task in resolving conflict. How can the rich potential of stories to engage relationship be tapped by trainers and third parties? Of the many possibilities, I suggest five. Stories can

- Engage our attention, bringing us into connection with each other and ideas
- Stimulate empathy through engaging our humanity
- Provide contextual information that helps us make sense of another's experience and ways of making meaning
- Convey messages indirectly, maintaining and creating harmony
- Engage us in deep listening

As we become aware of the possibilities offered by stories, we become more adept as third parties and trainers at working with stories to find the openings for change and transformation.

Engaging Attention

Stories have the power to engage our attention, to keep us present. Remember when you attended lectures at university or college. Did you sit with rapt attention, or did your mind sometimes wander? I tuned back in when there were stories. Stories quicken our interest; they help us feel connected to the speaker and to the ideas the story contains. In stories, we find places of relatedness and feel stimulated to act. Journalists, teachers, lawyers, mediators, preachers, and parents all instinctively know that while a picture paints a thousand words, stories are word pictures that lodge themselves just as powerfully in our hearts and minds.

It is with an awareness of the power of stories that we use role playing so frequently in our training. Practicing skills with the context provided by stories gets our attention, making it more likely that we will integrate those skills into our repertoires. In the 1980s, I trained many groups of lawyers who were curious or ambitious or wildly enthusiastic about adding mediation to their repertoires. Most were more curious than committed, intrigued by this new approach and its possibilities for business development. We taught interest negotiation through stories, including anecdotes, demonstrations, and role-play simulations. The lawyers had all been well trained in an adversarial mind-frame, so an approach to negotiation and conflict resolution based in interests and exploration was a different and challenging idea.

For every group, we would anxiously ask each other after the first day, "Are they getting it?" We searched their faces and their body language for indications of how the stories they enacted in the role plays touched them. Were they skeptical? Frustrated? Resistant? Or were they beginning to see that the story they had been told implicitly in law school—that all conflict is a contest and the best lawyers win the most—was just that: a story. Were they beginning to see that there was another story, one that might help preserve and even improve relationship, one that might be educational, empowering, even transforming?

We knew that they would not get it if we simply stood before them and told them it was a good idea. As they engaged in a negotiation about whether Styrofoam or china cups were more ecologically appropriate, they began to see how their habitual, competitive approaches tended to narrow and limit discussion.

Grappling with more complex fact patterns over the course of the training, they came to see choice points they had not seen previously. Putting themselves in the place of stressed small-business owners and disgruntled consumers, they experienced ways of constructing new stories of satisfaction and relationship in place of familiar frustration.

The power of the stories to engage emotions lent the simulations impact. Stories helped participants try on and integrate collaborative approaches into their repertoires. As long-accepted mental frames about conflict were disturbed, doors to new avenues of practice were opened for the participants. When participants worked with stories of their own, authenticity and cultural dimensions contributed to deeper learning.

Because stories themselves are not controversial, they are useful in initiating and framing dialogue and conversation. My story is simply an account of my experiences. You may disagree with the interpretations I have made of these experiences or with the actions I have pursued arising from them. Yet in an atmosphere of dialogue and inquiry, my story takes its place in the room, as can yours. As they are shared, our stories become more than parallel pillars; they touch us at sensory and emotional levels. This makes empathy possible.

Stimulating Empathy

Stories build connection through their capacity to generate or increase empathy. They communicate not only our human doings but our human beings. Stories take us out of ourselves, into that place where we can touch even those we would never have thought of touching. Pumla Gobodo-Madikizela, a black woman member of the Truth and Reconciliation Commission in South Africa, tells the story of Eugene de Kock, the head of a covert operations program targeted at those who opposed apartheid. His submission for amnesty detailing his political violence was the longest the commission received, numbering over a thousand pages.

During his testimony before the commission, Mr. de Kock recounted the story of the killing of three men, whose widows were in the audience. Meeting the widows privately, he apologized and received their assurance of forgiveness. Ms. Gobodo-Madikizela later visited him in prison to interview him about his experiences and his feelings. He cried as he talked about the pain he had inflicted. "If only they could see my heart," he mourned. Seeing his face contorted with pain and his hand trembling, his arms reaching out as if to carry the body of a husband back to one of the widows, Ms. Gobodo-Madikizela did something that surprised her. Her hand reached up and touched the right hand of this man who had been responsible for so much terror, injustice, and oppression of black South Africans. It was an unpremeditated expression of empathy.

The experience left her shaken; she kept coming back to it in her mind and reflecting on its meaning. A short while later, she saw Mr. de Kock again as he testified further in front of the commission. He asked to meet with her outside the formal session. She went to him in the upstairs tearoom where he waited with his guards. Addressing her, he said, "You know, Pumla, that was my trigger hand you touched."

This observation led Ms. Gobodo-Madikizela to reflect more deeply on the experience. She wondered about the pleasure he got out of her acknowledgment, about ways her empathy had been a betrayal of all those whose deaths had paid for the struggle. His painful story had evoked her humanness, and her hand had responded. Later came thoughts, questions, a flood of conflicting feelings. In the moment they touched, her heart acknowledged his humanity, despite the blood of others on his hands.

Empathy, like conflict resolution, is essentially relational. It is not a one-way decision by a listener to feel with a speaker. It is a transactional, dynamic event in which both parties feel closer and more in tune with each other. Pumla Gobodo-Madikizela's experience poses questions about the degree of "meeting" that took place, about whether Mr. de Kock's capacity for empathy had been impaired by his violent behavior over many years. Was he incredulous in his observation about her touching his trigger hand? Was he curious, gloating?

Robert Hare,[2] a world-renowned expert on criminal behavior and psychopathology, suggests that one of the most disturbing features of psychopaths is that they have a generalized inability to experience empathy. Was Mr. de Kock capable of empathy with the widows he had deprived of husbands or with Ms. Gobodo-Madikizela—a member of a group he had oppressed and hurt? Does empathy exist on a continuum? Can we practice it in degrees? Is there a point at which our actions so mire us in the need to split off from ourselves that we cannot return to a genuine experience of empathy because the dissonance would dissemble us?

Ms. Gobodo-Madikizela's story is powerful because of its complexity. It helps us understand why the literature about empathy is full of contradictions and alternative conceptualizations. Simply put, empathy is the capacity to think, imagine, and feel with another. It takes us out of our intellectual habits into other ways of knowing, discerning, and communicating connection. There is no recipe for how empathy is communicated; it draws more on intuition and feeling than any specific verbal or nonverbal behavior. Given that it is essentially relational, arising from a back-and-forth exchange in which words are only one part, it relies on a particular quality of listening that we will address in a short while.

Benjamin Broome[3] tells us that relational empathy is a way to build a third culture—one that encompasses the cultures of those at the table and gives them a new identity arising from their shared experiences. The Common Ground dialogues on abortion discussed in Chapter Eight work well for exactly this reason. There, groups of pro-life and pro-choice participants come together and begin by sharing their personal stories of how they came to their views. These stories often contain personal struggles and losses. Whether or not the listener agrees with the conclusions drawn by the teller, it is hard not to relate to the human feelings, experiences, and deep conviction contained in the stories. As empathy develops, commonalities are much easier to see. One Common Ground participant reflected, "We [on both sides of the abortion issue] are not apathetic. Those are the people I really worry about, the ones sitting on the sofa watching soaps and drinking Cokes." Through sharing personal stories, participants in this process came to adopt a new story for themselves—a story of connection rather than enmity, leading to collaboration on a number of community initiatives.

In conflict, our processes usually involve telling opposing stories. When we begin mediation with a time for each side to tell their perspective, we hear stories of justifications and rationalizations that situate the speaker positively, usually at the expense of the other party. Some mediators, troubled by the challenge faced by the second speaker whose space has been tainted by the first, listen to stories individually and then report a joint story to the parties at their first meeting. Most often, parties tell their stories in each other's presence, with the mediator listening for points of agreement and issues of contention.

Whichever approach is used, third parties encourage movement away from the contentious parts of stories in favor of connections and commonalities. This movement is facilitated by empathy. I remember a commercial mediation I conducted in which both the plaintiff and the insurance adjuster were obese. The issues of the degree of injury and liability were unsettled. As the plaintiff described his difficulty in completing everyday, routine tasks like picking up something from the floor, I could see the adjuster responding. She could relate to the difficulty from her own experience, though she had not suffered the same injuries. Although this did not lead the adjuster to assume 100 percent of the liability or acknowledge the full extent of the plaintiff's injuries, her ability to relate to the challenges he faced lent genuine civility to the conversation. This acknowledgment was pivotal in the plaintiff's accepting a settlement that reflected the weak links in his case yet compensated him for his pain and suffering. When the case was over, I reflected on how differently it might have gone if the adjuster had been unable to relate to the situation in which the plaintiff found himself. Empathy for his story was the lubricant that made the mechanics work.

Empathy arises when listening happens at levels beyond words, beyond cognition or rationality. It happens when we respond in physical, felt ways to stories. As in the stories just noted, empathy is neither planned nor contrived; it arises from an openness to listening. Some draw on their understanding of Spirit, or Source, for the capacity to empathize and the confirmation that it is desirable. Whether empathy arises from a spiritual or secular orientation, it is an acknowledgment of shared humanity, of connection. We will explore the conditions in which empathy takes place further in our section on deep listening.

Clarifying Context

The third way stories build connection is through providing contextual information. Even when we cannot empathize or feel with a speaker, we may feel less strong in our opposition when their view is contained in a story rather than a position or a demand. Of course, this is partly a matter of style and culture. Some cultures prefer a circular, narrative way of speaking to a direct, linear approach. Research suggests that women in the dominant culture in North America tend more toward telling stories by beginning in the middle, circling back to the beginning, and coming to the end. Men are more likely to tell stories in linear, sequential forms. The work of Sara Cobb and Janet Rifkin[4] suggests that mediation may favor men's stories for their appearance of straightforwardness and organization.

However a story is told, it carries more than facts; it conveys what is around the events and the people—what informs them, inspires them, moves them, explains them. Stories give us clues to all of these. Consider this. A woman is caught shoplifting in a local department store. She is sixty-something, her hair and clothes suggest inattention, and she has enough money in her purse to pay for the few things she has stolen. When asked why she did it, she offers no explanation, no story. Faced with little contextual information, we may try to imagine what motivated her. We can only make guesses that will probably be wrong, and so we shake our heads at the apparent irrationality of her behavior.

If she were willing and able to tell it, her story is one of despair and loneliness. Her husband of forty-seven years died weeks before, leaving her by herself for the first time since the 1950s. Her best friend just had a heart attack. Her memory is failing, exacerbating her lifelong sense of inadequacy and insecurity, reinforced by familial favoritism visited on a pretty younger sister. All of this is her context. It does not excuse her or necessarily evoke empathy, but it does help listeners imagine her in context. Seen in the light of these stories, the shoplifting behavior takes on a fuller meaning. The story invites us to draw on our emotional fluency to understand the woman in context. It may also suggest some ways to address underlying issues. Perhaps a way can be found for her to contribute as a volunteer in the community, countering isolation while saving face.

Stories provide context that lends legitimacy to parties in conflict. When people feel legitimized, they participate. This is not to suggest that the third party or trainer should bestow approval on everyone's story but that it is useful to find ways to frame the story that legitimate the speaker. To make legitimate is to provide context that gives a peek into the teller's way of seeing and being. It is not to judge, whether negatively or positively, but to situate in a way that invites others to see the teller in a context that makes the connection between the teller's way of making sense of the world and the teller's behavior.

How do we invest stories with legitimacy? Some of the tools to do this include positive connotation, empathy, and making intentional choices about the order and process of storytelling. Sometimes we need these tools most at moments when we least expect it.

Recently, I began a course on conflict and culture with a discussion of how we would proceed as a class. I was a guest instructor in the program, and many members of the class had studied together in other classes earlier in the year. Frequently, a discussion like this is a relatively noncontroversial exercise, with people making requests of each other relating to showing respect, refraining from side conversations, and maintaining confidentiality.

On this occasion, one speaker requested that everyone agree to stay present and stay engaged with each other, even in very difficult or "hot" moments. Her request was met by an angry interruption by another participant, who felt affronted and singled out. It turned out that the person who interrupted had left following an emotional discussion in a previous class. She interpreted the speaker's request as a thinly veiled reference to her earlier behavior and reacted out of frustration.

There was a range of choices open to the woman who felt singled-out when the suggestion to stay present was made. She could ignore it, dismiss it, or counter it in some way. Because the story implied in the request included her decision to leave after a hot exchange in an earlier class, she felt delegitimized and judged. For her part, the speaker making the request insisted that she did not mean to make a veiled reference to the past but to make a positive, future-focused suggestion.

Class members shifted uncomfortably in their chairs. One class member later wrote, "When things got difficult so quickly, I feared we were in for a rough ride. What was going on for these people that this issue was so incendiary?" Part of what was going on was the need for each of them to feel legitimate in the class setting.

The embedded story put the second speaker into a defensive mode, communicating a challenge to the legitimacy of her earlier decision to leave. She received this as a challenge to her legitimacy as a class member.

As facilitator, I was concerned that everyone have a place of legitimacy in the classroom. I used positive connotation to situate each person's perspective in the context of our collective desire for respect and effectiveness, emphasizing that each of them intended to contribute to the development of a constructive and authentic climate. We agreed that everyone would make an effort to stay present, while also attending to their individual limits and leaving when they felt they needed to.

Later, I spoke individually with each woman and heard more of the context from which the exchange arose. I felt empathy with each of them as I heard their stories and saw more clearly their very different ways of seeing what had happened and their roles in it. The first woman wanted to negotiate boundaries that accommodated her comfort with confrontation and conflict, as well as her desire to "walk our talk"; the second woman was concerned with psychological safety and respect for individual ways of coping. Each was in a very different life situation that reinforced confidence in the first woman and vulnerability in the other. Each was triggered by the other, and their interactions were characterized by tension and stiffness.

By the end of the week, the women disappeared from the group to have lunch together, returning to ask whether they could write the class paper jointly. They had found a way to listen to each other's story with empathy and caring. They came to this openness through the pain of conflict, conversations with trusted others, and a desire to put the principles of conflict resolution into practice. The credit for this breakthrough belongs to them; it was they who finally chose to craft a shared story. One of the things that helped along the way was the opportunity to talk in the class about issues we were studying, using a process derived from the Samoan Circle.

In this process, a question is posed and four chairs are positioned at the front of the room. Everyone in the class sits in a horseshoe around the chairs. Whoever wishes to respond to the question or participate in dialogue must take one of the seats at the front of the room. When all of the chairs are occupied, a new member may join the dialogue by standing behind the chair of one of the speakers, signifying a desire to participate. The speaker then finishes what he or she is saying and yields the chair.

This process slows communication down and helps people out of unproductive dyadic patterns they may get into by cycling others into the storytelling. It keeps things moving; it invites listening in a way different from the listening common to large group discussions. Attention is more directed to the speaker and the essence of what the person is saying than to an intended response, since the number of responses is limited by the number of chairs. Emotions are diffused because the communication is not primarily dyadic but is witnessed by the whole group. This sense of group responsibility and engagement and the silence that sometimes surrounds transitions in speakers decreases confrontations and personalization. As these two women found themselves participating in the circle dialogue about gender issues, their words were spoken side-by-side instead of at or toward each other. Somehow their words were able to coexist there in a way that created an opening for face-to-face dialogue later on.

Reflecting later on this difficult experience, I realized that I had used positive connotation, empathy, and process structuring to help legitimize the stories of each woman and other class members as well. As is often the case, stories that carry significant struggle seem to hold the richest learning. There is more openness to learning and also attention to the need to save face. Saving face is another potential that stories offer us as trainers and third parties in conflict.

Saving Face and Maintaining Harmony

Stories build connection by conveying messages indirectly, saving face, and preserving harmony. They are graceful and spacious, allowing your reality and mine to coexist in ambiguities or unspoken parts of stories. As Scheherazade shows us, stories can rescue both the creator-teller of the story and her audience from disaster. After all, Scheherazade knew that no direct appeal would work. She could not beg, plead, or bargain without evoking the king's rage and determination to effect his terrible solution. Only an indirect approach would work. Her stories worked to bring an end to a terrible, ongoing conflict without ever naming it.

Conflict intervenors know the importance of indirectness. If a conflict could be solved through straightforward naming, blaming, and restraining, it would not require intervention. Conflicts trap us in corners, constrained by the need to save face and maintain a positive image of ourselves and our motivations. We may be willing to contribute to a solution, but only incrementally in proportion to what is being given by the other side. Stories, like the metaphors they contain, help us advance by providing frameworks that acknowledge contributions without quantifying and comparing. They are flexible enough to accommodate positive self-image and acknowledgment of injury, to contain both continuity and change.

A moving example of the use of story to negotiate identity and change while maintaining harmony is told by Vamik Volkan[5] in his book *Bloodlines*. He relates his visit with Farouk, a young Palestin ian refugee living in Tunisia, whose parents, sister, and cousin were killed in front of him when we was five years old. Farouk was known in the camp as a leader for the other youth, someone whose resilience inspired. As they were speaking, Professor Volkan noticed that Farouk frequently rubbed a big scar on his right foot, the result of a cooking accident when he was a young child. His parents had put ointment on it to try to soothe his pain. Asked about the scar and his habit of rubbing it, Farouk said, "I almost feel my parents from within, inside my foot, inside my body." He had found a way for the scar to tell the story of connection and caring that sustained him as a leader for the other children where he lived, forming the root of his positive identity.

In cultures where indirect communication is the norm, stories are the lubricant that keeps relationships supple. Rupert Ross[6] tells of his experience of asking for advice in First Nations communities in the Canadian north. Inevitably, he would meet with non-committal responses to his questions about whether he should do a particular thing. "You could," he would be told, to his building frustration, as he noticed that this response was forthcoming no matter which option he posed. Over time, Ross came to see that views and opinions would be shared by those whose input he sought—but not directly. He learned to think out loud about subjects he sought advice about, posing alternatives but not asking direct questions. In response, his First Nations friends would share long stories involving other people, times, and places. Within the stories, certain facts or ideas were emphasized, pointing to a particular conclusion or view. Ross learned to listen differently and so received the guidance he sought but had been unable to elicit directly.

Stories come in many forms, and sometimes a novel form is surprising and energizing to a group that has worked together with patterned habits of communication. Process designer Craig Darling tells how a story in the form of rap music acted as lubricant when a process was stuck. In this instance, participants in a large-scale public process had worked over several months to come to consensus about complex issues related to land use planning on the west coast of Canada. The parties felt frustration and discouragement as they came to the difficult issues and choices that confronted them in the final stages of their work. There had been acrimonious exchanges, and it seemed possible that the process would break down. The group took a break.

One of the sectors represented at the table was youth. After a break, the youth asked for an opportunity to present something to the group. They situated themselves in the center of the circle and did a lively rap dance with lyrics addressing the contentious issues and points of view. It was a stress reliever, an icebreaker, and an injection of humor into a day that felt heavy. Participants relaxed. The rap "story" was the catalyst that broke the logjam, and they were able to move forward to resolve the contentious issues dividing them.

The stories we tell and the ways we tell them give us room to maneuver and see new perspectives about ourselves and issues. Stories told to Rupert Ross in northern Canada gave him input while according him respect for his autonomy in decision making. The story Farouk told himself allowed him to bring the love of his family into his present, even though they were gone. The story in the rap song invited everyone into the upper gallery, showing them the corners they had gotten themselves into as can only be seen from above. Stories depend for their power on the audience; they are not a one-way exchange. So we focus for a moment on the ubiquitous, yet rich and too-often neglected theme of listening.

Engaging Us in Deep Listening

From Steven Covey's hugely successful book *Seven Habits of Highly Effective People*[7] comes the wisdom: "Seek first to understand, then to be understood." Stories invite us to listen with our minds and our hearts. They touch our bodies with felt experience and sensations; they engage our imaginations. They require of us availability, concentration, and openness. Yet we often listen partially, our attention focused on something else at the same time, whether our reply to the speaker, our dinner date on Friday, or our irritating hangnail.

What is it to listen deeply? Consider this story from Japan related by David Augsberger in his book *Conflict Mediation Across Cultures*.[8] A Japanese husband comes home to find that the flower arrangement in the entryway is disorderly. Because his wife always arranges the flowers, he realizes that something has upset her. During the evening, he learns that she had a conversation with his mother. Because she could not speak negatively about his mother to him, she telegraphed her discomfort about the interaction through the arrangement of the flowers. Knowing this, he treats her with particular kindness and sensitivity.

The husband in this story is listening with his eyes and his powers of observation; he is listening to what is said and to what is not said. We need all of our senses to listen well, and we also need our capacities for concentration and empathy. As I described in Chapter Three, one of the ways I teach listening and empathy is to ask participants to sit back-to-back. One person then tells a short story to the other about something that happened in her or his life. The other listens and is given the task of communicating empathy. Then the process is reversed and the listener becomes the storyteller. Although it seems paradoxical to teach listening and empathy by removing most nonverbal cues about caring and attention, participants report that it helps them become aware of what they do by habit that may not help.

Listening back-to-back, we notice how our minds are concentrated on getting every word, in contrast to the way our attention may wander during "normal" face-to-face listening. We notice that our gestures of encouragement and response, like head nodding, may be reflexive rather than thoughtful and intentional. They may even be distracting to the speaker in ways outside our conscious awareness. We may also notice how we try to compensate for our lack of eye contact. Many people in this exercise lean into each other, using touching backs as a way to communicate connection. Our whole bodies are an important part of listening, not just our ears.

The other learning that comes out of this experience is reported by many of the storytellers. When we are assured that another is giving us the gift of undivided attention and when a dedicated space is created for whatever we have to say, there may be more freedom to plumb our own thoughts and convey them to another. Gone are some of the distractions of engagement: the fleeting feelings, thoughts, and responses on the face of the listener, the dirty smudge on her eyeglasses, the sense of impatience or distraction that seemed momentarily part of her gaze. In its place, there is space and intentional availability. How often do we give each other this gift? In my experience, it is more rare than we might believe.

Warren Ziegler talks about listening in a way that speaks to me in his book *Ways of Enspiriting*.[9] He says that the first step in truly listening is silence, not just refraining from speaking but "being silence." Being silence is not an action or inaction; it is a state that engages our bodies, minds, feelings, and spirits. When we are being silence, we are concentrating, still and calm. Our thoughts are silent. Our attention is in the present. Some people use meditation or centering as ways to be silence. Others use attention to breathing. Being silence becomes easier through practice. Listening back-to-back is one way of cultivating the state of being silence.

Ziegler suggests that giving attention goes hand-in-hand with being silence. Deep listening, he says, is a gift of the spirit. It is to give attention to the other so that "nothing else exists in the universe but this unique, singular focus of attention in being silence."[10] From this place, empathy is possible. It is empathy that lets us feel with others, even when they have not articulated their feelings. When we are willing to enter a space of listening without reserve or distraction to another, we will hear, know, and sense things both spoken and unspoken. There are many stories of people listening to each other and discerning feelings, even events that have not been explicitly named. We don't know how this happens, but we know that it does happen. It is as though the stories that are shared are doorways into many other stories, contained within each other like the layers of an onion. Once we enter that world with another, we can move among the layers and come to know the other much more deeply. This can lead to many things. One of them is change.

Changing Stories

Conflicts are not transformed when stories remain the same. Transforming conflict means that there is some shift—a shift of perspective or attitude, a shift in relationship, a change in stories. As third parties, we listen to parties with an ear for how they maintain identity, security, belonging, and positive self-image. This helps us think of ways to support and strengthen these aspects. Parties will change their stories when they are ready; before then, all of the urging or suggesting in the world will only make them cling to the stories with more resolve. We can, however, remind parties that stories are composed and not immutable. It is possible to tell different stories about the same events and relationships. In fact, we all do it. Have you ever told exactly the same story twice?

Although it may be difficult to tell the same story, given changes in feelings, mood, and thoughts and in shifting interaction dynamics, parties in conflict may get stuck in a rut. John Haynes[11] writes of a divorce mediation in which a woman whose husband had left her would not agree to his seeing their children in the presence of his girlfriend. Although Haynes proposed many different "stories" for how they could see the situation, they remained entrenched. He then moved to the metaphor of a downward spiral. Haynes suggested that the stories they were playing out would leave them with "a sackful of gorgeous grievances next Christmas," nothing more. Alternatively, he continued, painting a productive story featuring respect and constructive communication would protect the children they would be actively parenting for the next fifteen years. Hearing these contrasting stories proved a turning point for the parties, who started working more productively together. We will explore more ways metaphors give power to stories in the next chapter.

Finding Stories Big Enough

Let's play with the idea of story construction for a minute. Think of a time in your life when you had difficult things to deal with. Perhaps it was a time of transition or decision; perhaps there was loss or change. Take a minute and write down the events on a time-line, and then record the feelings associated with these events underneath. Now ask yourself what you know now that might have changed the way you experienced that time:

- Are there resources you have now that you did not have then?
- Are you more aware of your tendencies under stress so that you have more choices than in the past?
- Do you know ways to shift perspective now that you did not know then?
- How would you advise yourself in this story from all that you know now?
- As you allow new ways of seeing the story to arise, how do the feelings you recorded change?

When we start with ourselves, becoming aware of our own stories, we can become clearer vessels for helping others. When we neglect attending to our stories and how they play out internally, they may find a way to get our attention. Equally problematic, they may play themselves out in our interventions with others. My story, whether of abandonment or empowerment, frustrated ambition or success, will affect what I see, hear, miss, and interpret. It can operate in ways both helpful and hurtful, as my story affects my capacities to empathize and behave impartially. Empathy may come naturally when my story resonates with one of the parties' stories; it may be lessened when my experience and interpretations are at odds with one of the parties' stories. When an empathic chord is struck within us, whether harmonic or discordant, our impartiality may be harder to maintain. Through the lenses of my stories, I bring passion, determination, and concern to issues differently. When I am aware of this, I am better able to monitor my blind spots—ways I may be limited and times I should withdraw.

Sometimes our individual stories impede us, and we come face-to-face with dilemmas that are difficult to resolve. Then we can only get out by going through, by asking ourselves how we can compose a big enough story to contain paradox or contrasting parts of ourselves.

In Sue Bender's lyrical book *Everyday Sacred*, she tells how she was about to go on a book tour and was horrified to find her mouth "erupted in a moonscape of bumps like alligator's skin, that hurt every time [her] tongue touched [her] teeth."[12] She was anxious about how she would be able to speak, given the constant pain. In desperation, she went to a hypnotist. There she told the story of a battle inside herself between gentle, stoic Amish values and a striving, competitive New Yorker. The hypnotist listened deeply, then observed that she had the soul of the Amish and the blood of a New Yorker. Sue writes, "What she said had such a ring of truth to it that I stopped in the middle of my sad story and laughed. Her words changed something that had been unacceptable into something that could be tolerated. The 'blood of the New Yorker' which I had been rejecting was also a source of strength, allowing me to persist in the face of problems that in the past would have discouraged me enough to turn away from the project."[13]

Our job as third parties is to find stories big enough to contain the feelings, experiences, roles, and contradictions within and between parties. Sometimes this is as simple as finding a positive frame in which to put things. In Sue Bender's case, the story she told of a war within herself was transformed to one of balance, complementarity, and strength. This new story showed her that it was possible to accept both parts of herself for the gifts they offered. Conflict transformation shares this goal with therapy: we offer people new stories or ways to recreate old ones. Therapy focuses on the personal journey. Our aim in bridging conflict is relational—to create a container in which stories can be told that support and nurture positive and effective relationships. In thinking about this, we can learn from those who have had trauma or ruptured relationships in their early years.

Research suggests that orphans and others with traumatic childhoods are sometimes able to grow into even stronger leaders and helpers than those without such experiences. This is because they may develop a strong sense of inner self-sufficiency and find ways of drawing resources to themselves, including "adopted" family members. They also compose rituals to share with others—a topic we will explore in Chapter Eight. At some point, they move from telling themselves the story of victimization to seeing themselves as resilient. Choosing resiliency is a wonderful opportunity we can offer our clients, moving away from blame and pain to appreciation and resolve. We may not be able to offer all the scaffolding needed to achieve this transition. It may happen in a moment or it may take years. Therapists, friends, and unexpected events may all play roles. But we can suggest the possibility. One way we can do that is through telling and receiving stories, our own and those of others.

Stories as Resources in Conflict

Stories are rich with the potential to engage and to foster relationship, as we have seen. Thoughtful third parties will not use stories indiscriminately but will attend to timing, ripeness, and purposes of story sharing. When and how do we use stories?

When and How to Tell Stories

In our enthusiasm for stories, we may sometimes rush or pressure their telling. Some stories should not be shared because they are too fresh or painful; others need soft landings. While many mediation approaches derive the agenda or issues from parties telling "their stories," experienced mediators know that stories are tied to identity, values, self-image, and face. They may be revealed in bits and pieces over time, in private sessions, or not at all. Because they may be so much a part of us in our vulnerability or fragility in the face of conflict, it is important not to do too much to challenge stories, especially initially. Notice that Sue Bender's hypnotist took her story and found a way to make it palatable rather than suggest a variation or an alternative. This is the art of working with stories—to communicate respect first and choices second. One way to apply this in our training and intervention is to involve participants in sharing and constructing stories.

In a conflict resolution training session for interculturalists, I asked the participants to form groups of four and draw a story of conflict from their lives that related to the issue of power. I promised they would not have to reveal the substantive details of their conflict stories. My purpose was to get them to notice the patterns and thought-frames revealed by their drawings as these related to power and later to talk about these with fellow group members. In one group, a woman drew some stick figures that had meaning only to her but would not engage in the discussion. The conflict was too fresh for her and too painful. She could not separate herself from it to work with it. So, too, we have to ask ourselves as third parties when storytelling is cathartic, when it may be damaging or re-injuring to the teller or the listener, and when it is constructive.

The bias in dominant-culture approaches to conflict is frequently in the direction of disclosure. We want everything out on the table so that decisions will be fair and comprehensive. At the same time, there may be aspects of stories related to the conflict that need not be disclosed in joint sessions. Face saving, dignity, and respect may be preserved in indirect communication. Caucuses may be useful for hearing stories that the teller is uncomfortable sharing. There are other venues for stories to be heard and received, including therapy, pastoral settings, friendship, and support groups. Somehow we have to balance the need to get enough of the story to move forward with respect for cultural and personal desires not to reveal.

We will always hear only excerpts of stories. Whole, truthful stories can never fully be told. There simply is not enough time, nor are we faithful and unbiased enough in our telling. Telling is also dynamic and relational; it shifts as we change, unfolding with the multidirectionality of our conversations. If we let that be OK, then what needs to emerge may do so. For the woman in the group of interculturalists, her discomfort with sharing reflections on power related to her story led her to feel angry with me for asking her to do the drawing. As she voiced her anger, she got more and more upset. Group members spoke about the power of her refusal to participate. They had shared their drawings with each other but felt uncomfortable excluding her.

As I listened to her concerns without contradicting them or getting defensive, she suddenly stopped, hearing herself in a new way. Seeing the power of choosing not to participate for the first time, she also saw that the experience of power she had drawn was being played out again. She had drawn herself as a victim; she experienced herself as a victim of my instructions. This opened up an entirely new conversation for her and her group about moving away from victim identities. And the experience of hearing stories about power was powerful without the particulars of the stories ever being told.

Whether to Tell Our Stories

The question of how much of our own story to disclose as professional helpers is unsettled. Some mediators, facilitators, and trainers shy away from any personal disclosures, wanting to keep the boundary clear. Others disclose stories as a way of building rapport, developing empathy, or revealing a possible bias. Still others have no set view about the telling of personal stories but do it if and when it seems appropriate or helpful. We have all listened to teachers who tell too many, taking us away from the heart of the subject we have come to study. At the same time, when there is no window into who the helper is as a person, the lack of contact may feel clinical and cool.

My preference is to keep the telling of personal stories brief and to tell them when I can articulate a reason to myself for doing so. When I conduct divorce mediations, I always disclose that I am divorced. It is a fact—one that lets parties know I have more than just professional experience with the process. My experience has undoubtedly shaped my perceptions, views about roles, fairness, and participation in the process, as well as my perspectives about handling ongoing issues. To the extent possible, I have done the work of healing and bringing closure to my experience, hoping not to project my experience onto those with whom I work. But I still feel it is fair to let them know. Generally, parties respond favorably to this, feeling that I am more "with" them than someone doing something "to" them.

But it is also critical to be sure that the stories we bring with us do not impede the progress of parties. In a divorce mediation with Chinese Canadian parents, we were struggling with the question of how to make parenting arrangements for their child. Early on, one suggested sending their son to live with Grandmother in Hong Kong. Through the lens of my dominant-culture value that children of divorce need as much positive contact with both parents as possible, I downplayed that suggestion. We spent considerable time talking about their respective work schedules, personal commitments, and habits for interacting with their son, as well as how these could accommodate shared parenting. In the end, they again came to the idea of sending him to live with his grandmother. Both embraced it. My story about nuclear families had taken them away from their own—a story that "family" includes close relations who may be better able to look after children. Luckily, there was a happy ending, as I moved my story out of the way of what worked for them.

As this experience illustrates, our stories reveal beliefs, values, and worldviews. We cannot check them at the door of our processes, and we would not want to. As we have seen, they are rich resources for connecting, revealing, and transforming. At the same time, we must choose our stories carefully, with worldviews in mind.

I will not soon forget the negotiation training I delivered to the large international staff of a conservation organization at their Swiss headquarters. To demonstrate different styles of negotiation, a co-trainer and I staged a conflict in front of the group about the timing of breaks. We thought it was an innocuous subject and imagined that most participants would quickly discern our playfulness and exaggeration. With this in mind, remembering the success and fun we had experienced with a similar demonstration back in North America, we proceeded to contend with each other. We were, in turn, accommodating, competitive, avoidant, compromising, and collaborative. Following the demonstration, we briefly identified the conflict as contrived and invited the participants to consider the styles we had demonstrated during their break.

To our surprise, we were faced with several delegations during the break. The North Americans wondered how my co-trainer, a male, could have allowed a woman to "walk all over him" (I had played the competitive role). The Swiss and German participants felt the display unseemly and hoped for more professional proceedings. But the group that was most upset was the West Africans, who were concerned that there was a tear in the relationship between me and my co-trainer. We assured them there was not, that in fact we enjoy that kind of repartee. They were unconvinced.

We resumed the session holding hands, emphasizing our friendship and our intention to demonstrate conflict styles. But throughout the training, the West Africans continued to ask whether there was something needed to repair our relationship. To them, it did not make sense to pretend to be in conflict with your friend or colleague. We had crossed a line—violated their stories of how friends behave. And because our story of pretending in the interests of teaching did not fit into their experience, they kept trying to interpret our actions from their frame. And so they made repeated offerings of concern and even help to resolve our difficulties.

My co-trainer and I still work together. We choose our stories carefully. And still we know that we will probably run again into invisible cultural boundaries that you learn about only by violating them. Our stories, our processes, and our methodologies emerge from our experience and our worldviews. They do not make sense to everyone. Our job as trainers is to provide enough context that participants can learn from what we do and to be in continuing dialogue with participants about their stories to avoid the pitfalls of dissonant choices. It is especially important to be aware of this when we share our own stories in mediation or facilitation.

Teaching Tales

As we have seen, stories are rich vessels of culture; careful listeners will gain from them much insight into values, communication norms, and cultural dynamics. Astute trainers and third parties spend time listening to stories from parties and participants before and during processes. Of course, when we ask parties to tell us their conflict stories, they are not always forthcoming. Asking about conflict is a bit like asking about sexual behavior; it can be personal, intrusive, and difficult. Even if someone wants to be helpful and reveal his or her "cultural common sense of conflict," this is something that is often not transparent, even to the subject. So we find the stories where they lie, sparking crystals on the beach when the sun shines at a certain angle, invisible moments later. And we pay attention.

Some of our richest learning moments in teaching come when we work interculturally. A trainer tells a story of presenting a course on interest negotiation to a First Nations community on Canada's west coast. Noticing their polite attention but few verbal comments, she paused to ask the golden question, "How do you deal with conflict when it occurs in your community?" Here is the story they told:

> There was an elder who had a dog, and that dog barked all night long, every night, kept the whole neighborhood awake. It was a really yappy dog, and nobody could stand it much longer. One afternoon, an elder went over to visit the dog owner without being announced. They had tea. Talked about the weather and the upcoming pow wow. They told a couple of stories. Then the elder left. Still, the dog barked at night. A few days later, the same elder dropped by for another visit. Same thing. They talked about the weather and the brushfire down in the coulee. Then the elder left. Still, no relief. A day or two later, the elder visited again. They had tea. Talked about the weather, the way the government negotiations were going. And the elder left. After that, the dog was kept in every night. Never caused anybody trouble anymore.

After the story was over, there was silence. The trainer's dominant-culture mind struggled. What had happened? Why did the dog stay inside after the third visit? The other participants in the group were nodding their understanding. Clearly, there were ways to communicate indirectly in this community that avoided confrontation and saved face. The trainer was beginning to learn about them, and so were those of us with whom she shared her experience.

Then came the challenge dealt with by many intercultural trainers: How do we accommodate the stories of other groups into the conflict processes and approaches we teach, coming as they do from their own set of cultural understandings? The first step is to make them explicit—to listen for the ways that stories display the tellers' common sense of conflict and to name and explore it. Only then do we have a foundation from which to begin to co-create new stories that speak to more than one cultural way of knowing and being.

Co-Creating Stories

The first step in co-creating stories is to uncover and acknowledge where and how our own stories are situated. This exploration will give information about us, but also about the way we conceive our relationship with the world and with others. Stories are relational containers. They tell not only about the teller but about the relationships in the teller's domain. Listening to stories, we hear information about who we are seen to be in the eyes of the teller. This opens up the possibility of dialogue ultimately leading to co-creation. An example illustrates this point.

I was recently teaching a class on intercultural conflict resolution to thirty graduate students. Twenty-seven of the students were white; three were black. During discussions about neutrality, several of the white students spoke of class members and conflict resolution practitioners as "we." "We try to be neutral," one of them observed, going on to explain why neutrality was important and how it might be accomplished. One of the black students objected, pointing out poignantly that the assumption of shared experience obscured the distinctly different experience of students of color. In fact, as the black student went on to articulate, his experience of daily identity negotiation suggested to him that neutrality was unattainable. To be implicitly included in the "we" that was meant to refer to conflict practitioners was to include him in a story that was not his. His story was a story where racism and daily indignities communicating "otherness" reminded him that the "we" of white men and women did not capture nor communicate his experience.

Some of the students in the class found this exchange uncomfortable. It is unsettling to have our assumptions, our stories about shared identity, challenged. It is difficult to talk about conflict practice in a way that reflects the complexities of race, gender, class, and other forms of privilege. Yet as we find ways to have conversations that admit complex stories of identity and meaning, we can move meaningfully toward the goal of developing an inclusive field. From this place, we can work with clients to co-create stories.

There are many ways to co-create stories and the processes that flow from them. John Paul Lederach gives us a way of gathering and using stories in his book *Preparing for Peace*.[14] He suggests using storyboarding—a process originally developed by Walt Disney for outlining and producing cartoons. Participants write an idea, word, or image on an index card related to a particular theme. The cards are then linked and grouped together in ways that make sense according to commonality or sequence. From this exercise, a new story emerges that is related to the process being developed or the problem being addressed.

Lederach's accounts of his work in Latin America remind us that stories are a part of cultural webs, giving us access to systems of understanding essential to addressing conflict in different cultural settings. Even in a setting where there appears to be cultural homogeneity, co-creating stories has the potential to transform conflict. Personality differences, including ways of taking in and processing information and making decisions, along with learning styles and small "c" cultural differences, mean that co-creating stories is essential in arriving at truly collaborative outcomes that address deep divisions among us.

Appreciative inquiry also provides us with inspiration about co-creation. This approach is centered in the idea that we will not solve our problems by focusing on them, dissecting them, and unraveling them. If we want to create more generative, satisfying relationships in the workplace, in communities, or at home, we must begin with a vision of where we want to go. A friend who races bicycles competitively tells me his experience: he must look for where he wants his wheels to land on the trail, not at the rocks that pepper the way. If he looks at the rocks, he will hit them. By looking at the clear places, he is more likely to miss the obstacles. So appreciative inquiry suggests centering our attention in sharing and clarifying what is positive and where we want to go.

Doing this may seem dissonant when we are feeling the weight of conflict. It hurts, it irritates, and we want to fix it. Yet centering our attention in appreciation and the positive helps us connect with parts of our stories that sustain and energize us. As we do that with others, it helps us to be productive and focused in building workplaces and communities that address and prevent the conflicts that challenge us. Other ways to co-create stories include future search processes, open-space technology, and dialogue. Each of these processes features listening, deciding directions together, and capturing learnings from shared stories.

Healing Stories

Another way stories can be used in teaching and intervening is to shift perspective or suggest alternatives. Very often, parties in conflict have a narrowed rather than a broadened experience of themselves, each other, and the issues. They tend to see a skinny range of possible solutions. They tend to see solutions that involve more movement by the other party and less by them. Stories reveal hurt and pain, sometimes from incidents that happened hundreds of years ago to people and sometimes from interpersonal transgressions or ruptures. Until some way of addressing these hurts is found, it may be impossible to achieve conflict transformation.

This awareness is contained in the hero's journey of conflict transformation that Louise Diamond[15] writes about. She suggests that we move to problem solving much too soon—that until histories, hurts, and unhealed wounds have been addressed, we will not be able to solve problems in deep or lasting ways. Indeed, Diamond suggests that it is through the process of healing, forgiving, and letting go of the pain of the past that a shift occurs. This shift frees up energy to engage in problem solving and see the relationship in new ways. Until it has happened, big parts of us are tied up with the past; our energy is not available for problem solving or moving forward.

Everett Worthington's[16] experience emphasizes that forgiveness can free energy and shift perspective in general, not just about a particular issue. He learned that his mother had been murdered during a house robbery just after completing his book *To Forgive Is Human: How to Put Your Past in the Past*. He was enraged, and wanted nothing more than to be alone in a room with the murderer and beat his brains out with a baseball bat. That night, he heard the words of his book: "empathy is the key to forgiveness." Though he did not know who had killed his mother, he re-created the scene. From what he knew about the robbery, he supposed that it had been done by more than one person and that they were probably young and unprofessional. He imagined two or three youths keyed up, on edge. His mother's house was dark, with no car in the driveway. They would have thought that the occupant was out at a New Year's Eve party. When she came upon them emptying her drawers, they must have been shocked and terrified of what would follow. They lashed out in panic, killing her with a crowbar.

Worthington replaced his story—"I only want revenge"—with a willingness to venture into the story of those who had ended his mother's life. He did not excuse them, nor did his anger disappear, but he did report that empathy changed the quality of his experience. Upon reflection, he noticed that he was willing to do to them what they had done to his mother: kill, but with more forethought and malice. His realization of his own darkness helped him forgive, and he reported that the effect extended to other relationships. "I haven't felt the hostility or desire for revenge that I had at times felt for people who have inflicted lesser hurts on me."[17]

Healing conflict may take time, or it may happen in one "long night of the soul," as in Worthington's example. In his case, I suspect that the preparation he had done made the speed with which he forgave possible. So it is important that we prepare ourselves to be clear channels for the stories that are shared and those that write themselves new through our processes. As we engage in our own work to process unfinished conflicts, envision generative relationships, and step into creativity, we are better able to assist others.

Stories as Spirals

With those close to us, stories do not have closure, but continue. Stories connect us to others, to our ancestors and our progeny. Stories are as old as human language and as rich as any invention we have conceived. As we acknowledge the legitimacy of stories as ways of communicating and negotiating identity and meaning, we see that they are essential to our processes. They are the fabric through which conflicts are constructed and the threads through which relationships can be rewoven. Remembering Scheherazade, we invoke the power of stories to help us contain damage and save our relationships and, ultimately, ourselves.

CHAPTER EIGHT

Commemorating Tools
Using Ritual

Two lovers stand at the top level of the Eiffel Tower. Paris is below and all around them, as the day begins its transition to twilight. It is a magical moment, and they want to mark it as a time apart from all that has happened in their lives back home. On the long climb up, they have been speaking of their lives together and how they got in their own ways at various times. There has been hurt, resentment, and frustration along with pleasant and exciting times. Seeing their negative patterns, they resolve to be mindful and intentional about moving forward together in constructive and mutually supportive ways.

No one remembers who thought of it, but when they finally reach the top of the tower, they each spend a few minutes writing the things they wish to let go of on scraps of paper. The items are both specific and general. They refer to past events and to things they wish to be forgiven for. Moving close to the railing, they feel the wind on their faces. In turn, each reads aloud the writing from one scrap of paper and releases it into the breeze. After the last scrap of paper is gone, they stand for a long time in silence, watching the sunset bring night to Paris.

Years later, the two of them remember the time at the top of the tower and the sense of freedom and relief they felt as they walked back down, free of unwanted things from their past. They remember it, using tangible, physical descriptions like "It took a load off my mind," or "I breathed more easily after that," or "We wiped the slate clean." It remains a powerful anchor for them as they recall the sensations, images, and feelings that accompanied it. The ritual serves as an inspiration to them—a confirmation of their continuing commitment to each other and to finding ways to release themselves from the negative valence of past conflict.

Although not many people have the experience of throwing unwanted bits of the past from the top of the Eiffel Tower, everyone experiences ritual. Ritual is currently a subject of renewed interest after a time of association with dusty, outmoded practices belonging to past generations. Ritual is breaking free of its traditional associations, as more rituals are being invented or improvised to serve specific people and times; it is being seen for the vital way of making meaning that it is, as people recognize rituals in their everyday lives. Gradually, students and practitioners of conflict are coming to see ritual as an accessible tool for helping with transitions, intercultural bridging, and transformation.

The use of ritual in the conflict resolution field is not new. Experienced practitioners use it to frame, mark, and celebrate progress in mediation and facilitation. Trainers use ritual to convene, cohere, and manage groups. One of the reasons it has gone unacknowledged is that conflict resolution itself arose as an alternative to the formal rituals of the courtroom. In rejecting formality in favor of informality and mystery in favor of accessibility, practitioners de-emphasized the need for ceremony and symbolic communication. With the realization that ritual offers a broad range of choices, it is now being named, reclaimed, studied, and intentionally used. In this chapter, we explore the nature of ritual, how it works, and how rituals can be designed to help shift difficult conflict dynamics.

Ritual Defined

Ritual is pervasive. All societies and individuals have rituals that give meaning, structure, and richness to their lives. In a classic definition, Victor Turner writes that ritual is "the social phenomenon of shared experience firmly embedded in human interaction and cultural performance."[1] Ritual is derived from the Sanskrit word *rtu,* meaning any act of magic toward a purpose. For our purposes, magic can be taken to mean that which is outside our usual expectations or experience. Ritual involves bringing what was internal into the open through a patterned set of actions that mark a transition just as surely as a train trip between Boston and New York is a vehicle for getting from one city to the next.

Some say that modern North American society lacks rituals. In *Bowling Alone,* Robert Putnam[2] pairs a decline in civic and social rituals with the move to more individualistic pursuits. Others point to a decrease in shared family meals and an increase in cohabitation without formal marriage as evidence of this decline. Actually, we have many rituals, though some traditional ones have been rejected or modified. Consider sororities, fraternities, military academies, sports clubs, book groups, families, congregations. All have rituals, some developed over time and others composed spontaneously in response to changing needs, experiences, and transitions.

The problem is that traditional rituals lack deep meaning for some of us. Religious ceremonies, civic events, and educational rites of passage are inviting to some but not to others. My absence from the graduation of my law school class reflected my sense of anonymity in a large law school and an even larger university. One way of seeing this is that I doubted the convocation ritual would be a vital container for the meaning I personally made of the law school experience. Ten years later, I attended the convocation ceremony of my counseling psychology master's class. I was moved by the plaintive music of the lone Scottish piper, his profile framed by the magnificent coastal mountains as he led us to the podium. I was graduating from an institution where I had been acknowledged, where I was more than a number, where the academic work I did had immediate, tangible connection to my life's work. And so I welcomed the ritual as a meaningful observance of the connection and the transition to new identities.

Rituals involved with technology, financial gain, or formal institutions may leave our desire for connection and relationship unfulfilled. We turn on our computer and check our stocks as a first act in the morning; we attend a drive-in church and buy clothes through the mail. All of these activities traditionally involved contact with another human being and some acknowledgment of shared community or purpose. As the pace of change has increased and our lives have become more governed by efficiency, some rituals have been rendered shells from which life has disappeared, and others are shapeshifting to meet the demands of a new era. The courtroom as a forum for resolving conflicts, for example, continues to operate. Alongside formal, traditional processes, courts increasingly offer mediation, conciliation, early neutral evaluation, and other less formal ways of addressing conflicts.

What constitutes a ritual? A ritual is a time when senses are heightened, moments are distinct and marked, and participants feel connected to each other and to the meaning of what they are doing. Rituals have three elements: purpose, method, and outcome.

- *Purpose* refers to the intention of those involved in constructing and enacting the ritual, or why they have come together.
- *Method* is the way participants accomplish their intention, or how they plan to be together.
- *Outcome* is the projected result of the ritual, or the shared hopes, dreams, and expected outcomes of the group.

Ritual is a circular process, as the shared hopes and dreams of a group may inform new intentions and lead to new or ongoing rituals.

These elements are best understood with a concrete example. In the case of a dialogue among pro-choice and pro-life activists, participants agree in advance to meet with the *purpose* of learning, understanding that no one will try to resolve substantive issues. For most of them, the pain of "doing what we've always done" is a motivating factor to try something new. Debates and reciprocal attacks have only escalated the conflict. How do they come together? Facilitators use a *method* in which participants are asked to agree in advance to ground rules about respectful communication, listening, and refraining from personal attacks or attempts to persuade or convince. Participants are invited to bring open minds and a spirit of curiosity. Their minds are not open about whether or not abortion should be legal and available. As advocates, their minds are strongly made up. Their minds are open to the possibility that they might discover something unknown about those who are on the other side. In other words, their minds are open to relational possibilities, even while remaining closed about the substance of the issue.

They come together with openness to *outcome,* united by a desire to change the destructive course that the issue has taken.

Some of their dreams are shared and some are unique. They share dreams that abortion will become unnecessary, that every child will be wanted and have adequate nurturing. They hope that the feminization of poverty will be reversed. They hope that listening to each other will help them work together on issues where there is agreement (for example, adoption). They hope that the risk of "talking to the enemy" will be outweighed by the benefits of the process. Thus a dialogue about abortion becomes a ritual, as a group of people come together for a set period of time using a patterned process with openness to a new relationship or understanding of each other.

Ritual as a Way to Make or Mark Meaning

Of course, talking with "the enemy" may be viewed with suspicion or outright condemnation by advocacy groups. This discomfort relates to our reflexive tendency to move away from those with whom we experience difference rather than engage them in exploratory dialogue. Ritual is a way to help us do what is uncomfortable but needed. Viewed this way, ritual need not be associated with tedious and outmoded ways of behaving or old social customs. It is simply an intentional action outside the ordinary flow of events in which physical sensations and feelings are emphasized over rational analysis and logic. Ritual is essentially relational, whether the relationship is with another, the self, or with a higher power. Because rituals have to do with marking or making meaning, they are part of everyone's lives. Visiting a grave, lighting Hanukkah candles, writing New Year's resolutions, kissing a friend good-bye— all of these are rituals when done thoughtfully and intentionally.

Victor Frankl, in his classic book *Man's Search for Meaning*,[3] tells us there are three ways that the human need for meaning is satisfied. The first is through creating something, or work. The second involves encountering someone, or love. The third is through exercising the option to decide how to view a situation or an event, or choice. Rituals celebrate what we create, bring us closer in relationship, and give form to our chosen intention.

Rituals satisfy our human need to express meaning and connection. This need seems to accompany us, even when we are questioning and discarding rituals that we have observed in the past.[4]

We can see this in the case of the Puritans who came to the New World to escape the ritualistic religion of the Anglican church but who brought some of their own rituals with them and invented more new ones when they got here.[5] More recently, a movement in Judaism to compose blessings that speak to women shows a desire to match form with meaning.[6] When friends enjoy rituals of greeting or parting, when members of a club participate in a secret handshake, and when one-time enemies sign a peace treaty, all are communicating meaning and affirming connection.

Ritual gives us a way of enacting or becoming meaning. Because it evokes the symbolic level at which meaning is made, ritual is an important part of marking life passages. Ritual breathes the power of physical action and feeling into the creation of new meaning for those involved. The new meaning may involve a change in status and relationship (as in a wedding, a graduation, or a retirement celebration) or identity (as in a ritual to mark the passage from victim of abuse to survivor) or purpose (as in the dedication of a memorial).

Ritual functions to mark rhythm, repetition, structure, synchronicity, and pattern in life. It helps hold dissonance together by creating new frameworks for thinking and holding together ambiguous or different ideas. Ritual changes cognitive systems by giving us new felt experiences of others and ourselves outside the assumptions that previously limited us. It also makes it possible to feel secure in times of change or transition. Princess Diana's untimely death was marked by many rituals of connection and grief, including the state funeral that was televised and watched around the world and books of remembrance that were signed by millions. Both traditional and spontaneous rituals were important in mourning her death.

Ritual as a Tool for Transition

Ritual is more than an ordinary action that may be repeated. It is more than a habit; it is attended by distinct qualities of attention, intention, and awareness. An action becomes a ritual when it takes on a marked, symbolic meaning for one or more people. It involves entering into a space of mind apart from business as usual. Ritual is a versatile vehicle that draws on liminality or the power of standing "in between," apart from habit. From liminal spaces, we can look out onto the past and toward possible futures of our lives and see more clearly. In liminal times, we have the freedom to imagine ourselves in new ways and to build the foundation on which we will become them.

Liminality is a feature of both conflict and ritual. As conflict is a passage between times of harmony, ritual is a passage between different identities, purposes, or states. In liminal times, the usual "givens" are suspended. As this happens, we are free from constraints as well as old ways through which we derived security. Creativity can flourish if we can let go of the dizzying feeling of moving from what is known. As liminality is a generative state, it's good to resist the impulse to move through it too quickly, thus missing some of the richness available in that state. So part of our task as conflict intervenors is to compose rituals that liberate old patterns and help people negotiate, celebrate, and assimilate change.

Recently, I taught a class on conflict reconciliation where we were exploring the experience of liminality. I asked participants to sit quietly, bringing the sensations and feelings of a particular transition they had experienced into their awareness. After they had located these sensations in their bodies, I asked them to convey their experience to a partner without using words. Drawing materials were available; many chose to convey the experience through movement and physical expression. Some participants danced; others drew themselves into balls on the floor; still others sat in their chairs and let their facial expressions and gestures speak to their partners.

As the exercise began, a seventy-year-old African American participant pulled his chair across from mine and sat expectantly a few inches from me. I had not thought that I would participate in the exercise I was facilitating, but his behavior made his request clear. I can still see the taut veins in his hands as he conveyed the frustration and struggle of a transition that he had experienced. I stopped breathing for a moment, as he seemed to come to a breaking point before all of the tension dissolved and he came to terms with the changes in his life. When it was my turn, I felt his support and his strength as I mimed for him my feelings at a time when I was vulnerable and uncertain.

Many class members commented on the depth of their experience with this exercise. Graduate schools in many disciplines feature few experiences that invite a focus on sensing and feeling over analysis and reason. What is remarkable is that, having suspended rational analysis to engage in a felt, sensory experience, participants in the class had a much richer discussion of the nature of ritual and liminality than I have witnessed in groups who did not do the exercise. The importance of ritual is powerfully understood by reference to our lived experience.

In helping us to negotiate and mark life transitions, rituals become both the vehicle and the marker, a way of pausing with others to observe the passing of one role and the assumption of another. These transitions may relate to identity, role, status, loss, achievement, or the transformation of conflict. Because rituals happen outside ordinary time and habits, they become an anchor for what we have experienced deeply and what we wish to live into being. Anchoring may be aided by the use of special clothing, patterned speech, traditional actions, old conventions, or special venues. In my experience with the liminality exercise, enacting the experience of coming through a liminal time to a time of more clarity and security served as an anchor for the hope and achievement that attended these outcomes. Even now, I need only bring to mind the experience with my partner and I feel a sense of warmth related to our shared stories.

Ritual as a Vehicle for Creating Community

Community rituals invite others to participate in the process of enacting change. Many indigenous societies have longstanding communal rituals for addressing conflict, such as Ho'oponopono for Hawaiians and the talking circle used by First Nations people in several parts of North America. Ho'oponopono is a community process in which each person present speaks to an issue, and consequences or resolutions are developed jointly among all present. In the case of an offense, the person who committed the act is a part of the process, as are his or her parents, friends, and neighbors. Together they meet with the family and community of the victims and arrange a resolution through a set pattern of communication. The First Nations talking circle is a process in which everyone present is given an opportunity to speak for as long as they wish. The talking circle may be used in the case of community conflict or important decisions. Sentencing circles used in native communities and the

family group conference, based on Maori teachings, that originated in New Zealand are other examples of rituals used to address
conflict.[7]

Family group conferences are carried out in New Zealand, Aus-
tralia, and Canada. In these conferences, young offenders who
have committed minor offenses are brought together with their
family and supporters, along with the family and supporters of the
victim(s), in the presence of a facilitator. A supporter of the
offender can be anyone who has had an interest in his or her life,
including family, teachers, coaches, ministers, or neighbors. To participate in the process, the offender must accept responsibility for
his or her actions. The focus of the conference is to involve everyone in designing a consensual consequence for the young person
that corresponds to the crime. Family group conferences promote
sharing feelings rather than conducting legal analysis; they discourage recidivism by creating ongoing daily accountability for the
young person in her or his community. They also contribute to the
restoration of harmony in a community in a way that spending
time in jail does not.

The ritual of the family group conference helps bring about
conflict transformation through its relationship to moral territory.
This moral territory is a place where consensus is built and
expressed about how best to move forward in the service of community harmony and values. The territory itself, like ritual space
or time, is not inherently sacred or moral but becomes a place
where action is negotiated through voluntary participation and
commitment to relationship. In this way, ritual and art are the
same: they are each designed to stop us in our usual tracks, to get
us to pay attention. Ritual is a focusing lens, where nothing is accidental and everything is potentially significant.

Dynamics of Ritual

Ritual is a very special way of coming together. It involves a shared
intention to suspend ordinary ways of being with a specific purpose
and boundaries related to time, place, participants, and focus.
Those who participate are committed to a process while willingly
suspending what is known or assumed. They are open to mystery
regarding possible outcomes of the ritual event. Together, partici-

pants enter a space of connection and concentrate through a patterned way of behaving, moving from an emphasis on conscious, rational analysis to an emphasis on felt and enacted experience. In the end, transformation may be the result. Transformation may be internal for those participating, as in the experience of coming to peace with a death during a memorial service. Transformation can also occur on the level of identity, as former enemies emerge from negotiation rituals seeing each other as potential allies in a peace process. Finally, identities and status may be transformed, as in rituals marking graduations, divorces, marriages, or coming of age. The dynamics of ritual involve a whole that is greater than the sum of its parts. Each part contributes significantly to the whole, beginning with intention.

Intention to Engage

Intention is central to ritual, as it imbues the process with meaning that is personal to the participants and yet bigger than any of them alone. When two or more people come together to engage in a ritual, they cannot know exactly what the outcome will be, but their shared intention is synergistic and powerful. An intention to consciously reach out of the everyday realm and into meaning making is a way of jumping to a meta-level, above what is transient or ordinary. Whether the ritual is a simple meditation in the morning or a marriage covenant, the intention to honor life purpose runs through it.

Shared intention invites all involved to move in the same direction and to become attuned to the purpose. Paradoxically, a clear purpose must be held at the same time as an awareness that mystery, or something unanticipated, may be manifest in the process of the ritual. This is illustrated by the class experience of liminality described earlier. Participants brought a shared intention to explore ritual experientially without specifically knowing what shape that exploration might take or what the outcome might be.

Can ritual occur without a specific intention to engage in ritual being present? Most people can probably recall a time of deep feeling in which time seemed to stand still, and a significant event was marked that was not necessarily conceived as a ritual before it occurred. Examples are siblings singing a childhood song around the deathbed of a parent or the many bouquets of flowers placed in the streets of London immediately after the death of Princess Diana was announced. In both cases, grief led to moments both poignant and meaningful. Ritual may be spontaneous and informal, as well as planned and formal.

Suspension of Ordinary Habits

Everyone has habits of attention. A preoccupation with image, fear, or the suppression of anger in day-to-day interactions may make it hard to seize opportunities for authentic communication and relationship. Rituals are a patterned way of moving away from our habitual ways of being in the world. They invite us to do something differently so that we will get different results.

In the case of ongoing conflicts, we tend to repeat scripts and ways of behaving that impede forward progress. We do the same dance again and again, using a familiar style, getting familiar results. Conflict theorists use the term *conflict-habituated system* to describe this pattern when it involves groups of people. Ritual processes invite a suspension of the usual steps in the dance, changing the music so that something else can happen in the dance of relationship. For example, in mediation the presence of a third party who structures communication to facilitate listening will cause most people to modify their ordinary ways of being. Couples who had habitually interrupted each other and engaged in personal attacks now find themselves adopting the discipline of repeating back what the other has said. The quality and accuracy of their communication is enhanced.

Observance of a Specific Purpose and Boundaries

Everyone has had the experience of responding to a perceived weakness in themselves by resolving to change. Fagan, in the musical *Oliver*, resolves twice during the story to turn over a new leaf and refrain from his life of crime. Yet each time he lapses into "reviewing the situation," in effect rationalizing his continued pattern. So it is useful to have a specific purpose and boundaries for a ritual process. Transformation may mark the eventual outcome, but transformation is too broad and assumptive to be a part of the initial purpose. In deeply divided societies, progress may mean bringing people together to know each other as human beings with many facets rather than simply by the label "other." Rituals function best when there is a clearly articulated, shared purpose that is spelled out in advance or arises from the practice of the ritual itself.

Suspension of Knowing

We have said that liminality attends ritual. This means that ritual is literally a way between two places where the terrain is more familiar or secure. Ritual provides a route, but the exact nature of the journey along the way and how it will feel is not known in advance. Some writers suggest that the mystery of ritual arises from the unconscious; others speak of suspending knowing so that a deeper understanding can arise from the wisdom of the group. Many accounts of ritual include reference to shifts or new awareness that bring insight to participants.

Suspending knowing is a difficult task for many conflict intervenors. We have been trained to bring an authoritative presence, to hold the vision that resolution is possible, and to believe that we will be instrumental in bringing it about through the activities we have planned. A colleague tells a story of how his training and expectations were challenged. He was the convener and facilitator of a workshop held some years ago to bring together American veterans from Vietnam and Soviet veterans from Afghanistan for the first time. Planners thought that building relationships among these men could contribute to a lessening of Cold War tensions.

But the workshop did not get off to a smooth start. All the icebreakers the facilitator had planned got a lukewarm reception. The distrust and unease in the room were palpable. The facilitator felt like someone who had planned a bunch of party games that the guests refused to play. Sitting through the uncomfortable silence, he was surprised to see one of the Americans get up and stand in the center of the room between the two groups of men. The man pulled up his pant leg, revealing a prosthesis attached to his leg at the knee. He began to speak of the horror of the experience that ended with lasting loss. After a while, a Soviet man joined him in the center of the circle and answered by pulling up his pant leg to reveal his prosthesis. Others slowly joined them, revealing scars and disfigurement. Before the shocked facilitator could figure out what to do, men from both sides had converged in the center, channeling their pain into a physical pile-up involving kicking and punching. The atmosphere bordered on ugly, yet somehow limits were observed, even as limits were being pushed. Without causing each other lasting physical injury, the participants were enacting their pain and deep-seated frustration arising from years of struggle and rejection.

This ritual spontaneously created by the group cleared the air, making it possible for the men to engage in the quality of dialogue that the facilitator had hoped for. Witnessing it with fear and surprise, the facilitator had little choice but to suspend knowing. Through a mysterious and unanticipated route, space had been created for conversation, as the men enacted their pain and found empathy underneath it.

Connection in Community

Remember a ritual that you have experienced in a community. Although not as dramatic as the one just described, it may have been a wedding or a funeral; perhaps it was a bat mitzvah or observance of Veterans Day. How did you feel about those who were there with you, or about those you were commemorating? Rituals create an experience of connection in which we feel kinship, appreciation, and closeness with others who have come together in a shared purpose. This connection may be felt to other people in attendance or absent, to a Deity or revered figure and what She or He represents, or to the self.

In conflict, ritual space invites us to consider other parts of our identities than those that are in opposition to each other. Rather than an enemy image of the other, we come to see each other as mothers, fathers, shopkeepers, teachers, readers; we come to see each other as the complex beings we truly are. So in the Soviet-American workshop, closeness was the result; participants came to see each other as like them in having experienced the devastation of participating in a war that was protracted and unpopular at home. This closeness transcended the initial distrust and led to the group meeting together annually for many years.

Concentration on Patterned Behavior

In order to participate meaningfully in a ritual, focused attention is needed. Patterned behaviors may help us focus attention on the present moment by taking our awareness away from analysis and reason. In a time of emotionality, patterned behaviors help us engage with others and still maintain a sense of calm. So the sequence of actions in a wedding or a funeral is designed to provide a structure or pattern for the expression of feelings.

Patterned actions help everyone present participate. They provide enough information about the terrain that people are less likely to stumble on the path or be jarred out of concentration on the deeper meaning of the events. In mediation and facilitation, a structure is outlined to participants at the beginning of the process that allows them to focus on communication with the assistance of a third party, who will help maintain calm and a constructive focus.

Focus on Felt and Enacted Experience

In North American culture, we tend to rely heavily on rational analysis. It therefore seems natural to emphasize rational decision making in conflict resolution. We sometimes talk and write as though we are disembodied heads sitting around a table. Rituals allow us to literally move through a conflict, using the body as an instrument to enact change and to receive somatic messages as guides for action. Rituals engage our emotions, stimulating and containing feelings related to the event being observed. As we have seen, emotions are actually powerful guides to action when considered as valuable companions to rational analysis. As we invite emotional and somatic intelligence into the process, we bring more resources to the process that both inform us and increase our empathy for others.

Again referring to the Soviet-American workshop, the release of emotions allowed for a way forward in what was otherwise a stilted and limited conversation. The physical altercation that occurred made it possible to release emotions that the "ordinary, polite conversation" had kept trapped.

Openness to Transformational Outcomes

Not every ritual is attended by transformation. I could attend a ceremony and find it unmoving if it did not touch me in ways I make meaning. The American and Soviet veterans could have had congenial and interesting discussions and not felt the desire to meet again. But something happened among them that led to transformed relationships. Changes occurred within the participants and among them that ultimately had the potential to affect the way the societies they represented perceived each other.

When rituals speak to us personally, then transformation is a possibility. We can transform our identity, our status; or we can negotiate new meaning through rituals. In these cases, transformation may be signaled by the ritual but may actually take some time to become complete. A couple does not take on a complete identity as married or divorced immediately after a ritual signifying the change in status. The change is integrated over time as each person takes on and grows accustomed to the role.

Consider the ordination of a member of the clergy. An ordination is a communal, public series of actions involving patterned speech, prescribed music, and special clothes to mark a transition in identity. It is a time of celebration of what has been achieved and of the mission that the ordained person is assuming. The person walks into the church a candidate and out of the church a minister.

Through the ritual, the minister is welcomed into the role and promised the support of those who attend and officiate. Even so, she or he does not fully transform identities during the course of the ritual. Few new ministers wake the next morning thinking only of prayer or the needs of the congregation or the will of God. The mantle of the new identity settles slowly, over time. As others observe and reinforce it, it begins to feel more like a suit of clothes that fits.

Ritual opens up the passage to another state or way of being. So in conflict, mediation is a ritual in which parties are introduced to new identities and ways of communicating. If their relationship is ongoing, the onus will be on them to integrate these shifts into their ways of relating.

Anyone who has gone through a divorce or a major upheaval in life will know that integrating and sustaining change is not easy. Ritual as a reference point anchored in lived experience thus needs to be very strong to counteract habits of mind that might lead to further conflict. Because ritual offers the opportunity for us to connect deeply with others and with ourselves, our values, and our purpose, it helps us to align our behavior in a way that honors these connections. Ritual is a way of embodying our deep values and creating them as patterns through intentional, shared action. In ritual, doing is both believing and remembering.

Using Ritual to Change Identities

Rituals help us remember that our identities are multifaceted, something that we may forget when in the throes of conflict. When one aspect of identity feels threatened, it can become "magnetized" so that it takes on a pervasive quality, coloring all of the other identities and experiences that make up a person.

For example, I have many identities, including mother, Canadian, professor, woman, daughter, white, lawyer, counselor, writer, and Westerner. If one of these identities feels threatened, for example my female gender identity in an all-male work environment, then I may begin to focus on that identity primarily. My actions from this point may take several forms. I may seek alliances with other women. I may deny the differences between us and try to take on more "male" behaviors in order to fit in. I may bring up my concerns with my male colleagues directly or look for an advocate in the hierarchy of the university to set a tacit boundary for the men.

All of these actions relate to my identity as a woman. The security of that identity may need strengthening when it feels threatened or used as the basis for exclusion (even if this use is not conscious on the part of the men but is simply a function of the men working most easily with those who are like them). One strategy that may alleviate some of the conflict, both internal and interpersonal, would be to relate to my colleagues from other facets of our identities than gender.

I can relate as a lawyer, a researcher, a parent, a musician, a teacher. And so can they. In this way, some of the discomfort related to the gender conflict may be lessened. When this occurs, the relationships may improve so that I will have a better foundation for working on the gender dynamics with my colleagues as supporters. In the service of this strategy, I seek rituals that reinforce awareness of multiple identities. Attending a concert or a child's sports activity may help broaden the base of identities from which we relate, bringing us closer to the collegial state I imagine and desire.

Rituals transform by bringing together the world as lived with the world of our imaginations. They give form to a new story about the past, as well as an intentionally constructed picture of the future. Using this definition, mediation may be a ritual. The mediation session itself becomes liminal space in which antagonism shifts to mutuality. As parties share their experience and engage in structured conversation to resolve differences, new and more complex stories replace those peopled by the classic triangle of victim, aggressor, and rescuer.

Triangles in Conflict

Conflict frequently involves role triangles. Fairy tales and myths are exemplars of triangles in conflict, containing the age-old story of an oppressor who victimizes someone weaker. In these classic stories, the victim needs a rescuer to break free of the bonds of oppression. The rescuer arrives, the victim is rescued, and the oppressor is destroyed or at least stopped for the present. Each person's role remains the same; the victim has been rescued but may be victimized sometime later by the oppressor or some new bully. Only if a conflict is transformed do these roles change. Transformation means that the victim and the oppressor move beyond these roles or images to new ways of seeing themselves and others. Mediation is a process through which such transformation may occur.

Although fairy tales portray clear victims and oppressors, the roles are often much less stark in real life. It often happens that each side thinks of him- or herself as a victim of the other. Each may feel in need of a rescuer or someone to help equalize the power and bring about a just resolution. Power in these cases is not clearly distributed to one side at the expense of the other, but each side has sources of power and choices to make that can affect the balance of power in an ongoing, dynamic way. When a mediator assists with these conflicts, the stories that have been told and the way they have been told are interrupted to make way for new stories. As new stories are told, each person present becomes more nuanced in the eyes of the other, marking a transition from the roles each has played and has been perceived to play in the conflict.

Consider a matrimonial conflict in which both the husband (Patrick) and the wife (Jocelyn) are apt to see themselves as victim and the other as oppressor. This is the case, even when one has left or had an affair, because the one who initiated the break-up may justify the action as a reaction to oppression or longstanding unfairness. The role each assumes as victim presupposes that the other is not only acting as oppressor but that the other should be held responsible for acting in oppressive ways. The history of Patrick and Jocelyn is likely to be a series of actions related to these identities, escalating the conflict and further reinforcing a negative view of the other.

Their relational system may have been maintained over years, stabilized by a third role. This third role is the rescuer from the fairy tales of old. The rescuer in these classic tales does not fundamentally change the identity of either the victim or the oppressor. The victim remains weak, reinforcing her or his need to be rescued. The oppressor remains ill intentioned but, at least for the moment, is neutralized for the victim. For Patrick and Jocelyn, this rescue may have been limited, as when one of their friends listened to the complaints each made about each other. After venting to their friend, Patrick or Jocelyn would return home feeling somewhat relieved, even though neither had addressed the source of their frustration. They were rescued, but only temporarily. The roles they had assigned to "self" and "other" had been reinforced. After time, the frustration would surface again and build, not disappearing until addressed directly or again diverted.

The way out of this system, which may become habitual, is generally when the pain of continuing becomes so great for one or the other that they summon the courage to do something different,

which may take the form of marriage counseling (seeking constructive engagement) or family mediation (seeking constructive
disengagement). When the disengagement option is chosen, it is
important that the mediator resist the role of rescuer, thus challenging the roles in the calcified system. A rescuer does not question the original roles, but may actually maintain them by
reinforcing reciprocal perceptions of victimhood. A mediator
implicitly questions existing roles and interrupts patterns of communication, inviting everyone to step out of the victim-oppressor-
rescuer triangle. Rituals can help facilitate the transition in roles.

Mediation as Ritual

Mediation becomes a ritual container for holding a new and complex awareness of roles for each party, as the roles emerge when
communication patterns change.[8] The mediator, who may be seen
at first as a rescuer by each side, resists alignment with either side
in favor of fidelity to a fair process. Each person has the opportunity to tell his or her story of the conflict. Initially, they both situate themselves as well-intentioned victims. As mediation proceeds
and each is heard by the other, these roles become less pronounced. Attachment to the roles lessens as the mediator, functioning as witness and guide, helps the parties see each other as
nuanced, complex individuals with the potential to act as allies, if
not in their future relationship at least in addressing the immediate conflict. This transition in roles is depicted in Figure 8.1.

Mediation is a forum in which the focus on feeling and sensing can take precedence over logic and thought, at least during
some portions of the process. This opportunity to access emotional
resources and envision new ways of behaving in a setting where
negative communication habits are challenged can be liberating
and transformative. Mediation sessions act as catalysts, incrementally building trust and capacity to enable and sustain the shifts in
identity that are necessary to make bridging conflict possible.

Mediation as a ritual marries traditional approaches to conflict
resolution with modern influences from labor-management negotiation and the movement to develop alternatives to crowded,
expensive, adversarial courts. It is a forum where feelings can be
shared and motivations expressed in ways not allowed by judicial

Figure 8.1. Escaping the Victim Triangle

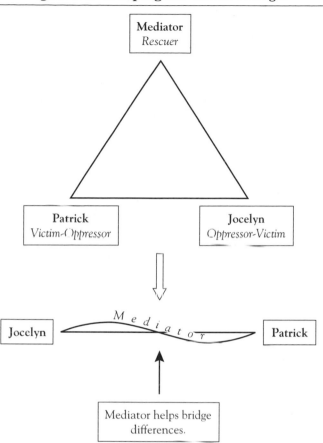

rules of evidence. People divided by conflict are offered the opportunity to braid strands of their lives and relationships back together in a way that is anchored in an experience of authentic communication and mutual recognition. When mediation is conducted with cultural sensitivity, it opens up additional ritual opportunities that draw on both tradition and innovation.

Some of these rituals are improvised and informal; others are traditional and formal.[9] The metaphor of dancing is often used to describe negotiation, with its continuous feedback loops and coordinated moves. Mediation is like a couple dancing with a master dancer alongside, ready to intervene, to assist with posture or questions, holding the picture of the disputants as graceful in their unfolding composition.

Rituals in mediation may look different, depending on the context, but they fulfill similar needs and purposes. Rituals include the things we do as mediators in convening and facilitating the process to address parties' felt needs for control, recognition, and relationship. The use of a round table without sharp edges or sides invites parties to see a situation holistically. Offering tea or coffee, asking parties to sit in silence before beginning to speak, or writing the ground rules on an easel all serve to mark ritual space and to allow feelings to emerge, as they contribute to a sense of safety necessary for the power of ritual to work.

Mediation functions as ritual in all kinds of matters, from commercial to public policy, from family to international. A motor vehicle case that I mediated functioned as a ritual passage for the plaintiff from seeing herself as a victim to identifying as a survivor. I will use the name Manjit to refer to her. Manjit attended the mediation with her lawyer, faced by an adjuster and her lawyer on the other side of the table.

Manjit did not experience a miraculous remission in her symptoms, nor was the settlement so generous that she was in a celebratory mood. For the first time, however, she had been listened to by a human being from "the other side" in conditions where ordinary patterns of communication were varied. Although some controversy hovered about the extent and seriousness of her injuries, she received acknowledgment that she had been injured and that the insurer's representative was sorry, as a fellow human being, to hear of her pain. As a mediator, I worked with the insurer's representative to distinguish the importance of demonstrating caring about the pain suffered by the plaintiff from accepting legal responsibility for all alleged symptoms. The representative listened attentively to the plaintiff, letting her know, as a fellow human being, that her experience was heard and that the difficulties she reported in resuming her usual activities would be frustrating to anyone in such circumstances.

Did the matter settle quickly or easily after that? There was no magical meeting of minds, but as the plaintiff had to put less energy into resisting an image of herself as a malingerer, she began to imagine herself on the other side of the claim. As the insurer's representative listened to understand rather than to undermine, the plaintiff's behavior became less extreme and the representative felt less concerned about ongoing, inflated demands. As the plaintiff moved from the identity of aggrieved, uncompensated victim to seeing herself as a survivor, both parties were able to hold a picture of the accident that contained enough of their own perspectives for each to let go of extreme positions.

During long negotiations, medical examinations, offers, and counteroffers, the opportunity for resolving the conflict had seemed ever more remote. Manjit worried that she would never "get out from under" the burden of the physical symptoms and the psychological stress of unpaid bills, missed employment, and the thicket of the lawsuit. Her story about the accident had been told and retold to friends and professionals, strengthening her resolve to achieve a fair outcome as shaped by her lawyer's advice. Very little of her time had been spent considering what it would really be like to be free of the two-year-long drama. She had come to identify as a victim at the same time that she resisted the injustice of the role.

The ritual of mediation helped her move away from this identification. Her transformation was facilitated by the demonstration of empathy and genuine listening, drawn from the essential human capacities of the insurer's representative. The representative, a repeat player in commercial mediations like this one, knew the format of the session and the "common moves" of mediator and plaintiff. Her choice to step out of the business-as-usual mode to demonstrate authentic concern for the plaintiff was not the norm in commercial mediations and would not have worked if it were contrived. It was marked and named by me, as mediator, as I slowed down the process and asked Manjit to phrase back what she heard to emphasize its significance.

Through this exchange, Manjit came to see herself as active rather than reactive, strong rather than wounded, dignified rather than shamed. She literally changed her mind—not abandoning her claim but entertaining a picture of her life beyond it. Ritual became a drama in which she was the audience as well as the participant; her patterns of thinking were changed. If Manjit had been able to think or talk her way into the transition from victim to survivor, there would have been no need for the ritual of mediation.

She needed a ritual space in which the usual competitive rules were held in abeyance long enough for genuine listening to liberate her need to hang on. She needed the dialogue that accompanied the ritual of storytelling so that an agreement could be crafted that met her needs, both for a fair settlement and recognition.

Dialogue as Ritual

As we have seen, the ritual of storytelling is used in a different but no less powerful way in dialogues about abortion.[10] In a facilitated process, pro-life and pro-choice advocates are invited to tell personal stories of how they came to adopt their views. They share their heroes and heroines. In doing this, they depart from the discussions they have had in the past in which the well-worn paths of each other's positions have been traversed again and again. As they hear each other's stories, their "enemy" image of each other begins to shift. Sharing the process of arriving at a deeply held value is personal and vulnerable. Threads emerge in common among the stories of those on both sides of the issue. Everyone present describes deep feelings about the subject. Commitment and energy can be respected in all present, even when the commitment is directed to achieving a different end.

In these dialogues, listening to stories without discussion of positions is an improvised ritual with some formality. While participants spontaneously share their stories, they are reminded by the facilitator not to stray into the territory of debate or advocacy. The formality of the form functions to make the improvised storytelling possible. It is an agreed-on departure from the way each person has spoken about the abortion issue in the past. Participants intentionally suspend ordinary ways of being with the specific purpose and boundaries negotiated in advance and monitored by trained facilitators. Those present open to the unknown in each other, for the first time clearing a space in which the beginnings of relationship are possible and empathy can be built.

Whether in a commercial matter or a dialogue about a difficult social issue, rituals make progress easier and mark it, once it has been achieved. Although some convening and ongoing rituals may repeat in different processes, parties and intervenors also make up their own improvised rituals as needs dictate. I believe that mediators who are good at helping parties compose rituals will be more effective than those who do not see this as part of their job description.

Creating Rituals in Conflict Situations

Improvised or created rituals are important to conflict transformation because they can be tailor-made to meet the exact needs of the group at a moment in time. This section addresses the paradoxical activity of developing improvised rituals, which by definition cannot be planned or imposed. Some of the most powerful rituals arise spontaneously from parties in conflict.

Lisa Schirch quotes a conflict trainer working with Greek and Turkish Cypriots to build relationship and understanding who reported:

> At the end of the banquet, two guitars surfaced, appeared out of nowhere, and the Turkish Cypriots started playing and singing folk tunes. A few minutes later, I heard the same songs being sung in Greek. All twenty had learned the songs at their mother's knee and they were singing together. A half hour later, the guitars were passed and the Greeks started playing and they both started dancing. I looked up a few minutes later and I saw Turkish and Greek Cypriots arm in arm, dancing around the room.[11]

This was an improvised ritual, and a surprising one given decades of division and violence marked by very little communication between the two communities. Through it, they acted out cooperation and peace, thus integrating the skills taught during the workshop. Schirch noticed something else significant about the effect of the ritual. During the evening, "the participants seemed to view each other by identities [other than Turkish and Greek Cypriots]: mothers, fathers, fellow victims of the war, teachers, musicians, dancers, etc."[12]

In this situation, like many others, relationship was built through an initiative arising from the group in the form of an improvised, informal ritual. Seeing the other as more than a label widened the ground on which relationship could be built. As mediators and trainers of mediators, we may try to orchestrate such moments, probably with varying success. Mixers, getting-to-know-you exercises, and warm-ups are all ways of proposing improvised rituals. These rituals are successful to the extent that parties are willing to suspend their inhibitions and buy into the process. They may be difficult to implement in situations where patterns of conflict and distrust are deeply ingrained.

Designing Nontraditional Rituals

So how can improvised rituals be designed? Simplicity is the first hallmark of the process. For example, when a large group is meeting, there is a need to have a shared way of reconvening after work in small groups. Sometimes this is done by letting a silent hand signal be the indication that everyone should finish their conversations and focus on one speaker. As each person sees others stop talking and silently raise a hand, focus is achieved easily and respectfully without the third party needing to talk over or interrupt participants. The signal provides a transition in which thoughts are collected and group members can take graceful leave of their conversations. After repetition, the signal becomes a reflex that leads to silence without negotiation or analysis.

Rituals work best when they are personal to involved parties or when they catch the spirit of a group. So a ritual relating to healing may work well with physicians, whereas a ritual involving harmony may work well with musicians or environmentalists. There is also a certain cache in novelty; the ritual may be completely out of the participants' experiences. When this is the case, it is preferable to propose the ritual after rapport has been built within the group and between the group members and the third party. Rituals of drawing or acting out experiences require participants to let go of inhibitions and preconceptions about what is relevant and what is likely to be helpful. Once they do, groups of lawyers can often learn a great deal from drawing; groups of executive officers may construct Tinker Toy towers enthusiastically. These activities are sensory channels that allow for reflection on group dynamics, facets of concepts, and unarticulated assumptions.

For example, in a course for a group of lawyers where power issues were a dominant theme, I asked the participants to form groups of five. I requested that they work in silence, spending two minutes drawing their images of power. Once they had drawn them, I asked them to pass their drawing to the person immediately to their left in the circle, without comment. With the new drawing in hand, I gave them a similar instruction: "Take in your colleague's drawing, capture the essence of their experience of power, and then add to their drawing." After two minutes, I asked them to rotate the drawings to the left, and so on, until each person had spent two minutes working on each drawing in the group.

Once the drawings had rotated to each person, I asked the originator of the drawing to spend some time looking at the new product. Were patterns revealed? Did the sum of the parts add up to new insights or a gestalt that spoke to her or him of the subject in unexpected ways? How did the others respond to the original work, and what did this say about the consensus or different experiences of group participants relating to the issue of power? Finally, I asked group members to discuss the experience and the products together, posing these questions:

- Were the drawings diverse, or did they contain similar themes?
- What was the experience of adding to others' drawings like?
- What surprised you about the experience or your final product?
- What did the exercise teach you about the nature of empowerment and its relationship to support, cooperation, or vulnerability?

The ritual of drawing and passing the drawings was not intuitive for the lawyers, given the individualistic flavor of their training and the uncomfortable unfamiliarity many of them felt with drawing. Yet because they had worked with me for three days at that point, they were willing to suspend their disbelief at the risk of appearing silly or less than proficient. They were quite surprised at the outcome. The pace of the ritual helped them move beyond a focus on their own limitations as artists; the final products were useful as springboards for a discussion rooted in their felt experiences.

Several people commented that the drawing process gave them an opening to communicate differently with each other, in ways complementary to the rational discussion mode used in much of the course. Others expressed surprise that the drawings captured the essence of their experience so well, especially given the rough nature of the original drawings. One lawyer who had looked at me incredulously when I described the assignment said that she went home and tried the activity with several members of her extended family, with the result that they had more fun and closer discussions with each other than they had had in years.

Although this drawing ritual took on meaning for many participants in the group, it is important to note that rituals cannot necessarily be imposed on groups. Rituals may encompass group members in a powerful experience; they may also fizzle or fail to capture the imagination and engagement of the group. What makes the difference between an improvised ritual that works and one that does not? Once a group has worked together for a time, group input into the design of the ritual is essential. This involvement not only builds ownership in the process but ensures that the process arises organically from the experiences of the group rather than being imposed from outside.

Group involvement in planning rituals also prepares participants to make the transition to leaving the training or workshop setting. In a recent workshop, I had used Nepalese chimes to convene the group after small-group exercises or discussions. Toward the end of our time together, participants began to ring the chimes themselves when they wanted the attention of the group. This simple action marked an appropriate transition toward more group initiative and less focus on the leader.

Composing Rituals

Beyond involving parties in the co-creation of rituals, there is no recipe for composing rituals as a third party. Most rituals used in mediation are likely to lean to the informal, nontraditional end of the spectrum. To begin, a mediator might ask her- or himself, "What is needed now?" Answering this question in a way that takes the symbolic, unstated dimensions of the situation into account may suggest a ritual. For example, I was once invited into an organization to help address a set of problems related to structural inefficiency, communication, and conflict. Destructive conflicts had left a legacy, and trust was low. I talked with employees and managers and heard about the negative effects of recent large-scale staff departures and new hirings, perceived management insensitivity, and perceived staff unresponsiveness. There was a shared desire to do something to address these. But there was also an atmosphere of retraction and delicacy. Before we could address communication or structural organization, my answer to the question, What is needed now? was to move away from issues and problem solving to an emphasis on the relational experience of those in the organization. How could all staff members truly hear each other's experience in an atmosphere of caring and inquiry rather than distrust and suspicion?

I asked the staff and management to gather in two separate rooms according to their time in the organization. They called their groups "recent arrivals" and "old timers." The old timers were given a set of tennis balls and a piece of music and asked to devise a repeatable routine involving passing the tennis balls to each member of the group in time to the music. After they had developed and practiced it, I invited the recent arrivals back into the room and started the music. The recent arrivals' task was to integrate themselves into the routine, understanding it and helping with it as best they could.

This departure from a linear, direct mode of communication into invention and sensory attention gave everyone new perspectives to share. Managers spoke about how frustrating it was to try to continue their routine with the new staff members who did not understand the way things were done. Recent arrivals shared their feelings of being overwhelmed, confused, unsure of protocols, and frustrated. These conversations arose from the ritual rather than from being grounded in the problems of the organization, so they provided a neutral way to build empathy and engagement.

Another way to devise a ritual is to use the idea of liminality. What are the parties between? What have you seen and heard about what they hold important that might help them move from where they are to another, more comfortable place? A ritual devised in this way may be as simple as a piece of music mutually chosen, played at the beginning of a family mediation session to bring to mind the parties' shared past. Even as the relationship is being renegotiated, the music may act as a reminder of what once was and provide inspiration for continuing in a way that respects the past.

Another question that arises from the realm of ritual is, What would have meaning for these parties now? In one estate mediation, this question led to conceiving and designing an educational scholarship program. Two Chinese brothers had come to impasse about the division of a final class of their father's assets. Their resourceful mediator built on their desire to venerate their father and their shared value of education to offer them a way through the liminal state of conflict into agreement and satisfaction. The process of designing the scholarship that would carry their father's name—identifying a discipline, requirements, and qualifications for recipients—became a ritual vehicle for the brothers to respectfully acknowledge his legacy.

But not all interventions are rituals. Although we have defined ritual broadly, seeking to enlarge its usual usage to nontraditional and informal experiences, it becomes meaningless if we cannot also answer the question, What is *not* ritual? Although symbolic dimensions are always present in conflict, interventions that do not emphasize them, that do not engage the senses in imaginative inquiry, or that do not draw on the senses or emotions as a resource for addressing conflict are not rituals. Rituals are what happens when we are not on autopilot. Composed with the parties or proposed by the mediator, rituals invite quickening, artistry, connection to something bigger than the self. They touch a chord of meaning. Much of conflict resolution is not ritual; it is slogging through details, hammering out particulars, negotiating outcomes. It calls on our capacities for patience, concentration, problem solving, and analysis.

Ritual helps us when those are not enough. It is the container for genius or spark; it is that which stands apart from the before and after; it is that which releases, progresses, marks, and captures. Composing rituals calls on mediators and trainers to find the poetry in the passage or the rock in the road and to invite participants into it, drawing on their artistry to dissolve or move it out of the way of problem solving and negotiation.

Invoking Culturally Appropriate Rituals

Depending on the cultural backgrounds of those present, it may be appropriate to invoke ancestors with all of their wisdom, strength, imagination, and courage as resources for the process. First Nations people often do this by way of prayer and other spiritual rituals. Asking parties to remember heroes and heroines in their lives not only helps them see their commonalities but brings to mind the qualities that each admires and finds inspiring. This inspiration can rub off on the process. Things that are shared in ritual space have amplified power related to shared intention and the quality of attention ritual invites.

I was recently asked to work with members of a nonprofit tribal organization who were experiencing challenges related to growth and reorganization. Of the two dozen staff members, two-thirds were from Native American tribes, and the others were from a variety of ethnocultural groups. I learned that they did not use native rituals during meetings or office functions, though many in the organization followed individual spiritual paths.

When we met together in a retreat, I asked some of the staff members to begin with a native ritual. We stood in a circle around a blanket on which we each placed something of value to us: rings, pictures of loved ones, feathers, pieces of pottery, and images of a key staff member who was away on sick leave. The process of placing something valuable on the blanket conveyed to everyone present the trust and importance they were investing in the process. Sweetgrass was passed around for those who wanted to "smudge," motioning the smoke toward the body in acknowledgment of its clarifying and cleansing properties.

This ritual had a powerful effect on the process. As the retreat ended, several of the participants spoke of the way that this beginning had set a tone for truth and had engaged everyone present in a unified spirit. Planning, conversing, and visioning were richer for the ritual that infused every moment of the day like the smoke of the sweetgrass that pervaded the room. Although rituals like this one had been avoided by the leaders, who worried about imposing a traditional ritual on the diverse group, those present left with a new realization. The ritual spoke of the values and ideals of the organization that had attracted employees to it in the first place. Remembering this helped contribute to a constructive spirit that enabled those who had been in conflict to speak with each other respectfully and flexibly. The ending of the retreat was marked by a similar ritual.

To mark ritual space as a time apart, it important to have a purposeful ending. The end can be signaled with an action. Participants may read a passage, share an image for the experience, or sit in silence. It is important to make a transition back into ordinary time and space, allowing time for integration and for digestion. Closure is also important because it contains the experience, preserving its integrity. As Frank Zappa tells us, the most important thing in art is the frame. You otherwise cannot know where art stops and the real world begins.

Finding Windows of Opportunity

Does the idea of composing a ritual still sound too unusual? Perhaps the admonition of R. Buckminster Fuller, who wrote *Dare to Be Naïve*,[13] is in order. The question I would ask is, What might the cost be of neglecting the important capacity of ritual? This question is explored in a scene with Elaine and John.

> It is the end of a long and taxing divorce mediation session. There is a pause, a poignant moment in which both Elaine and John step out of advocacy on their own behalf and take a deep breath. In the breath is an acknowledgment of the difficulty inherent in the life passage called separation and divorce. There is awareness of the loss, not only of material goods but the loss of something more precious. It is the loss of a dream, of a sanctuary that once each had invested in the other. And there is sadness and regret where the blame has flourished. If both are honest, there is self-reproach and fear about the future. Even though they know they do not wish to go back again to the conflict that increasingly characterized the marriage, they also know that there is a hole in each life. And the hole is harder to bear because it is borne alone. Not only are they no longer supports to each other but all of the joy and approval that others declared at their coming together has turned into sometimes awkward conversations and lost routines.

Elaine and John are experiencing a loss of ritual. Together they had devised ways of marking and observing occasions and communicating their caring in small daily observances. In the eight years they were together, they went every spring to the seashore and every autumn to the mountains. He searched for the smooth round stones she loved while hiking; she brought him tea on Sunday mornings. There were precious things in their relationship, and there were also things they could not resolve. And so they found lawyers and started the formal part of uncoupling.

The lawyers had suggested mediation, and so they met several times and resolved nearly everything. The mediation had its own unique shape: it began slowly, tentatively, and then transposed into a period of struggle, marked alternately by raised voices and unbending rigidity slowly yielding to a solution that revealed itself incrementally, unevenly. The mediator had held a space for calm, measuring her words, urging, encouraging, and challenging by turn. At last, all three of them sat in the quiet of the office.

The mediator saw that the moment was ripe, not ripe for negotiation but for the kind of act that marks a rite of passage. Nothing trite or sentimental would do: She could not imagine Elaine and John lighting candles and promising to set each other free. As she sat with the question of how to mark the moment, the moment passed and John and Elaine were on their feet. The question went home with her. She wondered about ritual and the missed chance.

But the loss was not only hers. Elaine and John had ongoing conflicts about small items in their property and the timing of actions. The tension between them resurfaced and played out in a dozen ways that seemed absurd, even to their friends. Of course we will never know, but it is possible that they may have come to a place of deeper peace had they marked their progress and acknowledged their losses through ritual rather than playing them out through other issues.

What could this mediator have done besides think more quickly? She could have addressed the opportunity for ritual early on with Elaine and John, asking them to think of what might be meaningful. She could have made suggestions based on what she learned of their values and ways they made meaning together and individually. She might also have pointed out "ritual" experiences that arose spontaneously during the sessions, normalizing their presence and inviting a more intentional exploration of what might be possible and useful. These actions may have helped Elaine and John through a difficult transition in both of their lives.

Rituals and a Relational Approach to Conflict Transformation

Rituals are significant for their capacity to make transitions possible. They help us hold things together that do not necessarily seem to fit, whether these things are different ideas or identities that seem fractured. Rituals show us a way to make amends for wrongs done or hurts suffered without losing face. They help us tap sources of wisdom within and among us. As we tap this wisdom, rituals help make intentions manifest in the world. They gather us and rally us, helping us "set relationships right" when there has been a disturbance or an imbalance.

Rituals have a transformative potential, helping us get out of the corners that we find ourselves in when in conflict. As Sharon Devlin writes: "The purpose of ritual is to change the mind of the human being. It's sacred drama in which you are the audience as well as the participant, and the purpose of it is to activate parts of the mind that are not activated by everyday activity."[14] As we activate these parts of our mind, we find creative and communal resources to help us transition.

Rituals are central to a relational approach to conflict transformation because they extend our capacities to connect deeply with others. As we engage with each other in ways that matter deeply, the relationships of those in conflict and the conflict itself necessarily shift.

PART FOUR

Third-Party Roles and Practices

With our exploration of metaphor, story, and ritual as intervention and teaching tools, we began a conversation that becomes richer as it continues. Many other creative approaches to bridging conflict that would enrich our toolkits are used in a variety of settings. Drama, improvisational theater, and other interactive methodologies engage people in creative problem solving and invoke emotional intelligence. Exploring myths or proverbs are ways into cultural meaning making. Events like music or arts festivals that bring people from different sides in conflicts together are powerful ways to build shared experience and relationship. The possibilities are limited only by our imagination and our willingness to try unusual approaches.

Creative tools contribute to more meaningful processes and deeper relationships, yet conflict continues. Recognizing that conflict is always with us, we return to the seven mountains we traversed in Chapter One. Each of the seven mountains symbolizes perspectives that are helpful in engaging conflict from the heart. Together they remind us of interconnection and caring as the center of our processes. In this final chapter, we reflect on how somatic, emotional, intuitive, imaginative, and connected ways of knowing help clarify our vision as third parties and teachers. Coming full circle, we reflect on our learning and its implications for third-party roles and practices. We generate new questions for the future, trusting that together we will live into the answers.

CHAPTER NINE

Revisiting the Mountains
Third-Party Creativity

We shall not cease from exploration
And the end of all our exploring
Will be to arrive where we started
And know the place for the first time.
T. S. ELIOT[1]

Climbing mountains. It takes perseverance, courage, planning, and resources we did not know we possessed. It takes teamwork and the ability to anticipate the unexpected and respond when predictions are inaccurate. It takes the chutzpah to imagine that the quest is both possible and significant and the humility to know that our personal agendas may not prevail. Climbing mountains takes grace, openness to learning, and willingness to enter into a conversation with what speaks to us, even when that conversation demands everything we have to give.

On the mountain, it is clear that our life may depend on our receptivity, our attunement to ourselves, each other, the environment, and on our creativity. In the conflicts of our twenty-first century, the same may be true.

Conflicts, like mountains, call us and challenge us. When we meet these challenges with determination and discernment, matching our rhythm to the environment, conflict leaves us deepened. Its footprints on our lives are unmistakable, but they are not just surface scars. They become places in the earth where welcome rain is caught in otherwise dry landscapes. They are the tracks in which others may follow as they navigate their own conflicts, responding to their own deep calls and the unexpected trials and revelations that come in any shared quest.

Bridging conflicts, like climbing mountains, involves paying attention to more than one level at once. From the trail, we get periodic glimpses of a panorama or a stunning peak. Mostly we see the path, trees immediately around us, snatches of sky. We simultaneously engage the small picture and the big one. We ascend from below, attending to details and making step-by-step, incremental progress. Guided by the spaciousness we seek, we suffer terrain that would block us, canyons that would swallow us, and avalanches that would bury us. So in conflict, we include past, present, and future in the circle of our attention, making incremental progress in restorying the past on the way to manifesting an imagined future. Conflicts buffet us, testing our resolve, yet they also create openings for us in ways we little understand.

Conflicts are much more than bad or good, desirable or deniable. They are the stuff of our dreams, nudging us toward who we can become. They are the sand in our oysters, calling us to immediacy and exquisite attention to alignment—alignment with our purpose and with what breathes meaning into our lives. They are the insistent tapping of what we know but have forgotten or of what we do not know but need to imagine if we are to extricate ourselves from the knots that confine us.

Gifted by conflict, we come full circle to celebrate the views from the seven mountains we have climbed. Like any adventurer, we look to what we have learned, what we will take from our learnings for the future, and where new adventures call us, even as we pack our gear for the trip home. Arriving home, we see the place with new eyes, embrace loved ones with fresh appreciation, and pause to mark all we have experienced: the conflicts, the surprises, and the achievements. All have been our teachers.

Through the pages of this book, we have traversed many accounts of change and transformation. Recognizing the inherent wisdom of those who own a conflict, we have noticed times when third parties are helpful. Moving away from an emphasis on discrete skills or a particular process, we have identified capacities that help conflict resolution professionals (like the readers of this book) develop the flexibility, sensitivity, and adroitness that bridging conflicts calls forth.

Drawing on their emotional, somatic, and imaginative intelligences, third parties bring creativity to conflict resolution processes. Relying on connected ways of knowing, they notice opportunities invisible to others and seize chances to deepen relationship. Realizing the importance of symbolic, meaning-making dimensions, they develop fluency with metaphor, ritual, and stories as resources for bridging differences.

In this final chapter, we turn our attention to the terrain of the third-party role. What does a third party need in the way of resources for the journey through conflict? Which practices help develop the wisdom needed to bridge differences? How does an effective third party demonstrate leadership across a range of conflicts, from complex to apparently simple, remaining true to self while acknowledging group wisdom? And how do third parties help compose imaginative interventions that magnify creative capacities (their own and others') while attending to the theories and research that inform their choices?

Answers to these questions emerge as we consider the enterprise of climbing mountains. Climbers need to stay oriented and aware of their goal. They need to train. Colleague Mark McCrea warns would-be third parties to try climbing local Buck Hill before setting out for Mount Everest. With the dream of higher mountains in mind, the work of daily training is willingly embraced. Climbers know that they need to develop flexibility and familiarity with many roles before they are ready for serious climbing. So it is with conflict: the ways of knowing we have explored breathe life and possibility into the many roles we take as third parties.

Just as this book has offered ways of knowing and being complimentary to existing theory and practice, so this exploration of third-party roles and practices offers unique and creative perspectives. Others have written extensively about the science of conflict intervention. Recognizing that the art is at least as important as the science, we conclude with a survey of third-party roles and practices designed to inspire, invite inquiry, and expand.

Third-Party Roles and Practices

Third parties intervening in conflict fulfill countless roles. They are listening ears, agents of reality, balancers of power, and designers and managers of process. They steer a course between building rapport and maintaining perspective, between impartiality and caring. They draw on hearts, minds, and intuition. They know some paths up the mountain; they realize that new groups of climbers need to find their own paths. As they gain in experience, they increasingly recognize that all their life experiences prepare them for the expeditions they lead. How these experiences are kept supple in memory, ready to be drawn upon, makes all the difference.

Third parties in conflict help parties arrive at a variety of destinations. For some the goal is agreement, for others acknowledgment or apology. Sometimes the outcome is a new structure; other times the desire is for positive peace. Whatever the goal, third parties need imagination and courage to guide the journey. Imaginations are nourished by pictures collected from life. For this reason, successful third parties are connoisseurs of life experience. They notice what works to salve conflicts; they notice how harmony is maintained. They seek to bring fresh minds to conflict processes, marrying rich images of what has worked with dreams of the possible. Creative third parties intentionally gather experiences of success. They also work with failures, using them as learning fields from which to harvest tools for the next expedition.

How do third parties keep their memories supple and their limbs limber to support creative conflict resolution? How do they plumb the riches of their experiences, both successes and failures? Some helpful practices include reflecting and conferencing, attending to secondary effects, and creating a portfolio. We'll explore each of these briefly before returning to the mountaintop views of third-party roles.

Reflecting and Conferencing

Learning does not come from just being in the vicinity of an event, even as a third party. I have seen lessons I needed to incorporate into my life, heard others describe their journeys, and watched struggle take place—and then resumed my old patterns. Some-times I become preoccupied with one aspect of a conflict dynamic and miss the bigger picture. Watching a practitioner who is more effective at balancing both levels does not necessarily lead me to change my behavior. Learning comes from engaging with others and having experiences; it comes from dialogue, reflection, and individual work directed toward integration.

Coming home after an intervention, or in the room itself after everyone has gone, I record my questions, observations, connec-tions. It helps to have a focus; I sometimes concentrate on an area where I want to learn and grow. Perhaps I attend to emotional expression; perhaps I'm attuned to somatic messages that contain rich clues about the shape and appetite of the conflict. Reflective writing soon after a session often reveals dimensions I was unaware of. Coming back to it later, I piece observations together like a jig-saw puzzle, creating a template for paying closer attention next time I meet with the parties. I note ideas that arise for the next intervention. I note questions I want to share with a colleague.

Another form of journaling that has worked well is an exchange with a colleague. In this practice, I exchange my prac-tice journal with a colleague who has kept a journal about her or his recent intervention experiences. Sometimes we write comments on each other's work; other times we come together and talk about our questions and observations. Always, this contributes to insight, extending my field of view and enriching my choices.

A variation on exchanging journals is conferencing with col-leagues in practice circles about current cases. Coming together, we talk about themes that have arisen in our work, ethical or process questions, successes, and challenges. We seek to weave the-oretical understandings into our dialogue, always grounding our exchanges in actual experience. Practitioners may belong to more than one practice circle, depending on areas of focus and interest. The practice circle process is affirming and expanding. Because we are committed to each other and to developing creative prac-tices, we help each other remember to access many ways of know-ing in sifting through the learnings from our work.

Each of these practices is centered in reflection. Each makes the link between raw experience and learning, fostering integration and synthesis. All of the practices enlarge the scope of individual experience by drawing connections between our own past learning and the perspectives of trusted others. They keep memories fluid and available to inform future decisions. However reflective engagement is practiced, it enhances learning by drawing attention to valuable nuggets that might otherwise be lost in the sheer volume of experiences we accrue in any one day.

Attending to Secondary Effects

People in conflict are often tense, distracted, off-center, traumatized. Practitioners who work with people involved in protracted and highly emotional conflicts report that they feel the effects of their work physically. It takes a toll on bodies and psyches to enter relational systems that are strained containers for pain. This is called secondary trauma. Shifting from residual tension and assumed emotions helps prevent the ongoing effects of secondary trauma. To avoid burnout and other negative effects, resilient practitioners consciously shift their emotional focus and take care of their physical needs following contact with stressed or tense parties in a conflict.

There are a variety of ways to do this. Invoking somatic intelligence, it is helpful to tune into our bodies following work as well as during processes. Where are we storing pain or tension? What is being internalized that does not belong to us? Yoga and movement therapy, as well as running, walking, meditating, and swimming, are all options for letting go of what is not ours, for moving through the physical effects of conflict. As we move, we break through the bodily armor that might otherwise develop around painful memories, keeping them accessible and available for continuing responsiveness to learning.

Movement respects our bodies' need to complete a process. It is an important and often-neglected part of our work. We come full circle when we tap into our somatic intelligence to notice the effects of our work on our bodies and then do what feels good and nurturing in response.

In addition to these physical ways of responding, it is important to know when to take a break; it is helpful to have colleagues and friends with whom to debrief traumatic experiences. Whether the conflict system is our own (for example, Palestinian-Israeli dialogues led by Palestinian-Israeli facilitators) or whether we are outsiders (for example, a meeting between a school board and parents facilitated by someone from another state or province), it is important to have time and space away from the intensity. Even when it is impossible to leave a geographic location, taking time for mental, emotional, and physical regeneration is essential. If we do not, we may lose our perspective, becoming a part of the conflict dance in a way that impairs our effectiveness.

Creating Practice Portfolios

We also enhance our effectiveness when we stop to celebrate our successes. This is one of the most neglected aspects of our work as conflict resolution professionals. A colleague told me that he puts tremendous dedication into planning, engaging, and critically reflecting on his work. But he loses resolve when it comes to marking it with a ritual or celebrating it. Instead he is on to the next project, the next goal. This deprives him of something precious; it may also preclude parties to conflict from the closure and satisfaction that comes from celebrating achievements.

One way to mark closure is to develop a portfolio—a multidimensional collection of materials from practice. A portfolio includes products using a range of media that document and reflect on practice. It may include connections to literature and research, an ongoing list of questions arising from practice, or materials related to themes like emotional intelligence or connected ways of knowing. It may reflect experiences that integrate theory and practice, generating creative observations or new questions. Journal entries are often part of portfolios. One of my portfolio entries records the visit of my class to the Hirshhorn Museum of Art, where docent Fanchon Silberstein led us through an exploration of connections among modern art, conflict, and spirituality.

Portfolios are excellent places to record observations, conflict assessment notes, effective and ineffective questions, process choice-points, and surprises. They may also include journal entries, peer responses to journal entries, and photographs or sketches done to reflect on interventions. Practitioners who create portfolios of their work are often surprised at their breadth and richness.

Shared in community, portfolios help us refine our practices, increase competence, and mark learning.

The portfolio idea comes from my work in an academic setting, where I realized that standard academic papers were too narrow to contain the dynamic, multifaceted dimensions of conflict resolution practice. Alongside written assignments, I began asking students to develop nonverbal products relating to themes of the class. Despite initial resistance, students produced an amazing, creative range of products that contributed to their learning in ways they had not anticipated.

They have made terrariums symbolizing the biosystems of conflict where attention to nutrients and balance is needed; they have woven cloth with multicolored threads reflecting the complexity and aesthetic beauty of conflict in diverse groups. One student wrote and illustrated a children's book about conflict; she was surprised at the challenges and dividends that came from capturing the essence of her work in simple language. Connecting the process of creating these products with conflict practice turns out to be a versatile vehicle for integrating theory and research with practice, stimulating dialogue with colleagues, and supporting learning. Creating products like these becomes a ritual, connecting our senses, feelings, bodies, and spirits to the analysis at which we are so much more practiced.

As we step outside a linear approach to training and intervention, taking time to journal and reflect, process somatically and create products to mark learning, we recognize again the multifaceted nature of the third-party role. Conflict is so consuming that it engages all of ourselves. So intervention requires nothing less. Returning to the mountains we surveyed in Chapter One, we see a range of third-party roles important to mindful, heartful conflict resolution.

Questing and Questioning

Whenever we intervene in conflict, we ask questions. Experienced practitioners know that all questions are not created equal. It is an art to come to ask good questions—questions that interrupt negative, stuck ways of seeing, that open the doorway to connections previously unseen. Questions are at the heart of the work of Mirror Mountain, the place from which we see that conflict shows us our connections, as well as places where the fabric of relationship has been stressed. From the summit of Mirror Mountain, we see the things we missed when we first glanced at an issue or a problem, and we engage in inquiry from this place.

Questions are deceptively simple yet vitally important in revealing connections. In exploring their power, practitioner Laura Chasin quotes from Elie Wiesel's *Night*—a memoir about the Holocaust. Young Elie's spiritual master, Moche, tells him that every question possesses a power of its own—a power that does not lie in its answer. "Man raises himself toward God by the questions he asks Him," Moche explains, adding that this does not mean he can understand God's answers. Elie questions the purpose of prayer, if answers are not understood. Moche replies, "I pray to the God within me that He will give me the strength to ask Him the right questions."[2]

Mirror Mountain reminds us to cultivate a spirit of inquiry, playing with questions in our minds until the right one emerges. Our questions can implicitly emphasize interdependence, invite creativity, or propose new perspectives. They can interrupt conflict escalation, turning the focus back to personal responsibility. They can plant seeds—seeds that may bear fruit later as they turn and play in parties' minds. Questions can be posed with silence as bookends, drawing attention to the multiple levels they contain. Questions can blame, trap, and badger, but they can also support, enliven, and shape. From the peak of Mirror Mountain, third parties see the power of questions to reveal, as a mirror reveals. The mirror reveals the contours of our conflicts reflected in our faces, showing us the ever-present possibility of change.

Change into Being

As a child growing up in a middle-class home, my physical needs were well met. Yet I felt a concern for the millions of children for whom this was not true. I sat on the kitchen stool in my prairie home and felt a desire to help. I dreamed then that change was possible, one project at a time.

Conflicts give us the opportunity to change; indeed, they present us with the imperative of change if we are to truly transform the relationships and systems that give rise to some of the most destructive conflicts among us. Contemplating change, we climb Invention Mountain to find new ways to think of and be with the conflicts that most challenge us. At its summit, we see that our role is not only agent of reality but catalyst of imagination. As we hold a vision of the possibility of change, staying open to a wide range of outcomes, the unforeseen can happen.

In India, a story is told of a holy man who stayed in his monastery when the army was advancing through the area, killing all holy men. A general was surprised to find him in the monastery after all the others had run away. "Don't you know that I can thrust my sword into your stomach?" asked the general. The holy man replied, "Don't you know that I can place my stomach around your sword?"

Conflict processes ask us to shift perspective, to engage a range of ways of seeing and being. As we do this, we encounter paradox. On the one hand, clarity of focus and goals are important. On the other, Invention Mountain reminds us that journeys always give us the opportunity to engage and embrace ambiguity. One day after a mediation session, one of the parties came to me saying that the ideas we discussed were still churning around, stretching her ability to live with the ambiguity and complexity of real people full of contradictions. With her categories and ways of seeing disturbed, she was on the edge of change.

Only as we are open to ambiguity and complexity are we able to change. The process of change, far from orderly, can feel confusing, disorienting, and unsettling. As we engage it, ritual can serve as a compass. As Mary Douglas observes, "Ritual recognizes the potency of disorder. In the disorder of the mind [and] in dreams, ritual expects to find truths that cannot be reached by conscious effort."[3]

Ritual and other symbolic tools help us move through change processes, marking and integrating our learning so that change is durable. Listening for metaphors, we see ways we are holding ourselves back from what is possible. Telling stories, we celebrate the changes we have made and uncover the seeds of new stories yet untold. Drawing on our imagination and intuition, we encounter the unexpected in all its rich potential.

Dancing with Surprise

At the summit of Magic Mountain, we encounter surprise. It is not a coincidence that many stories in this book include something unexpected or unplanned contributing to the resolution of a conflict. Third parties may appear to be magicians as they work with what imagination and intuition reveal; actually, they are working with elements that have presented themselves in creative ways. The capacity to do this adroitly and expertly arises from familiarity with the unseen in ourselves. We become familiar with what we cannot measure or evaluate through connected ways of knowing, often via unfamiliar channels.

In Tibetan Buddhist tradition, a female figure called dakini is said to appear to practitioners, bringing wisdom that cannot be learned through conventional methods. Dakinis are said to hold the key to "otherness," to the wound that must be invited in to puncture the conventional mind. It is significant that dakinis are female in Tibetan culture where patriarchy prevails and public voices of women are little heard. Representing "the other," they bring what is not seen into view; they ask questions otherwise not given voice. Dakinis disturb patterns of thought and help recipients of their visits uncover hidden resources. Conflict professionals find dakinis of their own as they climb Magic Mountain, encountering people and experiences that challenge habitual, comfortable ways of thinking and knowing.

A story is told by Simmer-Brown[4] of a dakini who appeared to Naropa, a learned man known for his prowess at scripture, debate, and commentary. This dakini embodied intuitive wisdom. To be in her presence was to experience a sharp, penetrating quality of holistic knowing beyond books and logic. It is said that she had thirty-seven ugly features, including a deeply wrinkled and bearded face, rotting teeth, bloodshot eyes, and a crooked nose. Unable to escape her presence, Naropa joined her to climb his own version of Magic Mountain, not knowing what was in store.

The dakini quizzed Naropa about his studies, asking him if he understood the words or the sense of what he was studying. At first he replied that he understood the words alone, and she was joyful to hear the truth spoken. After a moment, he added that he also understood the sense of the words. The dakini was upset to hear him lie so boldly. Easily, she pointed out his superficial understanding, which arose from intellect alone. He had failed to see that knowing the sense of what he was studying had as much to do with the landscape of the heart as with the intellect. It had to do with the borderland where identity and meaning meet. It had to do with a quality of attention that listened to—but also around, underneath, and beside—the literal meaning of words.

As Naropa received wisdom from the dakini, she who symbolized the intuitive, sensing, and heart-based ways of knowing so different from his intellectual approach, so conflict resolution practitioners enhance their work by moving outside cognitive habits, engaging the unexpected and the unnamed. The idea of moving beneath positions to interests to solve a conflict represents an advance in this direction. It takes us from the material surface of the problem into what fuels it. But going one step deeper to uncover what is beneath the presenting surface is only to expand along a unidimensional plain.

From Magic Mountain, we see that moving from positions to interests is a beginning but is not sufficient. Inviting in that which we have not seen through the lenses we habitually use, we look not only at the words but inquire into the sense of the words. We stretch to explore the boundaries where our ways of being contest other ways of knowing and being and the broken places inside us that fuel the chasms that threaten to swallow us. When we do not acknowledge differences in the ways meaning is made, these very differences operate under the table like a series of bowling balls, ricocheting off shins, escalating the conflict. The differences may seem threatening, but their existence must be dealt with to achieve lasting resolutions. When we engage these differences, making friends of surprise and improvisation, we embrace the gifts of Magic Mountain.

Developing Creative Leadership

From the top of Goldmine Mountain, we see that we need all of our physical, emotional, imaginative, and spiritual selves to bridge conflict. Searching our theories, we see that they take us only part of the way up the trail. We can master the lexicon of conflict resolution practice, but we remain below the tree line. Surrounded by apparent material obstructions and communication barriers, we are challenged to remember that conflict is centrally about meaning. Until this is understood, attempts to solve material or communication issues will be hampered. To access meaning making, we move into the world of symbol and perception. We adopt a spirit of inquiry, leaving what we thought we knew by the side of the trail. As we do this, we access our multiple intelligences and our potential for creative genius.

Resistance to using our whole selves in the service of conflict resolution seems to arise from fear of vulnerability as well as a lack of practice. It is easier to stay in the well-worn trails that do not lead to the summit than to create a new path around an avalanche. Parties tell old conflict stories again and again, reinforcing a focus on identity, security, the righteousness of their positions, or the unfairness visited upon them rather than see themselves as inventors of new stories. As third parties, we also stay in well-worn, linear processes, even when they do not have the vitality or flexibility to breathe life into damaged relationships.

Why do we not experiment and innovate more in our conflict processes? Perhaps as third parties, this would evoke vulnerability and counter our investment in our own expert images. We resist creativity out of attachment to the ways we have ordered our "givens"—those things we rely on as fixed realities. We justify our resistance by imagining that acknowledging the boundaries between what we know and where we are stumped looks like defeat. Yet it is these very intersections that are full of energy and life. In acknowledging what we are sure of and what puzzles us, we make room for others to do the same. In exploring ways we do not understand the "sense" of words or events, we open up the possibility of working together to uncover multiple meanings.

Goldmine Mountain reminds us that creative processes not only yield surprises but entail risk. Some of the things we try may not work. We may design rituals that fall flat when we try to implement them. We may encounter trails that seem to taper off into impenetrable undergrowth. As we collaborate with parties to try a range of creative approaches, we become more adept at engaging serendipity, surprise, and synchronicity when they grace our conflict processes.

Becoming Wise Practitioners

Reaching Noble Mountain, we see that the project of building competence and confidence as a third party is not only an outside job. At the outset of our process, we often look away—to someone, a technique, a place, or something outside ourselves as a resource. Yet we are not empty receptacles into which trainers and coaches pour immutable knowledge. Because conflict is relational, the dances we do to unwind it are also relational, context-dependent, and fluid.

Although it may not be apparent to the newcomer to the field, becoming an effective conflict intervenor calls us to ongoing inner exploration. This exploration includes asking ourselves hard questions like

- Where does conflict live in me?
- Where are the edges of my relational fabric frayed or damaged so that it might not provide a secure place for others to anchor their trust?
- How do I identify with my work in a way that might limit parties?
- How does who I am in the world, and in my inner world, support or undermine the values I implicitly share with others?

From Noble Mountain, we see that modeling our beliefs is a strong component of conflict resolution leadership. Valuing collaboration, we engage parties in process design and ask their advice at choice-points. Committed to change, we uncover our own resistance before expecting flexibility from others. Nothing will undermine our work more quickly than failing to implement the principles of receptive engagement we promote among parties. Seeking congruence between what we believe, profess, and do, we focus on our own awareness and development, even as we seek to assist others. Thomas Merton points to the importance of this:

> He who attempts to act and think for others or for the world without deepening his own self understanding, freedom, integrity and capacity to love, will not have anything to give others. He will communicate to them nothing but the contagion of his own obsessions, his aggressiveness, his ego-centered ambitions, his delusions about ends and means, his doctrinaire prejudices and ideas.[5]

Setting ego aside, we engage in inner and outer quests with a spirit of genuine inquiry. We will find incongruence—places where ideals are not met, either by others or by ourselves. Where the incongruence is our own, we pause for exploration. What stands in the way of stepping into the ideal? Although it often seems that someone else is in the way, it may be something inside of us, dancing with someone else. We may not be able to change them, but we can shift within. And this creates change in ripples throughout the relationship.

Traversing Noble Mountain, we recognize that the invisible inner world is as specific in its contours as the outer physical world. As our sense organs are adapted to the physical world, so our inner ways of knowing perceive the invisible world. We cannot know ourselves from the inside with machines or with analytical tools. We are not patterns; we are living persons. Coming to know this internal terrain is an ongoing process extending throughout life.

Noble Mountain reminds us that as we monitor who we are in what we do, we will not encounter straight lines. Trails loop around, sometimes giving us glimpses of edges that cause us to draw in quick breaths of awe. These edges remind us to be mindful in our quests for ways of bridging conflicts. They remind us that conflict bridging happens not only in the "wide world of important work" but in our inner worlds simultaneously. Spider, a mythological creature, knows this intuitively.

Seeing Ourselves as Spider

Seeing ourselves as Spider may be less intuitive than adopting the mantle of sage, magician, or leader. Yet Spider carries a legacy especially well suited to the conflict practitioner. In Native American mythology, Spider is wise and revered. She is creative, centrally embedded in the patterns of life. She connects the past with the future, generating possibilities. Weaving threads that glisten in the morning sun, Spider embodies the values of industry, artistry, and relationship. Spider's webs, intricate in their interconnections, remind us that conflicts are never disconnected from context, nor are individuals ever discrete, autonomous units.

Spider makes her home at the peak of Circle Mountain. From there, the connection among all mountains is clear. Circle Mountain reminds us that conflict resolution requires the integration of diverse ways of seeing and knowing. Third parties who recognize interconnectedness as the principle of conflict, whether related to its inception, escalation, or resolution, embody the creative spirit of Spider.

What are the implications of this recognition for practice? Winslade and Monk[6] remind us that conflict communications occur in a dynamic system. Focusing on conflict narratives and our role in co-constructing them brings us to an awareness of how our internal selves, with all of their unresolved feelings, competing meanings, and passionate convictions, play into the ways conflicts unfold. From here, we dispel the myth that it is possible for third parties to remain hermetically sealed by neutrality from parties, issues, and outcomes.

Recognizing the third-party role as part of a relational system is to acknowledge that nonverbal messages communicate our views and feelings, even when we suppress words. It is to know that if we are bored with our work, we are probably not creating an environment in which clients can easily access their imaginative and intuitive intelligence. What we think and feel affects not only the process of conflict resolution sessions but outcomes. If we resist knowing the extent of our influence, downplaying parties' abilities to discern our views to which they respond either with compliance or reactivity, then we are screening out a large component of relational dynamics.

As we acknowledge the power of the third-party role, we have choices to make. How can we use it generously and gracefully, remembering the physician's goal to "do no harm?" Recognizing that we always have a perspective and that our perspective is influential, how can we still work with parties to arrive at a place that works for them? Using our tools of reflecting and conferencing, and including parties as collaborative partners in design and ongoing process decisions, we answer these questions in an ongoing way.

Welcoming Heart into Our Processes

Seeking answers, we climb the final peak of our seven: Heart Mountain. From here, another question is posed, extending from the field of conflict resolution into our wider Western world: How can we welcome "heart" back into the center of our work and our lives? It has been more than a thousand years since educational institutions separate from the church first appeared. But even with the founding of specialized universities focused on the intellect, churches and monasteries still had important missions. They maintained the responsibility to look after the development of "good hearts," teaching compassion and other human and spiritual values.[7]

Today we have largely maintained the distinction between education for the intellect and education for the heart, though we have come to neglect the latter. This has happened for a variety of reasons. The split between scientific and traditional worldviews has been accompanied by a privileging of the intellect and a gradual decline of religion-based education. Few educational programs integrate a focus on the heart and on compassion. Outside faith-based programs, little exists to connect contemplative traditions to conflict theories. As much of our theory and research have developed in universities, they reflect the scientific tenets operating there.

Our academics have been prolific in producing a range of theories and analytical maps, informing concepts from ripeness (the idea that conflicts are more amenable to resolution at certain points) to integrative bargaining (the idea that collaboration potentially increases gains for all parties). We teeter on the edge of repeating the error of the Enlightenment tradition: focusing on instrumental, isolated aspects of processes rather than the relationships that are the heart of conflict and its resolution. We are afraid of what we do not know, squeamish about venturing into the realm for which we have scant vocabulary and few objective measures. This has foreclosed from our theories and practices some of most important ways of knowing needed for our processes to work at the many levels they are needed.

To integrate our work into the social realities of the twenty-first century, to troll for all of the resources available to fuel our understanding and our practice, we are challenged to bring the heart back into our discourse. We are challenged to ask how conflict processes can address this void of the heart in a language that the religious woman, the agnostic man, and the atheist teen can all participate in, to entertain the question, How can we "do" conflict with good hearts?

His Holiness the Dalai Lama offers some assistance. Firmly opposed to imposing religious values or attempting to convert others, he advises, "Simply make clear the essential human values: a warm heart, a sense of caring for one another."[8] No one would disagree with this, at least not until they were asked to apply it to someone seen as an enemy, an "other." Then, having a warm heart and a sense of caring is not only a stretch but may be seen as disloyal, traitorous, foolish, or uncaring to one's own people. Developing and articulating an ethic of care, even toward those on the other side of conflict, is an important challenge for those of us who seek to bridge conflict.

The durable ideas of Carl Rogers point us in the direction of manifesting this ethic of care. I paraphrase them here, drawn from the book *On Becoming a Person*[9] that summarizes his life's work. Rogers stressed the importance of authenticity, observing that it does not help, in the long run, to act as though we are something we are not. As we are not neutral and not disconnected from others, acknowledging our biases and our connections may be helpful. As we acknowledge them, we seek to be fair, attuned to self and others with understanding.

Rogers saw enormous value in permitting himself to understand another person. Sometimes it was more of a stretch than others. These times are the teaching times—the times we remember because they call on us to grow. We block ourselves from understanding when someone reminds us of our own capacity for hurtful behavior or inflicting pain. It is helpful to remember that we may understand without condoning, empathize without agreeing. In the service of understanding, Rogers found it useful to invite others to share their private, perceptual worlds. As these worlds are shared, windows into meaning making and identity are opened, and shifts become possible.

Finally, Rogers included in his ethic of care the idea that it is not always best to rush in with a view to fixing things. In our field of conflict resolution, where we are so oriented to reaching agreements and coming to closure, this is especially pertinent. Rogers observed that he was less driven to fix things when he cultivated openness to thoughts and feelings, his own and others'. Paradoxically, Rogers noticed that when he let go of an urge to control or to change himself or others, a space opened from which change could arise.

Infusing our work with an ethic of care is not to sugar coat it or drown it in sweetness. Far from an invitation to hold hands and sing, this ethic arises directly from the interconnection acknowledged on Heart Mountain—interconnection that Thomas Merton calls hidden wholeness.[10] When we imagine ourselves as connected by inextricable threads of relationship, the process of addressing conflict is much different than if we assume disconnection and competition. Starting with the mutual respect that arises from acknowledging connection, we are inoculated against individualized perspectives that obscure interdependence.

The acknowledgment of connection is pragmatic and ignored at our peril; its denial ultimately leads to war and environmental degradation. War relies for its continuation on an enemy "other." If the other is seen as part of the human web of relations, then dehumanizing actions are limited and finding ways to coexist takes priority. Environmental degradation is justified if we imagine that the earth is there for the use of select peoples at a particular time without acknowledgment of responsibility and interdependence with future generations or people in other regions. Both war and environmental degradation leave us poorer, diminished in our resources and our sense of interconnectedness.

Perhaps the greatest measure of our work is the extent to which it adds to our humanity, to our consciousness of caring as the key to bridging conflict. Mother Teresa put it this way as she accepted the Nobel Prize for her life's work. "It's not how much we do, but how much love we put in the action that we do."

Full Circle

And so we return to the words of T. S. Eliot: "And the end of all our exploring will be to arrive where we started and know the place for the first time."[11] What do we know, having traversed new terrain and sought perspective from a range of peaks? What can we name that we experienced but did not recognize in our work of the past? What is familiar in the ideas we have canvassed that was only an inkling in our consciousness in the past? No doubt, the answers to these questions will be as diverse as the readers of this book.

From the mountaintop, we see a vast expanse. Worlds stretch out below us, revealing splendor, inviting minds and hearts to open. Small concerns slip away; we hold our conflicts with the gentleness inspired by perspective and aesthetic beauty. We let in a little awe, not the awe that inspires the ubiquitous colloquialism "awesome" but the awe that is truly amazed and engaged. Bring to mind an experience with bridging conflict that was deeply satisfying. Did it not, as M. C. Richards[12] writes, deepen the colors of your life? As you keep this memory with you, you see that there is no such thing as a past to be recalled with longing, only a perpetual present continually blending with the heightened elements of the past.

From the mountaintop, we realize that we see through a thin wafer of consciousness tossed about in a swirling sea. We move not only with conscious intention but in concert with deeper, more ancient motions, complex motives, primal forces, and unseen patterns. Our intuitive intelligence confirms this; our imaginative intelligence gives us momentary glimpses of the bigger picture. Relying on connected ways of knowing, we summon the courage to acknowledge that we live always on the edge—the edge of the unknown.

From the far borders of our awareness comes inspiration and innovation, unlimited by what we think we know. What would happen if we saw our work as convening conversations among imaginations? Poet David Whyte writes of experiencing a "sea formed not from the general's command but from the flow and turn of a thousand creative conversational elements."[13] In creative conversation, we discover not only what to do but who we are.

In conflict, *who we are* is the ultimate gift. As Carl Jung admonished Robert Johnson: "Please remember, it is what you are that heals, not what you know. In the beginning of my career, I knew nothing, actually less than nothing. But it still worked. And do you know why? It was because of who I was."[14] As we nourish our beings—beings that love beauty, music, and symmetry, even as they "befall each other constantly," we find integrated ways to draw on all of our gifts in bridging the conflicts that enliven and challenge us most.

Then our work and our lives move in concert to fulfill Jung's description of our ultimate purpose: "to kindle a light in the darkness of mere being."

Practice Tips: Integrating Multiple Ways of Knowing

Throughout this book, examples and illustrations show how a creative, relational approach informs conflict resolution processes. Here is a list of ways to integrate multiple ways of knowing into practice. These are meant for practitioners—mediators, facilitators, conciliators—all those who find themselves informally playing the "in-between" role. The list is also helpful when we find ourselves in a conflict, because our conflicts challenge us to keep a sense of perspective and to access creative tools.

Creating a Space for Sharing

- Center conflict resolution processes in individual and joint awareness of purposes and meanings by including opportunities for people to share what they care about and multiple aspects of their identities, not just things related to conflict issues.

Cultivating Fluidity

- Remember that the material, social, and symbolic levels of conflict (see Figure 1.1) are not easily extricable from each other. Most conflict has all three dimensions, and they are interwoven and dynamic in ways that make analysis and tracking challenging. Conflict is never a linear process. Recognize that any successful conflict process will involve moving fluidly among the three levels.

- Whichever level of conflict (material, social, or symbolic) is in focus, ask yourself from time to time what is going on at the other levels that affects what you see and what you cannot see. For example:

  > When working on material issues, consider how communication and perceptions are influencing progress.
  >
  > When aiming to improve social structures or communication, watch for the ways symbolic messages are conveyed and identities are affected.
  >
  > When engaging in story telling, sharing metaphors, or a spontaneous ritual, be mindful of their effects on the material and social aspects of the conflict.

Creatively Changing Modes

- Find ways to change modes when the going gets tough. Creativity experts tell us that creative genius comes not from working in any one mode but from a using a combination of ways of knowing. For example:

  > When stuck in problem solving, try physical movement to get the energy moving again.
  >
  > When intuition suggests there is more to a story, let silence reveal a way forward.
  >
  > As a counterpoint to analysis, share an experience such as taking a field trip, watching a video, or studying a map or photograph to illustrate the issues in different ways.
  >
  > When focusing on details, take opportunities to back up for a view of the big picture to situate progress and see what else needs to be taken into account.
  >
  > Notice and celebrate the rituals that emerge in the group to provide experiences of connection and relief from intensity.
  >
  > Try a new angle when everything seems fixed or stuck.

Recognizing Impasse

- Don't keep pushing through an impasse when doing so may damage relationships or reverse progress. Taking a break or changing the focus can give everyone the space they need to come back to the process with fresh eyes.

Attending to Body Messages

- Attend to messages received in the body about moment-to-moment conflict dynamics, nonverbal behavior of others, and physical needs and comfort. Practice doing a mental inventory of physical sensations and decoding these messages to assist you to identify turning points, intuitive and imaginative insights, and emotional signals.

Validating Face

- Pay attention to facework by validating participants' identities and worth as part of the process.

Welcoming Surprising Moments

- Cultivate mindfulness and openness to the subtleties and surprises of imagination and intuition—yours and others'.

Befriending Emotions

- Welcome emotions for the energy, passion, and commitment they bring to the process. Encourage emotional fluency while maintaining boundaries against emotional "dumping."

Working with Metaphors, Rituals, and Stories

- Attend to and work with metaphors, rituals, and stories for the windows they provide into meanings and identities.

Invoking a Creative Climate

- Into your conflict resolution processes, invite

    Spaciousness
    Openness to a range of outcomes
    A spirit of curiosity about self and other
    Empathy

Genuineness

Attention to connection and shared meanings, even as differences surface

Variations in timing, setting, intensity, and modes of communication

Aesthetic sensitivity and appreciation

Opportunities for people to express what really matters to them

Celebrating

- Mark small achievements, milestones, turning points, and surprises, affirming everyone's capacity for resilience and integration, even as room is made to mourn what is lost and acknowledge pain. Find a ritual that makes room for everyone's experience, while celebrating accomplishments.

NOTES

Chapter One

1. Ramsey, S., and Smith, J. "Accessing Creative Potential." Seminar sponsored by the Crestone Institute, Washington, D.C., June 2000.
2. Rilke, R. M. *Letters to a Young Poet.* (S. Mitchell, trans.). New York: Vintage Books, 1986.
3. Elgin, D. *Voluntary Simplicity.* New York: Morrow, 1981, p. 31.
4. Bowling, D., and Hoffman, D. "Bringing Peace into the Room: The Personal Qualities of the Mediator and Their Impact on the Mediation." *Negotiation Journal,* 2000, *16*(11), 5–28.
5. Kolb, D. *When Talk Works: Profiles of Mediators.* San Francisco: Jossey-Bass, 1997.
6. Williamson, M. *A Return to Love.* New York: HarperCollins, 1992, p. 165.
7. May, R. *The Courage to Create.* New York: W. W. Norton, 1975, p. 13.
8. Quoted in May, 1975, p. 21.

Chapter Two

1. Gardner, H. *Multiple Intelligences: The Theory in Practice.* New York: Basic Books, 1993.
2. Goleman, D. *Emotional Intelligence.* New York: Bantam Books, 1995.
3. Goleman, 1995, p. xi.
4. Suttie, I. *The Origins of Love and Hate.* London: Routledge, 1999.
5. Abdalla, A. Personal communication, Apr. 2001. (For more information on this topic, see Abdalla, A. *Interpersonal Conflict Patterns in Egypt: Themes and Solutions.* Unpublished doctoral dissertation, Institute for Conflict Analysis and Resolution, Fairfax, Va.: George Mason University, 2001.)

6. Kochman, T. *Black and White Styles in Conflict.* Chicago: University of Chicago Press, 1981.
7. Gardner, 1993, p. 9.
8. Cameron, J. *The Artist's Way: A Spiritual Path to Higher Creativity.* New York: Putnam, 1995.
9. Bender, S. *Everyday Sacred.* New York: HarperCollins, 1995.
10. Gray, B. "The Gender-Based Foundations of Negotiation Theory." *Research on Negotiations in Organizations,* 1994, *4,* 3–36.
11. Gray, J. *Men Are from Mars, Women Are from Venus: A Practical Guide for Improving Communication and Getting What You Want in Your Relationships.* New York: HarperCollins, 1992.
12. The term *First Nations* is used in Canada the way *Native American* is used in the United States.
13. Goleman, 1995, p. 65.
14. Rogers, C. *On Becoming a Person.* Cambridge, Mass.: Riverside Press, 1961.
15. Fisher, R., Ury, W., and Patton, B. *Getting to Yes: Negotiating Agreement Without Giving In.* New York: Penguin Books, 1991.
16. His Holiness the Dalai Lama, and Cutler, H. C. *The Art of Happiness: A Handbook for Living.* New York: Penguin Putnam, 1998, p. 55.
17. Segal, J. *Raising Your Emotional Intelligence.* New York: Henry Holt, 1997.
18. Nin, A. *Wisdom Seekers,* 2001, *4*(160). [http://www.Groups.yahoo.com/group/ wisdomseekers/message/939] June 2001.

Chapter Three

1. Roth, G. *Maps to Ecstasy: A Healing Journey for the Untamed Spirit.* Novato, Calif.: Nataraj Publishing, 1998, p. 30.
2. May, R. *The Courage to Create.* New York: W. W. Norton, 1975, p. 15.
3. Rosenberg, J. L., Rand, M. L., and Asay, D. *Body and Soul: Sustaining Integration.* Atlanta: Humanics Ltd., 1987.
4. Goleman, D. *Emotional Intelligence.* New York: Bantam Books, 1995, p. 166.
5. Ury, W. *The Third Side.* New York: Penguin Books, 2000, p. 132.
6. Milner, N. "Linda Colburn: On-the-Spot Mediation in a Public Housing Project." In D. M. Kolb and Associates (eds.), *When Talk Works.* San Francisco: Jossey-Bass, 1994, p. 395.
7. Milner, 1994, p. 416.
8. Milner, 1994, p. 395.
9. Ferrucci, P. *Inevitable Grace: Breakthroughs in the Lives of Great Men and Women.* Los Angeles: Jeremy P. Tarcher, 1990, p. 161.

Chapter Four

1. cummings, e. e. *Untitled.* [http://www.geocities.com/Athens/Olympus/2601/cummings1.html]. Nov. 2001.
2. Parry, D. *Warriors of the Heart. A Handbook for Conflict Resolution.* Bainbridge Island, Wash.: Earthstewards Network Publishing, 1997.
3. Ferrucci, P. *Inevitable Grace: Breakthroughs in the Lives of Great Men and Women.* Los Angeles: Jeremy P. Tarcher, 1990, p. 43.
4. Bohm, D. *On Creativity.* London: Routledge, 1998, p. 42.
5. Volkan, V. *Bloodlines: From Ethnic Pride to Ethnic Terrorism.* Boulder, Colo.: Westview Press, 1998.
6. Parry, 1997, p. 19.
7. Hemery, D. *The Pursuit of Sporting Excellence.* London: Willow Books, 1986.
8. Siegel, B. S. *Love, Medicine, and Miracles.* New York: HarperCollins, 1986, p. 153.
9. Ferrucci, 1990, p. 44.
10. Siegel, 1986, p. 152.
11. Boulding, K. *Three Faces of Power.* Thousand Oaks, Calif.: Sage, 1989.
12. Cooperrider, D. "Appreciative Inquiry: Relational Realities and Constructivist Approaches to Organizational Development." Paper presented at the Organization Development Network National Conference, 1995.
13. Montville, J. "The Healing Function in Political Conflict Resolution." In D.J.D Sandole and H. Van Der Merwe (eds.), *Conflict Resolution Theory and Practice: Integration and Application.* Manchester and New York: Manchester University Press, 1993.
14. Winslade, J., and Monk. G. *Narrative Mediation.* San Francisco: Jossey-Bass, 2000.
15. Richards, M. C. "Separating and Connecting: The Vessel and the Fire." In M. J. Ryan (ed.), *The Fabric of the Future: Women Visionaries Illuminate the Path to Tomorrow.* Berkeley, Calif.: Conari Press, 1998, pp. 231–246.
16. Gleick, J. *Chaos: Making a New Science.* New York: Viking, 1987, p. 198.
17. James, H. "Preface to the Spoils of Poynton." In B. Ghiselin (ed.), *The Creative Process.* Berkeley, Calif.: University of California Press, 1985, p. 151.
18. Dewey, J. *Art as Experience.* New York: Minton, 1934.
19. Johnson, S. *The Rambler.* 3 vols. W. J. Bate and A. B. Strauss (eds.). New Haven, Conn.: Yale University Press, 1969.
20. Williams, E. M. *Miracles.* Excerpt from sermon delivered at St. Luke's Episcopal Church, Jamestown, New York, Feb. 6, 2000.

21. Artress, L. *Walking a Sacred Path: Rediscovering the Labyrinth as a Spiritual Tool.* New York: Riverhead Books, 1995.

22. Eliot, T. S. "Tradition and the Individual Talent." In *The Sacred Wood: Essays on Poetry and Criticism.* [http://www.eiu.edu/~literary/4950/eliot.htm], 1922.

23. Nin, A. [http://www.cyberquotations.com/sorted/qGrowth.htm]. 1997–1999.

24. Jung, C. G. "Commentary." In (S. Wilhelm, trans.), *The Secret of the Golden Flower.* New York: Harcourt Brace, 1931, p. 92.

25. Yeats, W. B. "The Fisherman." In W. B. Yeats, *The Wild Swans at Coolie* [http://www.geocities.com/Athens/5379/TheFisherman.html]. Nov. 2001.

26. Richards, 1998, p. 234.

27. Richards, 1998, p. 234.

28. Richards, 1998, p. 234.

29. Richards, 1998, p. 235.

30. Johnson, R. A. *Balancing Heaven and Earth.* New York: HarperCollins, 1998, p. 398.

31. Milner, N. "Linda Colburn: On-the-Spot Mediation in a Public Housing Project." In D. M. Kolb and Associates (eds.), *When Talk Works.* San Francisco: Jossey-Bass, 1994, p. 398.

32. Grudin, R. *On Dialogue: An Essay in Free Thought.* Boston: Houghton Mifflin, 1996, p. 210.

33. Buber, M. *The Knowledge of Man.* (M. Friedman and R. G. Smith, trans.). New York: Harper Torchbooks, 1965.

34. Zeigler, W. *Ways of Enspiriting.* Denver: FIA International, 1994, p. 21.

35. Zeigler, 1994, p. 19.

Chapter Five

1. Frankl, V. E. *Man's Search for Meaning.* New York: Pocket Books, 1984.

2. Follet, M. P. "The New State (1918)." [http://www.sunsite.utk.edu/FINS/Mary_Parker_Follett/Fins-MPF-01.html]. Nov. 2001.

3. Von Goethe, J. W. "Johann Wolfgang von Goethe: Famous Quotes." [http://www.brainyquote.com/quotes/quotes/j/q109110.html]. Nov. 2001.

4. Von Goethe, 2001.

5. E-mail correspondence received September 22, 2001.

6. Ferruci, P. *Inevitable Grace. Breakthroughs in the Lives of Great Men and Women: Guides to Your Self-Realization.* Los Angeles: Jeremy B. Tarcher, 1990, pp. 197–198.

7. Ferruci, 1990, pp. 203–204.

8. Ferruci, 1990, pp. 205–206.
9. Ferruci, 1990, p. 86.
10. Putnam, R. J. *Bowling Alone: The Collapse and Revival of American Community.* New York: Simon & Schuster, 2000.
11. Brown, S. L. "Animals at Play." *National Geographic.* Dec. 1994, pp. 5–7.
12. Erikson, E. *The Life Cycle Completed.* New York: W. W. Norton, 1985.
13. Friere, P. *Pedagogy of the Oppressed.* New York: Continuum Publishing, 1981, p. 79.
14. Newman, P. *The Canadian Revolution: From Deference to Defiance.* Canada: Toronto Books, 1995.
15. Friere, 1981, p. 81.
16. E. Williamson. "Macedonian TV Show for Kids Shows Life's Grittier Side." *Wall Street Journal,* Europe, Feb. 19, 2001.

Chapter Six

1. Lakoff, G., and Johnson, M. *Metaphors We Live By.* Chicago: University of Chicago Press, 1980.
2. Capra, F. *Uncommon Wisdom: Conversations with Remarkable People.* New York: Simon & Schuster, 1988, p. 77.
3. Schön, D. "Generative Metaphor: A Perspective on Problem-Setting in Social Policy." In A. Ortony (ed.), *Metaphor and Thought.* Cambridge: Cambridge University Press, 1979.
4. Docherty, J. S. "The Stewardship Metaphor in Forest Management Resource Conflicts: A Common Language Does Not Guarantee Consensus." In D. McFarland (ed.), *Conflict Analysis and Resolution: Challenges for the Times.* Fairfax, Va.: Institute for Conflict Analysis and Resolution, 1996, pp. 191–208.
5. Lakoff and Johnson, 1980.
6. Fisher, R., and Ury, W. *Getting to Yes: Negotiating Agreement Without Giving In.* New York: Penguin Books, 1983.
7. Fisher and Ury, 1991, p. 56.
8. Lakoff and Johnson, 1980.
9. Stoltz, J. "Gender, Culture, and Diversity in Conflict Resolution." Course paper written at the University of Victoria, Victoria, B.C., Canada, 2000.
10. Nudler, O. "In Search of a Theory for Conflict Resolution: Taking a New Look at World Views Analysis." *ICAR Newsletter,* 1993, 5(5), 1–5.
11. Deutsch, M., and Coleman, P. *The Handbook of Conflict Resolution.* San Francisco: Jossey-Bass, 2000.
12. Barrett, F. J., and Cooperrider, D. L. "Generative Metaphor Intervention: A New Approach for Working with Systems Divided by

Conflict and Caught in Defensive Perception." *Journal of Applied Behavioral Science*, 1990, *26*(2), 219–239.

13. De Bono, E. *New Think*. New York: Basic Books, 1967.

14. Schön, 1979, p. 261.

15. Acland, A. *Researching Practitioner Skills in Conflict Resolution*. Fairfax, Va.: Institute for Conflict Analysis and Resolution, George Mason University Working Paper Series (no. 12), 1996.

16. Blechman, F., Crocker, J. C., Docherty, J. S., and Garon, S. C. *Finding Meaning in a Complex Environment Policy Dispute: Research into Worldviews in the Northern Forest Lands Council Dialogue, 1990–1994*. Fairfax, Va.: Institute for Conflict Analysis and Resolution, George Mason University Working Paper Series (no. 14), 2000.

Chapter Seven

1. Winslade, J., and Monk, G. *Narrative Mediation: A New Approach to Conflict Resolution*. San Francisco: Jossey-Bass, 2000.

2. Hare, R. D. *Without Conscience: The Disturbing World of the Psychopaths Among Us*. New York: Guilford Press, 1993.

3. Broome, B. "Managing Differences in Conflict Resolution: The Role of Relational Empathy." In D. J. Sandole and H. Van Der Mewe, (eds.), *Conflict Resolution Theory and Practice: Integration and Application*. Manchester and New York: Manchester University Press, 1993.

4. Cobb, S., and Rifkin, J. "Practice and Paradox: Deconstructing Neutrality in Mediation." *Law and Social Inquiry*, 1991, *16*(Winter), 35–62.

5. Volkan, V. *Bloodlines*. New York: Farrar, Straus and Giroux, 1997.

6. Ross, R. *Dancing with a Ghost: Exploring Indian Reality*. Markham, Ontario: Octopus Publishing Group, 1992.

7. Covey, S. *Seven Habits of Highly Effective People: Restoring the Character Ethic*. New York: Simon & Schuster, 1989, p. 237.

8. Augsberger, D. *Conflict Mediation Across Cultures: Pathways and Patterns*. Louisville, Ky.: Westminster/John Knox Press, 1992.

9. Ziegler, W. *Ways of Enspiriting: Transformative Practices for the Twenty-First Century*. Denver: FIA Incorporated, 1994.

10. Ziegler, 1994, p. 18.

11. Haynes, J. "Metaphor and Mediation." Eugene, Ore.: The Mediation Information and Resource Center. [http://www.mediate.com<\\>], 2001.

12. Bender, S. *Everyday Sacred*. New York: HarperCollins, 1995.

13. Bender, 1995, p. 73.

14. Lederach, J. P. *Preparing for Peace*. Syracuse, N.Y.: Syracuse University Press, 1995.

15. Diamond, L. *The Heroic Journey of Conflict Transformation*. Washington, D.C.: Institute for Multitrack Diplomacy, 1996.

16. Worthington, E. L. "Is There a Place for Forgiveness in the Justice System?" *Fordham Urban Law Journal,* 2000, *27,* 1721–1734.
17. Worthington, 2000, p. 31.

Chapter Eight

1. Turner, V. *The Ritual Process: Structure and Anti-Structure.* Chicago: Aldine, 1969.
2. Putnam, R. J. *Bowling Alone: The Collapse and Revival of American Community.* New York: Simon & Schuster, 2000.
3. Frankl, V. *Man's Search for Meaning: An Introduction to Logotherapy.* Boston: Beacon Press, 1963.
4. Clark, M. *Ariadne's Thread: The Search for New Modes of Thinking.* New York: St. Martin's Press, 1989.
5. Holifield, E. B. *Covenant Sealed: The Development of Puritan Sacramental Theology in Old and New England, 1570–1720.* New Haven, Conn.: Yale University Press, 1974.
6. Falk, M. "Notes on Composing New Blessings: Toward a Feminist-Jewish Reconstruction of Prayer." In J. Plaskow and C. Christ (eds.), *Weaving the Visions: New Patterns in Feminist Spirituality.* New York: HarperCollins, 1989.
7. Ross, R. *Returning to the Teachings.* Toronto: Penguin Books, 1996.
8. Christiansen, Von J. "Ritual and Dispute Resolution: The Role of Reconciliation in the Mediation Process." *Dispute Resolution Journal,* 1997, *52*(4), 66–78.
9. Schirch, L. *Exploring the Role of Ritual in Conflict Transformation.* Unpublished dissertation, Institute for Conflict Analysis and Resolution, George Mason University, Fairfax, Va., 1997.
10. LeBaron, M., and Carstarphen, N. "Negotiating Intractable Conflict: The Common Ground Dialogue Process and Abortion." *Negotiation Journal,* 1997, *13*(4), 341–361.
11. Schirch, 1997, p. 2.
12. Schirch, 1997, p. 2.
13. Fuller, R. B. [http://www.geocities.com/~spanoudi/quote-11a.html]. 1994.
14. Devlin, S. In M. Adler (ed.), *Drawing Down the Moon: Witches, Druids, Goddess-Worshippers, and Other Pagans in America Today.* Boston: Beacon Press, 1979.

Chapter Nine

1. Eliot, T. S. "Little Gidding." *Collected Poems 1909–1962.* New York: Harcourt Brace, 1963.
2. Chasin, L. *Searching for Wise Questions.* Watertown, Mass.: Public Conversations Project. [http:www.publicconversations.org]. Sept. 2001.

3. Douglas, M. *Edward Evans Pritchard*. New York: Viking Penguin, 1980.

4. Simmer-Brown, J. "Commitment and Openness: A Contemplative Approach to Pluralism." In S. Glazer (ed.), *The Heart of Learning. Spirituality in Education*. New York: Jeremy Tarcher/Putnam, 1999.

5. Merton, T. "Hagia Sophia." In T. P. McDonnell (ed.), *A Thomas Merton Reader*. New York: Doubleday, 1989, p. 506.

6. Winslade, J., and Monk, G. *Narrative Mediation: A New Approach to Conflict Resolution*. San Francisco: Jossey-Bass, 2000.

7. His Holiness the Dalai Lama. "Education and the Human Heart." In S. Glazer (ed.), *The Heart of Learning*. New York: Jeremy P. Tarcher/Putnam, 1999.

8. His Holiness, p. 88.

9. Rogers, C. *On Becoming a Person*. Cambridge, Mass.: Riverside Press, 1961.

10. Merton, 1989.

11. Eliot, 1963.

12. Richards, M. C. "Separating and Connecting: The Vessel and the Fire." In M. J. Ryan (ed.), *The Fabric of the Future: Women Visionaries Illuminate the Path to Tomorrow*. Berkeley, Calif.: Conari Press, 1998.

13. Whyte, D. *Crossing the Unknown Sea: Work as a Pilgrimage of Identity*. New York: Riverhead Books, 2001, p. 231.

14. Johnson, R. A. *Balancing Heaven and Earth*. New York: HarperCollins, 1998.

About the Author

Michelle LeBaron first learned about resolving conflict in Alberta, Canada, where she was born into a family of homesteaders from France, England, and Denmark. Her first loves were art, music, literature, and dance, which serve as continuing inspirations for her work connecting creativity and conflict resolution.

LeBaron practiced law after completing her degree at the University of British Columbia, Canada, later adding a master's degree in counseling psychology from Simon Fraser University in Burnaby, Canada. She now consults in organizational, educational, public policy, and commercial settings, using a range of dialogic and creative approaches to address conflicts. Michelle has published on several conflict resolution topics, exploring connections between conflict resolution and multiculturalism, spirituality and conflict, and First Nations–government approaches to negotiation. Her training materials on public policy and intercultural conflict resolution are widely used in professional and academic programs, and she has visiting faculty appointments at universities in the United States, Canada, Asia, and Europe. She has served on the board of several conflict resolution organizations, including the Society of Professionals in Dispute Resolution and the Public Conversations Project.

LeBaron is a tenured professor of conflict analysis and resolution at George Mason University in Fairfax, Virginia, where she teaches courses on conflict as it relates to culture, gender, personal and organizational change, spirituality, and creativity.

Index